D1588109

MANZONI AND HIS TIMES

Manzoni, from a painting by Francesco Hayez, in the Brera Gallery, Milan

MANZONI

AND HIS TIMES

a biography of the author of
'The Betrothed' (*I Promessi Sposi*)
by
ARCHIBALD COLQUHOUN

*Ogni finzione che mostra l'uomo in riposo
morale è dissimile dal vero*—Every fiction
which shows man in moral repose is
dissimilar to the truth.—MANZONI.

*Illustrated with
sixteen pages
of photographs*

LONDON
J. M. DENT & SONS LTD

CONTENTS

ILLUSTRATIONS

FOREWORD

An English biographer of Manzoni has some grounds for hoping that his subject may appeal to other than specialists on Italian literature or history. He can scarcely avoid, as he delves into Manzoni's character and period, finding a variety of parallels which seem broadly applicable to-day. At times he must feel that he is exploring, in terms of an artist and a background little known to English-speaking readers, a corner of the modern conscience which is neither specifically Italian nor even European.

This book, then, is not only about a writer whom Italians consider as the chief figure in their literature since Dante, but about a type of mind and experience which we can find among us now. And the disquisitions on the various influences in Manzoni's life are intended, not as contributions to original research (which they could scarcely lay claim to be) but as attempts both to explain his development and to arouse speculation on problems which, in differing connotations, are actual to-day.

On Manzoni himself very little research, probably, remains to be done, though Dr Barbara Reynolds has recently made a remarkable confrontation of the numerous texts of his writings on language, and Professor Mario Ghisalberti is at the moment engaged in deciphering some of the original passages in the over-scored manuscripts of *I Promessi Sposi*. Possibly something can still be found in the comments which Manzoni wrote on the margins of books he read.

About his background and friends researchers such as Professor Bognetti are still making discoveries, and these can throw new light on passages in his works. But apart from these almost every conceivable aspect of his thought and opinions is covered in books, studies, essays, and articles which make up a good-sized library at the centre of Manzoni studies, the Casa Manzoniana, at his old home in the Via Morone in Milan. These range from full-length—and sometimes conflicting—interpretations which often mirror their author more than their subject, to detailed researches on Manzoni's attitude to education, agriculture, psychology, medicine, or music, and to every figure in Italian and many in European literature before and during his time.   Whole books have even been written about single characters in *I Promessi Sposi*.   The main body of commentaries, apart from those on his style and characterization, deals with his religious beliefs and opinions on the language.

The chief sources used for this biography have been Manzoni's own works and his correspondence.   Memoirs and reminiscences have also been used, but most of these date from his later life, when he had ceased to write anything but essays.   One or two stories linger in verbal tradition among Milanese who still talk of 'Don 'Lisander' as if he had only died a year or two ago, but these are now unlikely to find documentary corroboration.   The bibliography at the end of this book gives only the most important studies of him and his period.   They are only a small proportion of the books and sources consulted, and have been selected as those most easily available.

The illustrations are all reproduced from originals (except for one or two which have been lost) now to be found either in the Casa Manzoniana, the Villa Manzoni at Brusuglio, or the Brera Gallery in Milan.   Few have ever been seen in this country and one, of Cesare Beccaria in his old age, is here reproduced for the first time.

My thanks are due to many friends who have made suggestions, particularly to Giovanna Croft-Murray, Guglielmo degli Alberti, and John Willett; and to Freya Stark, Marina Luling-Buschetti, Joy Murchie, and Anne Willett for lengthy hospitality and encouragement at Asolo, Maser, San Martino, and Le Thil during the later, more dragging stages of this work.

I should also like to thank Dott. Emilio Sioli Legnani, Professor Mario Ghisalberti, the Librarian of the Institut de France, and the staffs of the Casa Manzoniana and of the Braidense and British Museum Libraries, for their kindness and help over many years of labours on Manzoni.

No one but myself, of course, is responsible for any mistakes, omissions, or misinterpretations in this book.

A. C.

June 1954.

CHAPTER ONE

MILAN BEFORE THE FRENCH REVOLUTION; THE SOCIETÀ DEL CAFFÈ

I

TRAVELLING through Milan with Hobhouse in October 1816 Byron jotted down an impression of the city which contrasts oddly with that of the visitor to-day: 'Milan is striking—the cathedral superb. The city altogether reminds me of Seville, but a little inferior.' Nowadays this silence of old streets between high, cooling buildings, is only to be found in one or two provincial Italian cities, such as Mantua and Lucca, certainly not in modern Milan. But off the crowded Milanese thoroughfares, with their clanging trams and hurrying industrialists, there are still streets, sometimes with, amid the cobbles, parallel strips of paving for the carriage wheels, which give a faint echo of what the city was like before the last industrial development of Lombardy overwhelmed it in the years after the Italian unification. The Borgo Nuovo, the Via Sant' Agata, the Via Bigli (and until recently the quarter between the Brera and the Corso Garibaldi which is now gapped with bombed rubble), remain in many ways as they were when Byron saw them a hundred and thirty years ago. The prevailing architecture of such streets is of the last half of the eighteenth century, and dates from the period of the first Austrian occupation, which the young Bonaparte's armies had ended by their sweep through Northern Italy in 1796. This was the city which Manzoni and Stendhal loved.

Old Milan was then enclosed by a system of canals, the Naviglio, connected with the sea through the River Po. From their banks houses, draped with washing and tufted ferns, were reflected in the still water. Inside the perimeter everything was within walking distance, from the palaces on the superb Corso Venezia to the popular quarter where, 'rising like lilies from their festering slums,' were some of the loveliest Romanesque churches in Europe. The Sitwellian phrase about Naples might have applied more, perhaps, to the ancient churches with a baroque overlay (such as the oddly named church of San Satiro—'Divo Satiro' is written in large classical letters across the portico) now to be found surrounded by modern buildings near the Piazza del Duomo.

In the early nineteenth century it was mainly a city of rococo. Even now in back streets, going past façades on which an occasional stucco twirl round a window can be discerned, one peeps into some of the gayest courtyards in the peninsula. Through frothy rococo ironwork screens are shaded groups of pillars and arcades, past which one may catch a glimpse of a grassy grotto, with frisking gods and goddesses lit in flashing sunlight. These courtyards, of which there are an extraordinary variety, are all lighter and less stately than those of Rome or Palermo, and show the strength of Viennese influence at the time of the first great period of building since the Renaissance. Much that is reminiscent of old Vienna has survived, even since the efforts of the architects of United Italy produced the city we see to-day.

The vast expansion of Milan in the last eighty years has made it a place of odd contrasts. The Piazza Belgiojoso, in which Manzoni lived, was very different from the curious modern inferno of the Piazza Duse, whose disproportionate buildings, put up in the 1920s, are topped by mock baroque figures waving hopelessly in their isolation, like some pastiche of an early Chirico. Nowadays in the Piazza Belgiojoso, which is just off the city centre, there is scarcely room to thread one's way among the parked cars—and there are more cars to the yard in Milan than in any other city in Italy, possibly in Europe, such is the concentration there of the national wealth. Emptying the square in one's imagination, one can see that its buildings are still those which Manzoni saw when he set off, accompanied by some priest or local schoolmaster in case the vertigo caught him crossing a street, for his long afternoon walks around the city. The façade of his own house in the corner he had covered, towards the end of his life—for he had little visual sense—with elaborate terra-cotta tiles. But the husk of the superb Palazzo Belgiojoso (the back of the vast courtyard was bombed) still dominates the square with its rows of hundreds of stuccoed windows.

They are stupendous, these Milanese palaces, even compared to those of Rome or Budapest. 'The King of France,' wrote young Alessandro Verri to his brother from Paris in 1766, 'is not more magnificently housed than the Marchesa Litta.' The Palazzo Borromeo, in what is now the Via Manzoni, must have one of the longest façades of any private house in the world, and the Palazzo Trivulzio still takes up to-day what appears to be an entire district in the centre of the city. And not only palaces went up at this time. The architect Piermarini, who designed many of them, finished his crowning work, the Scala Opera House, in August 1778—a date, it was to turn out, of considerable importance, for the Scala soon broke the musical hegemony of Naples over the peninsula, and drew whole new series of visitors to Lombardy.

This intensive period of building had direct economic and political causes. The end in 1746 of the Spanish occupation after nearly two hundred years had turned out unexpectedly profitable for the Lombard landlords. They themselves took some time to realize the advantages to themselves of the reforms ordered from Vienna. Land reforms, fiscal reorganization, census, were opposed by the Decurions, the old Milanese council of nobles, impregnated with the rigid Spanish mentality whose effects are traced so subtly in *I Promessi Sposi*. Yet by 1780, in spite of the slow and cumbrous administrative methods of the first years of the new Austrian occupation, the Duchy of Milan was yielding twice the agricultural produce of its neighbours.

By the end of the eighteenth century there was an immense division and subdivision of property in Lombardy—one reason why the Revolution, when it came, was less violent than in the more feudal south.

Yet perhaps only the Revolution was to shake the inertia hanging over nearly all classes as a result of the long Spanish occupation. The Heraldic Tribunal still regulated the life of the upper and middle classes to the smallest detail. The tassels on horses, the uniforms of children's nurses, the length of the trains on dresses, the bearing of torches before a coach or up the stairs, the use of footstools in church, even the sending of engraved invitations for weddings or funerals, were all laid down by stifling protocol. And in the working classes the long Spanish rule seems to have caused a profound modification of the Lombard character, which only the Revolution was to change. 'The ignorant nation,' wrote Cesare Cantù, 'called patriotism cowardice, moderation the weakness which is terrified of the idea of a courageous act, and religion the superstition which trembles before the unknown power of devils and witches.' And Cantù went on to refer contemptuously to the populace's incapacity for looking beyond its immediate interests —a docility which is perhaps understandable when one reads that, due partly to a fossilized system of guilds and fraternities, every working man was forced by law to follow the occupation of his father and grandfather before him. 'How the higher classes would have laughed,' wrote another liberal historian of the Risorgimento, Tivaroni, 'at any pleb who cut himself off from the paternal occupation in order to give himself up to books, without being a priest or a friar. . . . The steward or butcher who tried to make his children study would have been guilty of a crime against society.' The number of clergy in the city was prodigious. The habits of the religious houses dotted the streets, from the mendicant friars to 'that plague of the clergy, the abbés, informers, and clowns to the noble houses.' [1]

The routine of the upper classes was described by Goldoni: 'La mattina una messeta, l'apodisnar una bassetta, la sera una donnetta.' (A little mass in the morning, a little cards in the afternoon, a little woman in the evening.) In society the segregation of the sexes had been almost Moorish until one of the last Spanish viceroys introduced the *cicisbeo* or *cavalier servente* system, probably from Genoa. Benjamin Franklin, visiting Milan at this time, calculated that an army could be formed of the barbers, and maintained by the money spent on hair-powder. But Goldoni noted the gaiety and mildness of the Milanese populace, and their enjoyment of the pleasures available to them, particularly eating, without which (and in this respect there has been little change) no business could be discussed. 'The people are neither factious nor recalcitrant nor bad,' wrote the leading contemporary reformer Pietro Verri. 'The evils of our country are disillusion, falsity, and ignorance.' 'A quiet life,' summed up Cantù, 'modest resources corresponding

---

[1] Vernon Lee, *Studies of the Eighteenth Century in Italy*. Satchell, 1880.

to modest needs, even at the risk of everything being interrupted by a war for vain arrogance or foreign interests, made up the ideal of a people by now used and trained to the bit.'

II

The Austrian masters were determined to increase the yield of their new Lombard dominions. To this they were urged mainly by their own interests, such were the dilapidations to potentially valuable property by the last tenants. But this self-interest was mingled, for a time, with the reforming zeal of the leading innovator, the young Holy Roman Emperor himself. Joseph II was perhaps the most genuinely idealistic of the reforming absolute monarchs who were swept up in the wake of the Encyclopaedists. But he was not the most subtle or human of them. There was a touch in him of intellectual rigidity and superiority which made the iconoclast Gorani remark: 'He was a prince who pushed folly so far as to pretend to omniscience.' So sure was Joseph of doing good that in the manner of his reforms he was apt to be a little high-handed, a little like Voltaire's Mahomet 'who, with his scimitar in hand, was the most eloquent doctor in the world.' About the origins of his reforms he made no democratic pretence: they were all firmly imposed from Vienna. His 375 decrees to his favourite Lombardy were all carefully drafted by his own hand, and ranged from the abolition of torture to regulations for street lighting and the ringing of church bells. But apart from the resentment set up by Joseph's restless and despotic methods, most of his reforms were on too high and impractical a plane for the times. 'The good of a private individual is a chimera, I sacrifice it for the general good' was a chilling axiom for his individualistic Italian subjects, however much it was meant to improve their lot.

Joseph's efforts found support in what might seem an unexpected quarter. It was a period when in Italy, as in France and Germany, the most enlightened men of the time were collaborating with absolute monarchies from the highest of motives. Had not Voltaire in 1745 dedicated his *Mahomet* to the new Pope, Benedict XIV, and received the papal benediction in exchange? Even Horace Walpole had been stirred out of his cynical frivolity by this papal election, and found himself writing: 'Benedict is a pope loved by papists, esteemed by Protestants, a priest without insolence or interests, a prince without favourites, a pope without nephews.' Such hopes, particularly with the papacy, were usually short-lived. The reformers, in fact, were unconsciously in the paradoxical position —to-day it would be called dialectical—of supporting for their incidental benefits regimes which the logic of their theories urged them one day to undermine.   Joseph on the other hand was being just as dialectical in carrying out, as the historian Rota put it, 'the absurd policy of governing with the support of the very class whose grave he wanted to dig.'   But the Lombard reformers and supporters of Joseph were inclined to take a slightly detached view of the enlightened instructions pouring out in ever-increasing streams from Vienna.   'Under the rule of Maria Teresa,' wrote Pietro Verri, looking back on those times after the French invasion, 'the Milanese were as happy as it is possible to be happy under an absolute power.'   And when Parini, the greatest poet and satirist of his day (and the earliest influence on Manzoni), was asked to write a eulogy of Maria Teresa after her death, he withdrew to the country for a lengthy stay from which he finally emerged with the poem unwritten, saying: 'I cannot find any satisfactory idea round which to compose a eulogy of the empress.   She was only generous: and giving away the property of others is not virtue.'

III

They are very contemporary in feeling, this little group of enlightened Milanese, from whom Alessandro Manzoni drew his origins.   Pietro Verri, the leader of the group, was *de facto* if not *de jure* almost certainly his uncle; Cesare Beccaria, the reformer of the European penal code, his grandfather; Parini had been the tutor of his mother's lover; Giuseppe Gorani, an international adventurer more fantastic and considerably more intelligent than Casanova, was a family friend.   Young Alessandro could remember from family conversations in his early youth his mother's enthusiasm for Joseph II, 'which was then the common feeling among liberal citizens.'

The very fact that these liberal Milanese had a chance to collaborate with the emperor showed, so inelastic was the social system of eighteenth-century Lombardy, that the leaders belonged by birth to the higher ranks of the privileged classes. Count Pietro Verri was the son of the Regent of the Senate, the main officer of state under the Spanish viceroys. One of his forbears had been a close friend of San Carlo Borromeo; another had been a Commissioner of Supply under the Spaniards and might well have been the original of 'the unfortunate commissioner' whose misadventures are described in *I Promessi Sposi*. Pietro's father, old Count Gabriele Verri, was a rigid nobleman of the old school, a magistrate *d'une integrité proverbiale*, as his son's French biographer called him. For a young noble who combined liveliness and good looks with intelligence and an inquiring mind the wars were the classic escape. The Seven Years War was on: there young Pietro, disgusted by the intrigues and struggles for power at the headquarters to which he was attached, ran into a strange Welsh adventurer in the Austrian service, Henry Lloyd.

Henry Evans Lloyd, a philosophic soldier of fortune, was successively law student, lay brother, engineer, economist, spy, and soldier in the French, Austrian, and Russian services. Twice he surveyed the coasts of England with a view to invasion, once in 1748 dressed as a priest on behalf of the Young Pretender, and again in 1754 for the French. In 1779 he published in London *A Political and Military Rhapsody on the Invasion and Defence of Great Britain*, a book whose purpose—whether to illustrate the defence or the attack of the English coasts—is still uncertain. Lloyd also wrote commentaries on Helvétius and Montesquieu, and a book on the theory of money; he ended as a distinguished military historian, and a respected pensioner of the British War Office, with the rank of general. Pietro Verri, who saw him constantly on visits to Milan in the 1760s and 70s, thought him almost a genius, though touchy and erratic. 'He was my mentor,' Verri said of him. 'Thanks to him I began to reason.' It was Lloyd who first, during pauses between battles, talked to him of Voltaire and the new rationalist French philosophers. Stirred by the ideas injected into him by this curious companion, Pietro started off home. On the way, during a spell of duty as chamberlain at the Austrian Court and between duty dances with the archduchesses, he put in some intense reading of the advanced literature of the day.

Thus prepared, he returned to Milan in 1760 and, at the age of thirty-three, began his life's work for the political and moral regeneration of his country.

The group which he collected around him has gone down to history under the light-hearted name of the Società del Caffè. This came from the journal Verri started in 1764 called *Il Caffè*. Among the earliest collaborators on this short-lived enterprise (although it was one of the strongest leavening influences for new ideas in the second half of the eighteenth century in Italy, it only lasted for two years) were Pietro's younger brother, Alessandro, later to be one of the forerunners of Italian novelists; Frisi, a mathematician and friend of d'Alembert; and another unconventional and imaginative young patrician, the Marchese Cesare Beccaria.

Beccaria, when Pietro Verri found him in 1762 at the age of twenty-two, was not only at loggerheads with his family, but had been more or less ordered out of the home after a runaway marriage with the lovely—and sprightly—daughter of a half-pay colonel. Many of this lady's characteristics were transmitted to her daughter, Donna Giulia, the mother of Alessandro Manzoni, and so were to be a considerable influence on his life. Donna Teresa Beccaria was one of the causes, too, of the rift between the chief members of the group of reformers a few years later. Pietro Verri, who had now come into the family fortune, helped and befriended young Beccaria at this crisis of the young man's marriage. Soon Verri realized that he had acquired a protégé of unusual brilliance.

Cesare Beccaria was a remarkable, if unstable, character. 'His vivid imagination, together with his unusual understanding of the human heart,' Pietro wrote to his brother Alessandro on first taking him up, 'make him a really extraordinary man. As a result of his marriage—the Government held him under arrest for over a month to prevent it—he was flung out of his home with very little money; because of this he is so discredited that no one will have anything to do with him. He is a profound mathematician, a good poet, and has a mind adapted to try new paths, if laziness and discouragement do not suffocate him.' When Verri discovered him, poor young Beccaria was in a state of gloomy frustration, and finding it difficult to set his hand to anything for very long—such moods were to recur throughout his life. Verri encouraged him to write, and gave him the theme of his first little book, on monetary reform, published in 1762. His next started from discussions after some of Alessandro Verri's prison visits. Pietro then corrected and rewrote most of this book, which in 1764 suddenly made Beccaria world-famous, *Dei Delitti e delle Pene.*

Now, supported by the creative energy flowing into Beccaria from the new self-confidence of success, Pietro Verri started *Il Caffè.* The name was intended to suggest an imaginary coffee-house, where the customers, under the guidance of an old sailor, a kind of Uncle Toby, discussed freely and freshly an extra-ordinarily wide range of topics, most of them opposed to the accepted ideas of the day. To avoid the Austrian censorship the paper was printed in Brescia in the Venetian territory (it was before the days of Joseph's reforms). 'The paper's aim,' wrote Beccaria, 'is to make virtue attractive.' He meant social virtue. 'The purpose of this pleasing occupation is to do what we can for our country, to spread useful knowledge among our fellow citizens, and to amuse them too, as was done elsewhere by Steele and Swift, by Addison, Pope, and others.' But although Beccaria's mention of the writers for *The Rambler* and *The Spectator* was a tribute to their pioneering work in this form of journalism, the aims stated in the preamble to the first number of *Il Caffè,* of discussing 'things various, things unpublished, things written by a variety of authors, things all directed to the public good,' went far beyond those of the English reviews of earlier in the century. Also, though Locke and the French Encyclopaedists provided the theoretical basis, the emphasis in *Il Caffè* was on practical reform rather than general ideas. Put into a light and readable form, such as in a 'Dialogue between a Mandarin and a Solicitor on Civil Law,' were articles on adminis-tration, commerce, and agriculture. There were discussions on subjects now so perennial as the Italian forms of address, 'tu,' 'voi,' and 'lei,' attacking the inflated styles of the period such as 'Illustrissimo signori padroni colendissimi.' And another

Manzoni-ish touch can be observed in the ironic title of an article, presumably by Beccaria, 'On the Excellence, Utility, and Justice of the Flogging of Children.'

The response to Il Caffè throughout the peninsula was immediate. 'There is already in Milan,' wrote that original figure the Abbé Galiani of Naples to Tanucci in 1766, 'a group of young nobles who study and think and whom the people call atheists, as a century ago they would have called them sorcerers.' That the paper would arouse bitter opposition among the legislators of the old school was to be expected. Yet even Giuseppe Baretti, the friend of Dr Johnson, who represented the aesthetic Bohemian literary world of the day as opposed to the innovating and politically minded noblesse of the Verris and Beccaria, attacked it in scathing articles in his own short-lived journal, La Frusta Letteraria (The Literary Whip). His most ferocious attacks were on the antiquated literary style of Il Caffè, and its subservience to French ideas. Since both these touch on Manzoni's development and preoccupations, it is perhaps worth pausing over Baretti's points, buried though they were in his own invective.

One of the professed aims of Il Caffè was to simplify the language so as to widen the small public of readers who could understand the involved prose style laid down by the old Academies. But this was too vast a task to undertake, and the style of Il Caffè itself could not shake free of the Academies, whose influence over the whole of Italian prose was to remain considerable for some time. It was to take Manzoni the brooding of half a lifetime to renew the language to its foundations, and make it a vehicle of communication between the writer and the broad mass of the population. Yet the Academies, stultifying as their influence was apt to be, had certainly provided a means of intellectual intercourse between the few. Pietro Verri, always a great one for societies, had been a member of the Milanese Academy of the Trasformati ('Transformed Ones'), recently revived by a rich banker, Giuseppe Maria Imbonati, from the old Trasformati of the Renaissance. These Academies were scattered all over the peninsula. As Vernon Lee wrote in her enchanting *Studies on the Eighteenth Century in Italy*, where the Academies and the Arcadians are described in detail:

The Academies which grew out of the pompous receptions of car-
dinals and princes, and out of the disorderly concourses at literary
coffee-houses . . . fairly exhausted the stock of intelligible appellations.
There were the Gelidi ('Frozen Ones') of Bologna, the Intronati
('Stunned Ones') of Siena, the 'Erithrean Shepherds' of Naples, the
'Phlegmatics,' the 'Frigids,' the 'Fervids,' and the 'Drunkards.'

The universal appeal of the Arcadians, started at the end of the
previous century to oppose the literary pomposities of Marino
and the baroque school, had absorbed most of these Academies
by the middle of the eighteenth century. 'None of our *cicisbeos*
dare now peep out of his hut, but with a crook in one hand and
a flute in the other,' wrote Baretti in his *Manners and Customs of
Italy*. But so restricted then was the number of persons in
Italy with literary and intellectual interests that these gatherings,
in spite of their touch of not unengaging farce, did serve to bring
together congenial and sometimes inquiring spirits. Some of
these organizations, as, for instance, the Società Palatina, also
financed great historical studies, such as the chronicles of
Muratori.

If the range of these Academies' and Arcadians' meetings was
small, they must often have been delightful. One of the more
famous gatherings of the Milanese Trasformati was devoted to
composing verses on the death of a member's cat. Baretti has
left a description of a visit in 1761 to the Imbonatis' magnificent
villa at Cavallasca on Lake Como, where the Trasformati were
gathered. 'Songs, music, poetry, rare foods, delicious wines,
strolls by the lakeside, and games, from cock-crow to sunset.
The English, the French, the Austrians, the Prussians, and the
Russians can fight away and slaughter each other to their heart's
content, to us it doesn't matter a straw.' And like straws
which had put down no roots the Academies and the Arcadians,
careless of any struggles that went on outside their parks and
drawing-rooms, found themselves swept away a few years later
by the storm bursting over their heads.

If Baretti's invective about the style of *Il Caffè* and the Academies links to Manzoni's preoccupations in later life with the
Italian language, his onslaughts against the journal for its French
ideas touch on the great influences of Manzoni's youth and early
manhood.

In later life, when Manzoni had made a conscious rejection of the philosophic ideas of his youth, he once attacked the Società del Caffè in the overstated terms of conversation as 'a French colony, for they had nothing but the French ideas of their time.' Yet in the first draft of *I Promessi Sposi*, *Gli Sposi Promessi*, written at a time when he was reviewing his philosophical ideas in the light of his new-found faith, he acknowledged how much not only he, but all his generation, had absorbed from the French writers of the century before.

The reading of the distinguished French writers who were flourishing at that period in which Italian letters were at their most stupid and empty, began to work on Italians, to give them an idea of a literature fed on important researches, on serious reasoning, on sincere discussion, on inventions which resembled something human and real, aimed at passing on to the reader's mind the reasoned persuasion of the writer, at leading the way to a loftier point in the science of feeling, which a few had reached in private meditation. . . . Nauseated by the writings, intentions, methods, by everything in the Italian literature of their time . . . they began to put more care and precision in their writing, to seek out important truths . . . and they gradually diffused in the minds of their readers the good sense they had attained themselves.

Profound as it was, the influence of the French writers and thinkers of the Enlightenment on the group of *Il Caffè* was more general than detailed. Writers in the journal made little distinction between the conflicting views of the Encyclopaedists; Voltaire, incidentally, is only mentioned rarely, and then only in a literary connection. The tone of this Lombard movement, with its feeling of the inferiority of the Italy of the last two hundred years and the need for its regeneration, was less abstract than that of the French. It was, in part, the increasingly practical turn of the movement, and Pietro Verri's absorption for some years in administration, that were responsible, together with more personal factors, for *Il Caffè* ceasing publication in 1766.

IV

No events, perhaps, are ever purely public, and the effects on them of private character can be fascinating—as they can be

Cesare Beccaria in his old age. From a picture at the Casa del Manzoni, Milan

Cesare Beccaria. From a portrait at Brusuglio

horrifying when used by propaganda. The closure of *Il Caffè* was connected with the strange behaviour of Cesare Beccaria during and after a visit he made to Paris in 1766 with Alessandro Verri, to receive the homage of the French intelligentsia for *Dei Delitti e delle Pene*.

The effect of this book was compared by the leading thinkers of the day to that of the Gospels. Voltaire, Diderot, Helvétius, Holbach, and Hume all wrote commentaries on it. The Vatican rapidly put it on the Index—to Beccaria's horror, for when a religious paper attacked it as an offence to the authority of both religion and monarchy his nerves got the better of him, and he collapsed in terror of being arraigned for heresy and rebellion. 'Your work does good and will do more,' Voltaire wrote to encourage him in 1768. 'You are working for reason and humanity which have been so long crushed. You are freeing these two streams which have been stifled for sixteen hundred years. At last they begin to flow and make their voices heard; but since they have spoken, fanatics protest. They fear being humane, as much as they should fear being cruel'; and later, in an extravagant moment: 'Honest folk rest their sorrows on your bosom as on that of the champion of humanity.'

Certainly this small book by a young amateur—he was only twenty-six when he wrote it—had a profound effect on penal reform throughout Europe. His basic argument, that punishment should be a measure of social defence and not of vengeance, is familiar and accepted to-day. But Beccaria's development of it caused then the final abolition of numerous medieval punishments still on the statute-book, such as branding and burning for treason, or for the murder of husband by wife or master by servant. It led Leopold of Tuscany to abolish capital punishment in his dominions; and on reading it Catherine the Great wrote and asked its author to come and reorganize for her the penal system of the Slav world—a task which Beccaria, who had only too clear a knowledge of his limitations and disabilities, prudently refused.

Beccaria indeed was a curious character on whom to found such extravagant hopes. The combination of brilliance and laziness is only too common; but in Beccaria's make-up there was also a strong tendency to pathological melancholia, and even

to epilepsy, as has been studied by Lombroso. Some of these
tendencies were hereditary in the Beccaria family, and appeared
again in Cesare's son by his second marriage, Giulio, the last of
the name, and a contemporary of his cousin, Alessandro Manzoni.
There is no doubt that Alessandro himself also suffered from a
share of the family ills, which in his mother, Donna Giulia,
appeared only in the form of a gay and rather hysterical
instability.

These neurotic tendencies in Cesare Beccaria first came to light
during the journey to Paris in 1766. From the moment they
left Milan his behaviour was most extraordinary. He flung
himself about in the carriage, sobbing and weeping, bewailing
leaving his young wife. It was only with the greatest difficulty
that young Alessandro Verri, bent on enjoying the trip, prevented
him turning tail for home at every post-stage. Once in Paris
(where they arrived in the midst of the polemics between
Voltaire, Hume, and Rousseau, 'like a civil war,' noted Alessandro) the adulation went to his head. 'The votes of Europe
are in my hands,' he wrote home grandly. And to the irritation
of the Verris, who had considered the visit as representing them
all, Beccaria was apt to take the credit for the whole of the movement of *Il Caffè*. Young Alessandro, after writing back to his
brother: 'Beccaria will never forgive me for having been the
companion of his imbecility,' broke away and set off for a jaunt
to London; while the object of all the adulation, after unbalanced
behaviour which astonished the French philosophers (particularly
Morellet, who spent a night listening to him raving in the next
room), cut short his visit by three months and made for home.
On his return he found his wife with child. He then proceeded
to accuse Pietro Verri, in whose charge he had left her, of being
the father. Although from subsequent tendencies the child was
almost certainly Beccaria's, his wife's later history perhaps made
the suspicion of infidelity not unreasonable; she died of venereal
disease in 1774. But the dutiful, almost priggish, Pietro Verri
was just on the point of marrying a young girl; besides he disliked
the Marchesina Beccaria, who had, he considered, a bad influence
on her husband's vagaries. Relations between the two intellectual partners naturally cooled, particularly when Beccaria
followed this up by claiming the authorship of a commentary on

Dei Delitti e delle Pene, which was undoubtedly written by Pietro Verri. 'Beccaria is so wilfully suspicious and difficult that even his brothers fear he will go mad,' wrote Pietro to Alessandro Verri in May 1768. 'I shouldn't be surprised if the poor man really did go mad. . . . In spite of his faults I don't want heaven to vindicate me quite to that extent. . . . Perhaps I'm already vindicated without realizing it.'

For a time there was an open break, and, although Verri and Beccaria collaborated later, the personal breach was never really healed. As time passed Verri may have realized that he had been perhaps provoked into an irritating self-righteousness, and his tendency to insist on the past benefits of his friendship would surely have maddened the most balanced beneficiary. But what created a link again was public events, and the deterioration of their common reforming hopes. For from the late 1780s Joseph II and then his brother and successor, Leopold, disillusioned by the effects of their decrees and alarmed by events in France, abrogated them one after the other. The reforming movement collapsed in Italy as it had elsewhere. Beccaria withdrew to giving desultory lectures on law at Milan University; while Verri, abandoning even the Società Patriotica, which he had founded to help trade and agriculture, retired into private life to write philosophic essays. 'The clergy, the ministers, and the nobles,' he made Joseph II say in an imaginary dialogue written after the emperor's death, 'are the three bodies which oppress humanity and which bind the hands of the monarch; no happy resolution is possible unless these abuses are dealt with.' But Verri, understandably, was losing hope in benevolent monarchy. In the end he realized that only a formidable shake-up with all its attendant horrors might cure his country's ills. He and Parini were among the few Milanese of standing who hailed the invading French as liberators in 1796. Saddened, in spite of himself, by the excesses and racketeering of the new administration, Verri was about to retire again, when he collapsed from a heart attack at a sitting of the Commune in Milan in June 1797, and died in his chair, surrounded by respectful Jacobin politicians.

Verri, Parini, and Beccaria had been themselves denounced as Jacobins before the French occupation and, as the anti-Fascists learnt in Italy before the war, the raft of mutual persecution can bring together the most diverse spirits. It was after the first reconciliation between Pietro Verri and Beccaria that Verri tried to do his old protégé a last good turn.   He, possibly with Parini's help, arranged the marriage of Beccaria's brilliant and portionless young daughter Giulia—who was longing to get away from home after her father's second marriage—to a middle-aged country squire, Don Pietro Manzoni.   Like Verri's other efforts at helping the Beccarias this was also to go amiss.

V

All his youth the figure of his famous grandfather Cesare Beccaria was a central influence on Alessandro Manzoni. 'It is a title in which I glory,' he wrote from Paris in 1806, when insisting on having the name Beccaria added to his own on the title-page of his poem on the death of his mother's lover.   Even in his old age there is a touch of regretful admiration in a balanced summing-up made to Cantù, who was writing an essay on Beccaria.   'Beccaria had all the illusions of a young man, good faith, boundless confidence in the triumph of everything that appeared truth to him.   And what appeared truth to him seems to have been what contradicted the things he had learnt at school. He expressed himself like a Frenchman, without fine phrases and with much feeling.'   Was it, unconsciously, a disillusioned summing-up of his own youth?

Living in more complicated times when many of Beccaria's assumptions and conclusions seemed over-simplified, Manzoni, even in early manhood, had been critical of some of his grand-father's theories.   'Excuse me, mother,' he would say, after he and Donna Giulia had both been saying how great a genius their forbear was, 'but with all due respect to grandfather's memory, his arguments for the abolition of the death penalty have no validity.   Is that punishment not sanctioned by Mosaic law?'—and he backed up this unexpected argument by pointing out that anyway it was not valid in certain cases, such as during coups d'état.   More logically, perhaps, he saw some need of qualification in an opinion of Beccaria's (quoted by Helvétius, and very much of its period) that all men are born with the same capacities, and that everyone could be made to write and talk in the same way if they were given equal opportunities.

Such simplifications were not for one who, like Manzoni, based his life on the sober and ironic observation of the prismatic qualities of reality, however he might divagate in theory. But he retained much that had been filtered through Beccaria from the French Enlightenment. The combination of clarity and humanity, of sensibility and fantasy, the inquiring mind, all seem partly inherited from his maternal grandfather.

There were other heritages too. The occasional emotional instability, contained later in life by an iron will trained in the discipline of the Church, and transmuted into a subtle and pervasive ambivalence; the apathy alternating with bursts of nervous creative energy; the laziness (writing letters was an agony to both of them); the incapacity for long concentration; the breaking off of work at the slightest excuse. And, though most of their lives were spent in study, both founded European reputations on very few works.

But allied to the humanitarianism in Beccaria there was a certain careless—and rather endearing—epicureanism, which his grandson could not but have deplored. In an article on 'The Pleasures of Imagination' in *Il Caffè* Beccaria had written: 'A thing which you will find most apt to your purpose' (he was advising a young philosopher)

is to acquire a little philosophic indolence in human things, both in affairs and in the search for truth. Let men fight, hope, or die, you repose gently on that enlightened indifference to human things which does not prevent your enjoying the very lively pleasures of bring just and beneficent, yet saves you useless worries about the tormenting alternations of good and evil, which are continuously jolting those who are unwarily convinced that they are the major part of life.

His grandson, equipped both with the logical clarity of the Enlightenment and the turgid and compelling experience of the Revolution, was to be dogged all his life by this same 'useless worry about the tormenting alternations of good and evil.'

CHAPTER TWO

Background; Education; Early Influences, including that of Parini

I

Enlightened groups within the upper classes are apt to link themselves together in private systems of defence. Most of the members of the Società del Caffè, like the Ideologists under Napoleon, the Fabians in Edwardian England, or the anti-Fascist intelligentsia in pre-war Italy, seem to have been related or connected in various ways, or to have lived together so closely that their relationships, with their attendant dependencies, criticisms, and squabbles, took on the qualities of links by blood and family. With the Società del Caffè the same names, Verri, Beccaria, Imbonati, Melzi d'Eril, crop up again and again in the most varied connections, dynastic, political, literary, or even business.

These family links might be legal or not. Cesare Beccaria's second marriage in 1774, a month after the death of his first wife, to Donna Anna Barbò, made him a cousin of the Verris. But Pietro Verri had been for years the *cavalier servente* of his sister. Now a new and stronger link was to be forged, the result of which was almost certainly Alessandro Manzoni.

Pietro and Alessandro Verri had a younger brother, Giovanni, who, after serving some years in the Order of Malta and travelling the Mediterranean in its galleys, had returned home and dedicated the rest of his life to pleasure and the humanities. He was a man of some originality. For years after his brothers had abandoned their faith either in the principles or actualities of revolution, he persisted in his new beliefs, even during the disillusioning period of the Cisalpine Republic. Some historians have hinted that this may have been due to his character being both less acute and less reflective than his brother's. Be that as it may, we find him, under the date 'Mirabello, 7 Frigifero, Anno P.' of the Cisalpine Republic, publicly renouncing his Cross of Malta. As late as 1809, though by now he had succumbed to the charm of the Viceroy Eugène, he was writing:

18

'Divorce, marriage of priests, abolition of verbal confession . . .
these are my favourite opinions.' It was due to this provocative
and attractive person that the first family rows began in the
Manzoni household in October 1782, only a month after Donna
Giulia Beccaria's marriage to Don Pietro Manzoni.

Both Don Giovanni and the sprightly Donna Giulia had been
for years assiduous frequenters of the evening parties given by
various members of the Società del Caffè. As described in the
memoirs of Giuseppe Gorani these evenings sound both stimulating and varied. The mixed society of 'wits, savants, ex-
Jesuits, and ex-opera singers' also included Frisi, the greatest
mathematician in the peninsula ('very proud of his legs'), an
Irish beauty, Contessa Masserati, née Elizabeth Brady, who had
been brought up in Hungary and spoke eight languages, and La
Fogliazza, the mistress of the Imperial Chancellor Kaunitz and
the wife of Angiolini, one of the earliest choreographers of
ballet. There were also two particularly well-informed, gay,
and tolerant ex-Jesuits, members of the Arese family. In this
society 'the supporters of despotism, bigots, fanatics, egoists,
and above all the ignorant could not deceive for long.' 'Among
the members there was high thinking and mutual regard, and
never did boredom or discord appear.' Gorani describes an
evening at Don Giovanni Verri's in the early 1780s, at which the
two other Verri brothers and three members of the Imbonati
family were present. There too was 'Giulia, daughter of
Beccaria, married to a gentleman by the name of Manzoni. She
was the adored of the Chevalier Verri; and as she had a great deal
of wit, and as it was decorated with a great variety of knowledge,
she added much by her intelligent talk, and by the graces with
which she was adorned, to the pleasure given us by the amiable
and instructive conversation.'

Don Giovanni's role seems to have been that of mentor and
intellectual godfather, as well as lover to Donna Giulia. Though
physically such affairs are seldom enduring or satisfactory, this,
it seems likely, had one very lasting result. The evidence for
Don Giovanni being the father of Alessandro Manzoni is as conclusive as gossip can make it. The baldest and also the crudest
statement is by a neighbour and family enemy, Baron Pietro
Custodi, whose fragmentary memoirs, together with his vast

B

collection of—largely unsorted—historical documents of the period, are now in the Bibliothèque Nationale in Paris. Custodi's story is that Donna Giulia had decided to apply for a divorce from Don Pietro Manzoni on the grounds of nullity ('con il fondato motivo di essere Don Pietro inabile al matrimonio per mancanza di testicoli') when she was actually with child, and only the entreaties of her friends persuaded her to abandon the idea. These friends, including her next lover, Taglioretti, according to Custodi, acknowledged Don Giovanni as the father. Niccolò Tommaseo, whether or not he took his facts from Custodi, to whose memoirs he is unlikely to have had access, stated the parenthood quite openly in his account of conversations with Manzoni which took place in the 1830s. 'Manzoni,' he wrote, 'also talked of Pietro Verri with reverence, all the more as he knows, and his mother does not attempt to hide it, that he is a nephew, being the son of a brother of his who was a Knight of Malta.' At the time of Alessandro Manzoni's first marriage in 1808, Gorani, with his flair for plunging headlong into scandal, wrote to his old friend Don Giovanni Verri: 'So Donna Giulia has got her and . . . son off with the daughter of the Blondels,' leaving three dots for what can only be the personal pronoun—indicating Don Giovanni himself. Finally a member of the Visconti di San Vito family, who kept a diary throughout the late eighteenth and early nineteenth centuries, full of such hair-raising details about the provenance of most of the Milanese aristocracy from ostlers and footmen that the document has been hidden away and never thoroughly examined even to-day, wrote: 'This Alessandro was already born when the Beccaria became the mistress of Imbonati, and Giulia used to say that Alessandro belonged to the Cavaliere Verri, whose mistress she was for some years.'

If, as Tommaseo states, Manzoni knew this himself (and Donna Giulia does not seem to have been a woman capable of hiding anything), it provides a first clue to the paradoxical threads in the character of a man in whom nothing, including his very origins, is quite what it seems. The story is not belied by Donna Giulia's subsequent history. She had inherited, obviously, a good deal of her father's intuitive intelligence ('She could have been our Mme de Staël had she not been too modest,' an admirer and friend, Compagnoni, went so far as to say), but in her private life she took after her flighty mother, though perhaps with less experimental an urge, for she kept her affections within the circle of the Società del Caffè. After what turned out to be a short-lived affair with Verri (who spent the last twenty years of his life immersed in a *ménage à trois* at Como), and another with Taglioretti, she finally obtained a legal separation, not a divorce, and took off for Paris in 1796 with Count Carlo Imbonati, who was to be the great love of her life. He was the son of the Maecenas who had revived the Academy of the Trasformati a generation before, and had presumably been one of the Imbonatis present at the party described by Gorani. With him Donna Giulia lived in happy devotion, as well as riches and comfort, until his early death in Paris in 1805.

This liaison, by sending Donna Giulia off to settle in Paris, was to lead to her son's renewing and deepening the family links with France, and so to the great influences which were to shape his life.

II

Don Pietro Manzoni may have first come into contact with Count Pietro Verri through a mutual interest in new methods of agriculture. He was a childless widower of forty-seven when through the mediation of Verri, and possibly of Parini, a marriage was arranged between him and the almost portionless Giulia, then just twenty. This seems to have been imposed on Giulia, and the negotiations pushed through in spite of her by Verri and her father. The wedding took place in the Beccaria chapel in Milan on 12th September 1782. The match scarcely justified the cooing doves entwined on the wedding invitation. Disagreements began almost immediately. They were a peculiarly ill-suited couple. A sketch of her by Mrs Cosway,[1]

[1] Mary Cosway remained a lifelong friend of Donna Giulia. On separating from her husband, the miniaturist Richard Cosway, she had settled in Paris, where she became an intimate of Thomas Jefferson, then American ambassador. She remained in Paris throughout the Revolution and the Napoleonic Wars, until, having given up painting and taken to teaching, she founded in 1812 a girls' school, the Casa delle Dame Inglese, at Lodi. This precursor of many similar ventures by English ladies in Europe became the most elegant school in the north of Italy. Through Donna Giulia's interest two of Manzoni's daughters were educated there. In 1834 Mrs Cosway was created Baronessa Cosway by the Austrian emperor for her educational work.

painted either when she first arrived in Paris or when she visited
London a few years later with Imbonati, gives an impression, with
the reddish hair, mobile mouth, very white skin, and green eyes,
of an unusual if brittle vitality and charm.   And Don Pietro
was no Othello to conquer and hold a Desdemona by mature
masculinity.   His portrait shows a pale, indifferent face peering
out from under its incongruously lively *perruque*. He was, in
fact, we learn from Alessandro, a cold, withdrawn, and rather em-
bittered man, whose only interest was looking after his country
estates.   But his income was good, while old Beccaria could only
give his daughter five thousand crowns as a wedding portion.

The Manzoni family were solid provincial squirearchy, land-
owners, soldiers, merchants, and lawyers, settled for some
hundred and fifty years around Lecco on the lake of Como, where
they owned the country estate of Il Caleotto, and the fief of
Moncucco near by.   By origin they were a mountain clan from
the Valsassina in the Alps, and the name is found all over
Northern Italy in various forms.   There is a Palazzo Manzoni,
belonging to another branch of the family, on the Grand Canal
in Venice, and part of the village of Monforte in Piedmont is
called I Manzon, as at one time every inhabitant of the quarter
bore the name.   Though lords of all they surveyed in their own
part of the country, where they were notorious for their
haughty pride, Don Pietro's family were small fry in Milan compared to the superb patricians of the city, the Borromeos, the
Trivulzios, the Belgiojosos.   The Manzoni family had indeed
succeeded in having 'the quality of its blood' recognized by the
Heraldic Tribunal in 1771, yet the name does not figure in any
of the Golden Books of the Milanese nobility.   The title of
count, which is now often added to Alessandro Manzoni's name,
was applied for by Don Pietro just before the Revolution, and
the claim withdrawn; but Monsignor Paolo Manzoni, Don
Pietro's brother, persisted in his efforts until he was able to get
a copy of the family arms (in duplicate) accepted by the Town
Hall of Milan in 1821.   Yet in spite of Monsignor Manzoni's
insistence, Alessandro had refused to renew the claim of nobility
after 1815, when the Austrians were anxious to distribute titles
to prospective adherents.

About this he held consistently to the position he had taken

Donna Giulia Manzoni Beccaria. From a sketch by Mary Cosway in
the Braidense Library, Milan

up in youth.   There is a story that when he was eighteen, on his
way back from Venice in 1804, he strayed into a noble's club in
Vicenza in mistake for a café.   When asked by the waiter if he
were noble, in which case he could stay, he replied: 'There
aren't these distinctions in our country any more, and I don't
know if I was noble under the last Government, as it seemed so
unimportant that I never bothered to find out.'   Chilled perhaps
by so careless an attitude on a subject dear to most of the inhabitants of Vicenza, which boasted more nobles than any other
city in Italy, local historians have tried to show that this anecdote
must be apocryphal, as no café in the city at that time could
possibly have been mistaken for a nobles' club.   A few years
later Manzoni used to smile when the Napoleonic officers, lovers
of titles, called him 'Count.'   'I am not a count or even noble,
I am Alessandro Manzoni.'   And towards the end of his life his
final comment on the subject was: 'Those who call me "Count"
show that they have never read all my works through, which is
one of the sins that an author, however little self-esteem he may
have, never forgives.'

The advantages and disadvantages of class he saw with the
penetration of a La Rochefoucauld.   Sismondi, in his *History of the
Italian Republics*, had remarked: 'One can regard the privileges
of birth as unjust, but discrimination against birth is even more
unjust,' and Manzoni noted sombrely in the margin of his copy
of the book: 'Les privilèges de la naissance sont nécessairement
des privilèges contre la naissance.'   (The privileges of birth
necessarily work both ways.)

Round Lecco the Manzoni family had long had the reputation
of being the terror of the district, a memory perhaps of the
fearful Don Ercole Manzoni of a century before, who had constantly done away with guests through an oubliette in the dining-
room floor and finally, so tradition had it, vanished on his
death-bed, leaving a strong smell of brimstone.   His ghost still
rode the valley in the mid nineteenth century, and in 1850 was
said to have killed a peasant with fright.

> Cuzzi, Piovena, e Manzon
> Minga intendan di reson.

Cuzzi, Piovena, and Manzoni never listened to reason, went

the saying in the local dialect: Cuzzi being another famous local family of tyrants and the Piovena a raging torrent from the mountains. Massimo d'Azeglio, who was married for a short time to Manzoni's daughter, noted during a visit he once paid to the Manzoni estates at Lecco: 'They say the old folk of the family used in feudal days to have a great dog to which, when it went through the village, the peasants were obliged to doff their hats and say: "My respects, my Lord Dog."' From the first young Alessandro reacted against this crude provincial pride, so different to the enlightened self-esteem of the Beccaria circle. This repugnance was expressed in his description in *I Promessi Sposi*, clearly based on a visual memory, of Don Rodrigo's walk under the portraits of his ancestors after dismissing Fra Cristoforo.

Don Rodrigo . . . was pacing with long strides up and down this apartment, whose walls were hung with various generations of family portraits. When he reached a wall and turned round, he would find himself facing one of his warrior ancestors, the terror of his enemies and his own men, with his grim aspect, cropped straight hair, twirling pointed mustachios standing out from his cheeks, and receding chin: the hero was standing encased in proof armour, with greaves, cuisses, breast-plate, brassards, and gauntlets, his right hand on his hip and his left on the hilt of his sword. Don Rodrigo gazed at him; and on getting up to him and turning round, there he was facing another ancestor, a magistrate, the terror of litigants and lawyers, who sat in a great arm-chair upholstered in red velvet, wrapped in an ample black robe. Everything about him was black, except for a white collar with two broad lapels and facings of sable (it was the distinctive senatorial dress and worn only in winter, which is why one never finds a portrait of a senator in summer clothes); he was spare with frowning brows; in his hand he held a petition and seemed to be saying: 'We'll see about that.' On this side was a matron, the terror of her servants; over there an abbot, the terror of his monks—all people, in fact, who had inspired terror, and still breathed it from their canvases.

This early loathing of the haughty and the overbearing was deepened by an uncertainty of standing (overruled, of course, as he became more famous) due both to the differences of rank between provincial squirearchy and city patricians, and also to the series of family scandals in which both he and his mother openly flouted the rules of a superficially conventional society.

In *I Promessi Sposi* Manzoni seems to identify himself in turn with the independent confidence of the great noble, the 'Unnamed,' and the aspirations and renunciations of the young merchant, Lodovico. Renzo's anarchic simplicity must have seemed a blessed, though perhaps temporary and ineffective, relief.

III

Alessandro was born in Milan on 7th March 1785 at 20 Via San Damiano (now 16 Via Uberto Visconti di Modrone), over-looking one of the typical canals of the old Naviglio. Donna Giulia, it seems, insisted on setting up house in Milan to escape from provincial internment with her husband. Il Caleotto was always to hold unhappy memories for her of the short period of married life she had spent there.

In the eighty years since he died the Manzoni cult has grown to such proportions in Italy that there seems to be a commemora-tive tablet on almost every house in which he spent a night. The next plaque in date after that on his birth-place hangs on the Cascina Costa, a farm above Galbiate, a few miles from Lecco, where he was sent to wet-nurse for a month or two just after he was born:

> In questo casolare
> ebbe il primo nutrimento
> Alessandro Manzoni
> nell' anno 1785.

(In this cottage Alessandro Manzoni took his first nourishment in the year 1785.)

After his death the farmhouse became a place of pilgrimage, as can be seen in a picture in the manner of Tissot by Casimir Radice, showing a very old peasant who had played with the baby Alessandro recounting his memories to a group of young ladies in puckered pink. Still preserved there is a wattle cradle believed to have been used by Manzoni. 'It is the very cradle of a genius' (observed Professor Stoppani, when reverently collecting details for his book on Alessandro's childhood) 'who, almost as if conscious of himself even in the cradle, despises luxury and vanity, for they enervate the moral forces of man and use up his brain.'

The next six years were spent between this farm and the family home of Il Caleotto.   This is a good-sized country house with a long, formal façade hung at intervals with balconies, and facing out between cypresses over the lake and the sweeping mountains—the landscape which he was to make the background to *I Promessi Sposi*.

That branch of the lake of Como which extends southwards between the unbroken chains of mountains, and is all gulf and bays as the mountains advance and recede, narrows down at one point, between a promontory on one side and a wide shore on the other, into the form of a river: and the bridge which links the two banks seems to emphasize this transformation even more, and to mark the point where the lake ends and the Adda begins, only to become a lake once more where the banks draw farther apart again, letting the water broaden out and expand into new creeks and bays.

On one side, like a background by Bellini, stretches the gentle silvery countryside of Brianza.

Before long things came to a head at Il Caleotto between Don Pietro and Donna Giulia.   Quarrels between husband and wife had reached such a pitch that it was decided to send the child to school long before the normal time, to get him away from the family atmosphere.   From the first moments of the marriage Donna Giulia had found herself being watched by Don Pietro's brother, Monsignor Manzoni, and by a bevy of sisters, most of them nuns who were without convents as a result of the ecclesiastical reforms of Joseph II.   She was surrounded by criticism, all the more biting for being justified, particularly of her relations with Giovanni Verri.   Again and again Pietro Verri, who had some authority over her, intervened to keep the marriage going in the eyes of the world.   But by November 1791 Donna Giulia was writing to him, in her rushed, vivid prose, that she could not bear another moment of a household united against her. 'My husband, animated by a holy zeal, wants to get me into paradise at all costs by dint of making me suffer here on earth.' The nuns were spying on all her movements, the monsignor 'looking behind every picture.'   She ended by appealing to Pietro Verri to arrange a legal separation.   Verri finally faced the fact that he, the leader of Italian reformers, had arranged one of those 'Italian marriages of the horrible school of the fine world' which made Alfieri cry:

> Maraviglia sia
> Che in Italia il divorzio non s'adoperi
> Se il matrimonio Italico è un divorzio.

(How astounding that there is no divorce in Italy, when Italian marriage is itself a divorce.)

A few months after writing this letter Donna Giulia left home to visit an uncle, Don Michele de' Blasco. She was never to return to Il Caleotto until after Don Pietro Manzoni's death. She also refused to go back to her father's house, saying it had been made intolerable for her by his second wife. In a legal separation arranged in February 1782 Donna Giulia's little marriage portion was returned to her, and she was allowed to go on living with her uncle. But Donna Giulia was self-willed and energetic as well as beautiful and sprightly. To avoid dependence on her uncle she now demanded her share of a maternal inheritance left her under a sister's will, then being administered by her father. Beccaria refused to hand it over, saying that he was afraid of her wasting it. In 1794 Donna Giulia began a lawsuit against her father to gain control of the money. In the deposition she made for the court she reduced her age at the time of marriage to sixteen, and stated that she had been married against her will to a man who caused her 'aversion and disturbance.' Whether guided by Donna Giulia or not, her lawyer in his brief seemed to be trying to show that Cesare Beccaria's world-famous humanitarianism was at variance with his practice in the home. 'Family spirit,' poor Beccaria had written a few years before in an amiable generalization whose truth was now grimly to come home, 'is necessarily in contradiction to public spirit.' But the case never came to court, for on 28th November 1794 Beccaria suddenly died of an apoplectic stroke, brought on, some said, by his daughter's behaviour. The heir, her young half-brother Giulio, was much more amenable. Donna Giulia soon arranged her affairs with him and set up house on her own.

Don Michele de' Blasco, the uncle, with whom she had

* B

originally taken refuge, and the brother of the *capricciosa
marchesina*, Giulia's mother, who had come to such a sad end,
was devoted to his niece. It was he who encouraged and helped
her in a new and deepeningly satisfactory affair with Carlo
Imbonati (a help which Imbonati acknowledged when he made
his will at the time in 1795). A year later Giulia and Imbonati
set off together on their travels, and a new phase of her life
began—the happiness, finally, of fulfilled love. Such phases,
alas, are often short-lived.

IV

Meanwhile her son Alessandro was spending five miserable
years at the colleges of the Somaschi friars at Merate in Brianza,
and then at Lugano. When he arrived he had been the youngest
pupil. It had been agony to leave his mother, to whom he
remained devoted throughout life. One wonders if he did not
deceive himself slightly about her attitude to him, particularly
at this time when she had her own intense preoccupations. In
later life he used to recall how this parting had been so difficult
for her that she had slipped out while the headmaster was
talking to them in his study on their arrival. Suddenly the little
boy found himself alone with the headmaster, 'this unknown
whom I never had any desire to know,' as he later called him.
He broke into sobs; at this the headmaster turned and cuffed
him, growling: 'Why don't you stop snivelling?'—an introduction to school life which made a deep and lasting impression.
Revisiting the school in 1869, four years before he died, his eye
fell on the picture of Christ carrying a great cross, still hanging
in the same place in the headmaster's room, on which his eyes
had been fixed at the moment of that cuffing over seventy years
before. And the famous old man fell into a profound and
melancholy reverie.

In the holidays, during the long summers above the lake, the
little boy was left to himself. Don Pietro seems to have held
more or less aloof. He never visited him at school, only
occasionally sending over an old bailiff to report on the boy's
progress. The gulf between Don Pietro and Alessandro was
from the beginning far wider than the normal one between the

generations, or the abnormal one due to the family circumstances. Whether Tommaseo, who was notoriously inaccurate,
had reported truthfully that conversation about Alessandro's
knowledge of his parentage, we shall never know. Certainly,
even immediately after Don Pietro's death, Alessandro's references to him were extraordinarily cold. Even apart from this,
and from his passionate attachment to his 'advanced' young
mother, there were other differences. Don Pietro was an old
traditionalist: he looked back, while Alessandro already as a
schoolboy was looking forward, with that eagle eye of the early
portrait. And the gulf between youth and age must have
seemed far wider in the 1790s than ever before.

v

The irruption of the French Revolutionary armies into the
Milanese provinces in May 1796 caused Alessandro's sudden
removal to another college of the same Order in a safer area,
across the Swiss border at Lugano. He had watched the troops
pass through Merate amid the enthusiasm of the population, an
enthusiasm which had seeped into the school, for all the young
pupils cut off their pigtails, symbols of the old formal world, in
token of sympathy with the natural followers of Rousseau. One
of his priestly biographers goes out of his way to point out that
Alessandro was very sorry for this in later life, which may well
be; according, however, to the headmaster's letter to Don
Pietro at the time, he was one of the ringleaders. This seems
to have been an unusual self-assertion, for he was a quiet, withdrawn boy with nothing outstanding about him. Often later
he complained of the bullying he had had to endure at school
from his contemporaries, though older boys sometimes protected him from too much violence. 'But what will happen
then?' he would say to himself, according to an account he gave
a schoolmaster in later life. 'The protectors who arrogate the
power of protecting me will want to be paid back afterwards—
then they'll tire of me and leave me to the mercy of the majority,
who'll then take revenge on me for the protection I've been
given.' Whether this detached and somewhat dialectical
analysis was made by the boy at the time, or by the old man in

reverie over his youth, certainly his experience as a shy and
sensitive schoolboy gave him a lifelong sickener of cliques,
coteries, and self-constituted secret societies formed to impose
their power on others, and a loathing of those who settle problems by brute force.

A kindly memory from the second school was an old school-
master, Father Francesco Soave, one of the leading Sensist philosophers of the day and a prominent anti-Revolutionary Jesuit,
who was also at Lugano to avoid the French.   He was probably
the first to sense the quiet little boy's talent and originality—
which did not prevent him getting furious with Alessandro for
insisting on writing the words 'king,' 'emperor,' and 'pope'
without capital letters.   This was a tribute, like the cutting of
the pigtails, to the influence of his mother's circle.

Looking back Alessandro realized how little he had learned
at school apart from the classics.   'Good folk,' he said of his
teachers years later, 'though as educators one could have wished
that they had been a little more educated themselves.'   Alfieri
has left a description in his autobiography of his own schooling
in Turin a few years before this.   What had particularly struck
him was the falsity and confusion of all presentation of ideas,
and the masters' indifference as to whether they aroused interest
or not.

The lesson of peripatetic philosophy held after the midday meal was
a matter of sleeping sitting upright.   In the first half-hour in fact we
wrote the course dictated by the teacher; in the next three-quarters
of an hour, while the teacher explained this in Latin, God only knows
what kind of Latin, all we scholars spelt most soundly, each wrapped
in our huge cloaks; and the only other sound to be heard—apart from
the languishing voice of the teacher, who was nodding a bit himself—
was the various tones of the snorers, some high, some low, some
medium, making a most excellent concert.[1]

Studies at this school, as Manzoni told a friend in later life,
concentrated on mastering Latin and history, particularly Roman
history during the Punic wars.   So pervasive was the effect of
this that the boys even formed sides for Romans and Carthaginians, which would line up in the playground and fall on each
other.   Alessandro was always on the side of the Carthaginians

[1] From the anonymous English translation of 1810.

as, from what he had heard of the Romans so far, he found them too overbearing; but the Carthaginians, being the weaker side, were apt to get beaten. Although he ended this account by deploring the whole education of the period, the classical teaching of the Somaschi and Barnabite Fathers had been so efficient that it influenced his literary taste for life. Under their stern discipline he not only mastered Latin grammar, but acquired a lasting taste for Latin literature. Though he had an abnormally bad memory for everything else, so bad that he is said to have quoted his own works thinking he was quoting others, according to Cantù he knew all Virgil and Horace by heart, and even composed Latin epigrams for his own amusement. He was reading a Latin poem on his death-bed.

At the third and worst of his schools, the Nobles' College in Milan, now the Longone, he wrote a hymn of hate in Latin. This poem he kept until nearly the end of his life, when he destroyed it in his study fire after reading it out to the parish priest at Brusuglio. His verses seem to have made him a certain reputation at this last school, for on leaving his portrait was hung with those of other pupils distinguished by brains or blood.

But it was a miserable time. His adored mother he saw very seldom. Since her departure with Carlo Imbonati when he was eleven she had made only rare and fleeting visits to Italy. Don Pietro took no interest at all, and the food, supplied by robbing contractors, was filthy. This, as well as the literary fare, may have been in his mind when he wrote later:

> . . . nodrito
> In sozzo ovil di mercenario armento,
> Gli aridi bronchi fastidendo, e il pasto
> De l'insipida stoppia, il viso torsi
> De la fetente mangiatoia; e franco
> M'addussi al sorso de l'ascrea fontana.

(Nourished in the filthy pen of a mercenary flock, disgusted by the meals of dry husks and insipid straw, I turned my face from the foul troughs and went to drink at the fountain of Hesiod.)

Although years later he regretted to Cantù having used 'such bold and arrogant words in criticizing his priestly teachers,' his whole experience of school was so disastrous that he kept his

own sons to be educated at home—with, it may be added, no
very satisfactory results.

VI

One advantage of this last college, when it moved back to
Milan, was that he was able to get books from outside: these he
read through recreation times, munching a loaf of bread the
while to stave off hunger. The school texts for contemporary
literature were the Arcadians of fifty years before. Missing,
perhaps, amid all the paraphernalia of shepherds' crooks and
pipes, the polished technical charm of such authors as Frugoni
and Bettinelli, he acquired only a distaste for the Arcadians'
falsification of the simple life. His favourite reading was the
odes of Monti or the solemn invocations against tyranny of
Alfieri. Once, as he sat reading on the school steps, the headmaster passed with a group of distinguished visitors, one of whom
was Vincenzo Monti, the most celebrated poet of the day.
Monti, perhaps because the shy boy had been pointed out as the
grandson of Beccaria, stopped to say a few words. To one
sitting absorbed in reading the poet's stirring ode, *La Basvilliana*,
the visitor seemed like the apparition of a god.

But with Monti as with Alfieri Alessandro's period of un-
critical adoration was short. He had defended Alfieri in 1803
against the attacks of a school friend, Gianbattista Pagani: 'You
write to me of Alfieri, whose life, according to your way of
thinking, is a proof of his mad, proud fury for independence.
According to mine, it's a model of the pure, uncontaminated,
true virtue of a man who feels his own dignity and never makes
a step for which he could blush.' What made him first doubt
his hero was Alfieri's fanatical loathing for France. From then
on his criticisms broadened. 'His only feeling,' he said to
Cantù in the 1830s, 'was hatred of kings, whom he called
tyrants, and priests, whom he called impostors'; and when
Cantù protested that Alfieri 'wanted citizens to be virtuous so
that they could be free,' Manzoni shook his head and said:

Alfieri was not a liberal, was not a patriot, was not a democrat.
Just read his autobiography. He complained of not having any
children because of its always being sad to see an illustrious family die

out. He protested he was a citizen only of the world, yet when all the thinkers like Beccaria, Filangieri, Galiani, Ricci, and Verri were trying to obtain concessions from kings, all he did was curse them.

Perhaps the deepest and most lasting of his influences at this period were the odes and satires of the 'divin' Parini, the mentor and friend of so many of his relations and connections. They never met, and it was while Alessandro was reading one of Parini's odes at school that he heard of his death. Though the circumstances of their lives were very different there was some affinity of temperament and approach between them, particularly in their hatred of cant. Like Manzoni, Parini was visually and emotionally influenced by the landscape of the elegiac region of the Brianza, in which he had been brought up as the son of poor peasants. He had taken orders, like most of the poor literary men of the day, more out of convenience than conviction, and most of his life was spent in the unwilling service of the rich. A 'poor priest in a hot town,' tutoring at the Serbellonis' and the Imbonatis', he had watched and judged, as he sat ignored and snubbed in a corner, the fashionable world of Milan. His long poem, *Il Giorno*, of which 'Morning' and 'Midday' were published in 1763 and 1765 (the plan was adapted partly from Thompson's *Seasons*, translations of which were then very popular in Italy), showed up with a polished irony and a mastery of visual detail the follies and vapidity of a dandy's existence. Perhaps no other poem except *The Rape of the Lock* tells us so much about the details of social customs of the day; Pope seems also to have inspired some of the satire, with the young fop replacing Belinda. But Parini had read Voltaire and Rousseau as well as Pope, and the poem has a depth of purpose belied by the cumbrous latinisms and obscurity of the language.

At a gathering at Rosmini's in the summer of 1852 the literary gossip Ruggiero Bonghi asked Manzoni what he thought of Parini then. 'It's easy, perhaps, to judge badly in old age the things one has admired greatly in youth,' came the considered reply, 'but his odes seem the best we Italians have and among the loveliest ever written.' But Parini did not come off without a scratch. Another time in later life Manzoni criticized in a rather malicious aside his exaltation of the simple life. 'With all his democracy, with all his desire to sing of the diligent

peasant boy and the pretty peasant girl, and to bind himself, not
in cords of noble gold, but in simple themes close to nature,
the beautiful women he celebrated were always countesses or
marchionesses—La Castiglione, La Castelbarco. I made the
acquaintance of La Tron [the most famous Venetian beauty of
the late eighteenth century, praised by Parini]. She looked to
me like a big Venetian slattern, and I could not bring myself
to believe that she was the *donna d'incliti pregi'* (woman of
illustrious worth). But in spite of this understandable weakness Parini's hatred of privilege went so deep that at one time it
even included the noble reformer, Pietro Verri himself, whose
argument that luxury was necessary in order to provide work for
the poor is the object of a passage of biting irony in *Il Giorno*.

Verri and Parini only grew to appreciate each other when they
found themselves side by side in the new Milanese administration
at the entry of the French in 1796. Before he died Parini's
idealism, too, was disillusioned by the shortcomings of the Cisalpine Republic. That same evening at Rosmini's Manzoni told a
story of Parini at a theatre during the French occupation. The
play had been interrupted by a *radicale di dozzina* (twopenny-
halfpenny radical), who got up and shouted: 'Viva la Republica:
death to tyrants!' At which the old man rose up in his box and
shouted in reply: 'Viva la Republica: death to no one!' There
is another story of Parini entering his new office at the Milan
Town Hall after the French entry and asking why the crucifix had
been taken away. 'Because Christ has done nothing for
liberty,' was the answer. 'When citizen Christ doesn't enter,'
replied the old priest, 'citizen Parini doesn't either.' And he
put on his hat and walked out. He could have been so sure of
himself in such circumstances only if he was no bigot. In his
later approach to religion Parini combined many of the theories
of Rousseau with a broad form of Christianity, which has its
affinities with Manzoni's. As he grew older he left behind both
the crude and savage satire of his earlier odes and of the first part
of *Il Giorno*, and also the stock romantic emotions which owed
much to Young's *Night Thoughts*. His verses at the end of his
life breathe a simple humanity, an intimate lyrical message,
which made him, as De Sanctis observed, much more 'the new
man in an old society' than Monti or Alfieri ever were.

CHAPTER THREE

The French Occupation; First Contact with the World; Youthful Friendships with Monti and Neapolitan Exiles

I

The disillusion with the French in Lombardy after the first wild enthusiasm of 1796 had not been due so much to the widening gaps between theory and practice, the dishonesty of many of the French commissioners, or even the vast contributions levied on Italian towns, but to the personal behaviour of the French troops quartered on the inhabitants.

From his last school, which he had joined in September 1798 at Castellazzo, near Magenta, when it had evacuated its building in Milan for the Cisalpine soldiery, Manzoni had watched that autumn the retreat of the French troops before the Austro-Russian offensive. In behaviour there does not seem to have been much to choose between the French and the Cossacks. While the French general Duprez wrote home light-heartedly: 'Here everyone steals,' the Italian deputy-governor Melzi commented sadly. 'No one so brutal and rapacious has descended into Italy since the *Landsknechte*.' In April 1799 Russian troops broke into the wine-vaults of Il Caleotto at Lecco. They broached the wine-casks and, rolling drunk, were just about to kill the old custodian when he was saved by a French soldier jumping in through the window. In the French attack which followed the drunken Russians were massacred in dozens, so that the floor of the wine-vault 'was carpeted with their corpses.' Another story whispered in the family was of the terrible adventures of Donna Maddalena Isimbardi, Cesare Beccaria's sister, who had been in the hands of the Cossacks for three days before she managed to escape. The behaviour of the French armies, together with the Russian reprisals by Cossack troops, impressed itself so vividly on young Manzoni that the moving and horrifying notes on foreign occupation in *I Promessi Sposi* are undoubtedly drawn from memories of personal observations at this period. 'Finally they were going; they had gone; the sounds of their drums and fifes were heard dying far away. Followed a few hours of terrified quiet. And then another hateful rumble of drums, another hateful blare of trumpets, would announce a new squadron.'

When the French returned in 1799 rapid reforms were introduced to wipe away unpleasant memories of their first occupation. The Treaty of Lunéville in 1801, by confirming the Cisalpine, Ligurian, Batavian, and Helvetian Republics, aroused once more the flagging enthusiasm of many of the Italian middle and lower classes for the French, and won them into accepting a French protectorate over the peninsula. This, declared the First Consul, was designed to draw the various Italian states together in mutual economic interests and administration, and to be the forerunner of an independent Italy. But a delegation of responsible Milanese who went to visit him at the palace of Monza was chilled by hearing him remark that: 'The Italian people, enervated by centuries of bondage, are unfitted for liberty or independence.' But the wave of pro-French sympathy continued, particularly in Lombardy and the reconstituted Cisalpine Republic, as some of the excesses of the Austro-Russian reaction had been worse than anything the French had done. Even so the flogging of pro-French patriots and the forced labour of high functionaries of state ordered by the Austrians had been in no way comparable to the bestial Anglo-Bourbon reprisals on the Parthenopean republicans of Naples in 1799.

The heirs of the Società del Caffè took an active part in the new French Lombard administration. Among the four prominent Milanese who were summoned to Paris in 1801, to advise on the drawing up of a new constitution for Lombardy, were Melzi d'Eril, a lifelong friend of Donna Giulia, and the young Duca Serbelloni, liberal product of the tutorship of Parini. But there was a weakening of character since the days of the Verri brothers. The result of this conference in Paris was a compromise between the soothing of interests threatened by reform and the introduction of measures calculated to draw the approval of the rising middle classes. One of the rewards for radical support was a promise of independence—that will-o'-the-wisp of small landlocked peoples. But when four hundred and fifty deputies met at Lyons at the beginning of 1802 and proceeded, under the First Consul's guidance, to elect the chief officers of the new state, in their ingenuous enthusiasm they elected Melzi himself as head of the republic. The choice, they found, was strongly disapproved of; their guide, Talleyrand, gently enlightened the dismayed deputies—Bonaparte expected to be elected himself. The new president, duly elected, consoled them for the disappointment by announcing, at the last sitting of the commission in January 1802, that henceforward the name 'Cisalpine' would be substituted by 'Italian.' This experiment in semantics was greeted by wild applause, and even hailed by Alfieri as the first step towards that 'Italia virtuosa, magnanima, ed unita' of nationalist dreams.

This second Cisalpine Republic, under the control of Melzi d'Eril as Bonaparte's deputy, and of the Finance Minister, General Prina, turned out to be an able administration. Between them the two reorganized all the chief departments of state. The finances were reordered, public education reformed, and the universities of Pavia and Bologna, which had been closed by the Austrians, reopened. But by now the Lombards, particularly in the outlying towns and districts hankering after federation, were beginning to think themselves capable of keeping order in their own house, and there were continuous complaints against the French army of occupation. Some of the local Jacobin leaders found a sympathetic ear in Joachim Murat, the commander of the army of occupation, who encouraged them in intoxicating terms. 'You will be free,' he declared expansively, his splendid uniform glittering, his handsome face beaming, 'and you are more sure of being so than the French. Milan will be your capital, the Rivers Oglio and Senio your frontiers. You will embrace the two seas and you will have a fleet.'

Unimpressed, the vice-president, Melzi, noted: 'The feeling of animosity against the French is universal.' But Melzi was a great landowner, 'a citizen in Lombardy and a grandee in Spain,' who, according to the ever-malicious Custodi, 'hid the mediocrity of his talents and knowledge under a Spanish gravity.' Behind him now were grouping the conservative interests in Northern

Italy. The Jacobins complained to Murat, who reported to Paris that Melzi was disloyal. In reply Murat suddenly found himself withdrawn and consoled with the governorship of Paris. For Napoleon was now wooing the established classes, who might help him assume the Iron Crown of Lombardy.

II

Early in 1801, his formal education completed at the age of sixteen, young Alessandro found himself settled in Don Pietro's house near the Porta Tosa in Milan. Whether by carelessness or benevolent intention on Don Pietro's part, these next four years of adolescence were spent in comparative freedom. Alessandro alternated between Milan and lengthy periods, particularly during summer and autumn, at Il Caleotto. The long days amid the flowing, interlocked lines of landscape were to remain in his mind's eye from these summers of childhood and adolescence, to be recalled poignantly after Il Caleotto was sold and the lakes and mountains left for the dusty plain.

In Milan he followed the lectures at the Brera by Pietro Signorelli on dramatic poetry; he also attended the University of Pavia, particularly the flamboyant and rousing orations by Monti, who had just managed to get the appointment to the new Chair of Poetry. At Pavia, too, he listened to the leading philosophic Jansenist in Italy, Giuseppe Zola, recently reinstated by Napoleon. Attendance at these lectures was rather spasmodic, and he never took a degree.

The youth with the quiet manner and the fiery eyes also plunged into direct experience of city life. At home he found a teacher ready to introduce him to this branch of knowledge— an aunt, an ex-nun, one of Don Pietro's numerous sisters, who had been torn from her convent by ecclesiastical reforms, not entirely, it seems, to her disgust. 'I myself,' she would say, 'agree with Joseph II. Air! Air!' and she would wave an arm as if thrusting away something that prevented her breathing. If she was one of the sisters who had spied on Donna Giulia she did not visit the sins of the mother on the son. She seems to have been a temperamental woman, delighted to find someone in the house whom she could introduce to the ways of the world

which she herself had missed.   Alessandro used to recall his
innocent surprise at the liveliness of her instructions.   She was
carrying them on one day in the embrasure of a window when
they were suddenly interrupted by old Don Pietro and his
brother, Monsignor Manzoni, the canon of the cathedral.   The
smoothness with which she changed the subject astonished her
young pupil and introduced him to yet another way of the world.
This restless, frustrated nun made a great impression on him:
there seems a hint of her in the tragic Signora of Monza of *I
Promessi Sposi*, whose personal traits and character bear too warm
a stamp of experience to be drawn entirely from her wretched
historical original, Suor Virginia de Leyva.

With this aunt's encouragement, young Alessandro threw
himself into the brilliant life of a city which had just become a
European capital again for the first time since the Renaissance.
After the upheavals of the last few years there was something
feverish about the life of the cafés, of the balls and theatres, of
the clubs where, under the green-shaded lights, entire patri-
monies and new-formed fortunes were gambled away in a night.
Milan was already the first city of Italy in literature, industry, and
social enterprise.   Within a year or two, with Eugène de Beauharnais as viceroy, it was to have one of the most brilliant and
lively courts in Europe.   Italy was always Napoleon's favourite
country after France, partly because of his origins and partly,
perhaps, because of the adulation of him in certain circles in
Milan.   When he became emperor a Milanese senator was said
to have 'begged God to preserve the throne of Napoleon if He
wanted to maintain His own'—an opinion supported later by
the fresco of Napoleon's apotheosis on the ceiling of the Madeleine in Paris.   But there was always a small radical opposition
to him in Milan, led then by the poet Foscolo and by his mistress
of the day, one of the most beautiful women in Lombard
society, the Contessa Cicognara.   Once at a gala night at
the Scala for the First Consul, young Manzoni—it was 1801
and he was just sixteen—was sitting in her box, which was
directly opposite that of the hero.   For the entire evening
Napoleon gazed steadily across at them, so that Alessandro and
his companion spent some hours 'under the hawklike eyes of the
dominator of Europe.'   'What eyes!   What eyes that man had!'

Manzoni would recall in later life.   And in his ode on the death
of Napoleon, *Il Cinque Maggio*, there are lines which still recall
his emotion after twenty years: 'Chinati i rai fulminei!'

The sight of those fascinating and hypnotic eyes increased
Alessandro's admiration for Ugo Foscolo's moral courage.   For
a period he and Foscolo became close friends, and probably
Foscolo first introduced him to another nervous stimulant to
which the older poet was addicted all his life—gambling.   It
was while young Alessandro was in the grip of what he later
called 'that terrible passion that can in a short time turn a father
of a family into a parricide,' and gambling at the Ridotto of the
Scala, that he was clapped on the shoulder by Monti, with the
genial remark: 'Fine poems we'll be writing in the future if we
go on like this!'   Shaken, Alessandro went and told the story to
his mother, who was on one of her rare visits to Milan at the
time, and declared that he had resolved to give up gambling for
ever.   Donna Giulia, rather naturally, asked how he proposed
to keep this resolution, and, worldly woman that she was, suggested a trip to Paris with them as a distraction.   'What merit
would there be in that?' was her son's admirable but somewhat
priggish reply.   For a month he went and watched the gambling
at the Ridotto to steel himself against ever playing again—and
he never did.

Manzoni and Foscolo remained close friends for three years.
The youth was enthralled by the older man's independence of
mind and hatred of cant, his combination of thinker and man of
action, of poet, soldier, and revolutionary, his air of an anarchist
before his time.   'I have no friends and I don't need them,'
proclaimed Foscolo, when he found Monti, whom he had helped
and supported in an hour of trial, avoiding him at the time of
Napoleon's coronation; and it was probably Foscolo who first
made Alessandro turn a critical eye on his first mentor—an eye
which, for totally different reasons, he was soon to turn on
Foscolo himself.   Now Foscolo attacked Monti on literary
grounds too.

Gran traditor dei traduttor d'Omero,

he quipped about Monti's translation of Homer, and the criticism
was repeated by Manzoni.

The few years of Foscolo's friendship for Manzoni coincided with the young man's own period of open breaking of convention. Yet oddly enough what brought about the rupture between them was the coldness with which Donna Giulia received Foscolo when he visited Paris, as rather a seedy soldier, early in 1806. Donna Giulia's reaction to this frankly peculiar visitor may have been purely social, but Alessandro appears to have modelled his own behaviour on that of his formidable mother. Touchier than ever in misfortune, Foscolo was quick to take offence. 'By Manzoni I only want to be respected and nothing more,' was his first sharp comment. In 1816 he wrote rather sadly from exile at Hottingen to their mutual friend, Sigismondo Trechi:

I only regret his lack of constancy towards his friends. I put down to his youth, his weakness of character, and his mother's madness the coldness with which he received my visit—nor did he recognize in me the man who had, so to say, warmed his fine talent in my bosom; but I have forgiven him everything, and in the notes to my *Sepolcri*, written after my return to Italy, I did justice to his noble genius, and did not forget our former friendship.

In these notes, published in 1807, Foscolo had quoted some verses from the ode to Imbonati and called them 'the poetry of a young man, born to letters and warm with patriotism. I quote them in praise to show how much his distant friend remembers him.' They never met again, and this elegiac note did not prevent Foscolo making a bitter attack years later on Manzoni's verse-tragedies.

In Manzoni's conversations with his intimates during his last years there was very little mention of Foscolo, although his talk ranged over almost every Italian writer of the previous five hundred years. But once when Bonghi had said: 'I maintain that Foscolo is an unbearable writer' a murmured aside was heard from Manzoni: 'There are some things I think and don't say.'

III

Most of these early verses which Foscolo and Monti had seen and liked have now disappeared. They were probably burnt at the end of his life among the many early papers which, in sudden impulses of regret for the past, he would push into his study fire, and even sometimes, in summer, into the kitchen range. Even his later poems written before his conversion, such as *Urania* and *Carme in Morte di Carlo Imbonati*, would probably have suffered the same fate had they not already been published and distributed beyond recall. The early verses which escaped destruction throw considerable light on his interests and attitudes during this period. Among these were *Del Trionfo della Libertà*, a Parini-like ode in praise of the French Revolution, and a sonnet to one of the Neapolitan exiles from Bourbon tyranny, Francesco Lomonaco. In a curious little verse written between the ages of fifteen and sixteen, and only published some years after his death, he composed a portrait of himself, following in the footsteps of Alfieri and Foscolo. He began by observing his own physical characteristics with some approval: his dark hair, his round and coloured cheeks, his eloquent eyes, his high forehead, his nose 'not too small and not too big' (it was later to become too long); 'he now speaks slowly and now fast, never basely'; 'he speaks the truth openly or is silent'; 'he is young in years and young in sense'; 'he lacks boldness, is severe in manner but soft in heart, is good to the good, good to the wretched, but wretched only with him-self'; 'he is easily moved to anger but more easily to forgiveness.' 'La gloria amo e le selve e il biondo iddio.' (I love glory and the woods and the blond god.) And he ends with an adolescent's cry: 'Little known to others, little to myself: men and the years will tell me what I am.' The note of mild and somewhat lofty contempt for his fellows was in singular contrast, as an adoles-cent's reaction, to Stendhal's fierce memory of his own youth. 'J'exécrais tout le monde.'

Del Trionfo della Libertà was the first poem circulated by his friends in manuscript. From internal evidence it was written between the short Austro-Russian reoccupation of Northern Italy in 1798 and the Peace of Lunéville of 1801.

The poem reflects this period through the eyes of an idealistic youth. Manzoni seems to have kept a warm place for it in his memory, for he saved this from the flames, though he never allowed it to be published during his lifetime and it only saw the light in 1878, five years after his death. In a note in his hand-writing attached to the manuscript and found among his papers after his death (it was probably written in Paris in 1805, when he gave the manuscript to his school friend and fellow radical Pagani), he wrote:

I, Alessandro Manzoni, wrote these verses in the fifteenth year of my life, not without a certain pleasure and presumption in the name of poet. Rereading them now, with more understanding and perhaps with a subtler eye, I refute them; but not seeing in them any lie, obsequious praise, or anything unworthy of me, I recognize the sentiments in them as my own, as the follies of a young mind, and as the effusions of a pure and virile soul.

The poem is fiercely, almost demagogically, anti-clerical, full of the youth's aversion to religion, particularly to Catholicism. He blamed the Church for its pretensions to world dominion, the popes for using the mask of divine support to subjugate men's minds, undermine every moral law, and repress the movement of science. Later he made an attempt to explain such sentiments away, though in curiously tortuous terms. 'I protest,' he wrote of the early poems,

that here and in general I am writing of abuses. In fact anyone can see that I am not here touching principles of any kind. Besides, the Gospels praise meekness and the contempt of riches and power, and here I am attacking the cruelty and avidity of riches and power, all things diametrically opposed to the Gospel's principles, which are consequently diametrically opposed to those described here and to those people who find such abuses advantageous to themselves.

The ode was written in the manner of Monti and Alfieri. It is full of invective and sarcasm, of anger and contempt. The goddess Liberty descends in a golden coach bearing two banners, on one of which is written: 'Peace to all Men,' and on the other: 'War on Tyrants.' She drives into two evil monsters, Tyranny and Religion, and puts them to flight, while the poet addresses 'the force which makes heaven the instrument of vengeance and which the vulgar call religion.' He attacked the cardinals of the Curia as 'Druids in purple,' and then went into paeans of exaltation of the martyrs of the Parthenopean Republic massacred by order of Queen Maria Carolina. And the 'English

slave-traders' and the Russian 'Tartar cannibals' were not spared
for the help their fleets had given to the Bourbons.

But there were already signs of the balance which was to be
one of Manzoni's most distinguishing characteristics.   Although
at first, in the swinging and sententious manner of Monti, he had
invoked Etna to destroy the entire city of Catania, where the
Neapolitan Bourbons had their court at the time, on second
thoughts he limited the volcano's activity to destroying only
Maria Carolina and her clique.   Then he appealed to Brutus
to rid the world of such tyrants, who swear peace but never
keep their word:

> . . . la legge de' troni
> Son gl' inganni i spergiuri i tradimenti.

(The law of thrones is deception, perjury, and betrayal.)

The peroration boldly addressed Lombardy 'shaken in the
grip of one tyranny substituted for another as bad, although
tyranny in Italy was called liberty,' and called on the citizens to
rise, invoking, with a sudden sweep to bathos, the energy and
vitality which animated the 'Ferrarese genius' of the poet Monti.

IV

Both for the established poet and the enthusiastic pupil the
image of citizens rising was purely literary.   Manzoni's inflated
praise of Monti was partly, also, an attempt to defend his hero
from the attacks that were being launched on him as a turncoat.
But while the influence of Monti on literary-minded young
Italians of his day was as strong—though not so disastrous—as
that of Gabriele d'Annunzio a hundred years later, his character,
unlike d'Annunzio's, was too obviously swayed by self-interest
to hold their admiration for long.

Vincenzo Monti was then at the height of his fame and considered the greatest Italian poet of the day.   He had begun, like
Parini, as an abbé, though he had only taken minor orders.   As a
youth in Rome he had first been taken up by the elegant dilet-
tante Pope Braschi, Pius VI, to whose nephew he became
secretary.   He had recited his first poems in the lyric silvan
setting of the Bosco Parrasio of the Arcadians on the Janiculum.

During Alfieri's frustrating visit to Rome in 1781 to court the
Young Pretender's wife, the Countess of Albany, he had followed
his chiefs in attacking him as 'cynical, arrogant, and stateless.'
When the young envoy of the French Convention, de Basseville,
was killed by the Roman mob in 1793, Monti had written the
greatest counter-revolutionary ode of the day, *La Basvilliana*.
A year later he suddenly saw the light—or the trend of events—
and slipped secretly out of Rome.   Once in Florence he became
lyrical about the Revolution; feeling his way by stages, he reached
Milan via Venice in time for the first Cisalpine Republic.

Milan was in a state of uncompromising revolutionary fervour,
and he had some difficult moments.   *La Basvilliana*, he
avowed, had been written under duress.   But he must have had
amazing magnetism when reading his own poems, for as soon as
he began reciting, doubts were swept away.   Once he succeeded
in gaining the tribune at a crowded and hostile meeting of the
Cisalpine Convention, he swept all before him.   He followed
this by reading with equal success, at a dramatic recital at the
Scala, a long poem in commemoration of the beheading of
Louis XVI.   A niche was then found for him in the Foreign
Ministry of the second Cisalpine—now Italian—Republic, until
he was nominated to the Chair of Poetry at the newly opened
University of Pavia.

Now established as the official poet of Napoleonic Italy, he
produced stirring, beautifully phrased odes about the various
occasions and personalities of the new regime—on the Viceroy
Eugène, on the birth of the King of Rome.   But as time went on
he began to have considerable private doubts about Napoleon.
'He does things,' he wrote in a letter, 'that would cool a volcano.'
The growing number of Napoleon's enemies filled him with mis-
giving.   If things went on as they were, he foresaw, the whole
regime would collapse and he with it.   When the expected
happened and as a result his income was stopped, he appealed to
the new overlord, the Austrian emperor, declaring his hatred
of Napoleon.   'This man seems to have praised every successive
government in his country,' noted the Emperor Francis in his
own handwriting on the refused application.   From thence-
forward no one loathed the Austrian emperor more than Monti.
But as a final effort he wrote and had performed at the Scala

a long poem execrating Napoleon and exalting the Austrians. Alas, it was too late.   His old age was spent in poverty and blindness, with an engaging enthusiasm for the Greek War of Independence lighting his last years.

'A poet of the ear and in no way of the imagination or the head,' was Leopardi's judgment on him.   Ugo Foscolo, who had helped him on his first arrival north from Rome, and quarrelled with him later for his subservience to Napoleon, wrote at his death: 'He was really rich in poetic talent, but he lacked consistency, and sold his talents to the various governments; he praised or execrated all the principles of civic rights, according to the urge that was given him by money.'   As a stylist he is still praised.   Although his declamatory odes whipped his audiences into a frenzy, in style he was the last of the classical poets in Italian literature, an eclectic who preferred, as he said, a verse of Metastasio's to all the tragedies of Alfieri.

Young Manzoni, as he watched Monti's chameleon-like career, soon withdrew from that first fervid admiration of the last lines of *Del Trionfo della Libertà*.   But a recurrent warmth persists towards those who have encouraged us to creative activity in youth.   'You have often reprimanded me for being a fool' (in politics?) 'and praised me for being a good poet,' wrote Alessandro when sending Monti a short poem, *L'Adda*, in September 1803.   And Monti's reply was full of praise.   'I find they [the verses] breathe that Virgilian *molle atque facetum*. . . . All things considered I become more and more confirmed in my opinion that, if you follow this trend, in a short time you will be great in this career, and if you mingle a little more Virgilian sweetness with the fine vigorous coloured style that you already possess, I foresee it acquiring all the character of originality.' But he added, for he was totally without arrogance: 'I am far from being able to be a teacher to you.'   Soon the roles were almost reversed: by 1805 the youth of nineteen was openly reproaching the famous poet for the crudities of a literary quarrel between Monti and a mediocre poetaster, de Couriel.   This controversy, observed Alessandro, would harm rather than increase Monti's reputation; and then he slipped into a moral dimension, which was perhaps beyond his correspondent, by observing: 'Let not good writers forget that humanity which is

Alessandro Manzoni at the age of 17.   From a drawing by Gaudenzio
Bordiga in the Casa del Manzoni, Milan

the first fruit of letters.' There is almost a note of irritation in a letter from Manzoni in 1804 in Venice to a friend: 'If Monti wants to send me his *Persico* let him send it, for God's sake, to my father's in Milan.' Later he criticized more and more openly Monti's pretentious use of mythology. In *L'Ira di Apollo*, written in 1818, Manzoni put the most mannered language into the mouths of characters who were hardly flattering to his old friend: 'A hired journalist and a hack poet, both great admirers of the poet Monti.'

In 1806 Manzoni's school friend, Pagani, charged with publishing *In Morte di Carlo Imbonati* during the author's absence in Paris, thought to heal the breach between the two poets by dedicating the poem to Monti without referring to Manzoni. This so enraged Manzoni that he demanded a published denial. The annoyance, apart from the fulsome wording of the dedication, was understandable, for the poem contained an obvious and cruel reference to Monti: 'Poets who do a shameful trade in bought work and flattery, for whom there waits an ignominious old age.' But when this prophecy was fulfilled and Monti fell into poverty, Manzoni's affection returned, and persisted till the end. The old poet could not resist, however, getting an occasional dig at his famous successor. Just after the publication of *I Promessi Sposi* a young Florentine, making a literary pilgrimage round Italy, visited Monti with a companion, Papadopulos, from Venice. They had left Manzoni seated in the midst of a small circle of admirers, 'the leaders of the Milanese romantic school.' Monti was alone, sitting in his shabby arm-chair with his glasses on the end of his nose, reading a comedy of Goldoni's. On a table beside him lay a copy of *I Promessi Sposi*, presented by Manzoni with a flattering dedication. When the young man asked what he thought of it, the old poet replied that he had had some difficulty in getting through the first chapter, but was prepared to undertake the second; and Monti's comments to friends after he had read it all were somewhat contradictory. 'This book won't have much success,' he wrote in a letter, 'as it's too humble for the learned and too learned for the humble; the morality is hypocritical and so it cannot live.' But to the author himself he wrote: 'I've read your novel, and on finishing it I felt better in my heart and my admiration increased'; and in another letter: 'Meanwhile before my Don Abbondio sings me the *Profiscere* I want to thank you for the precious gift of your *I Promessi Sposi*, of which I say what I've already said of your *Carmagnola*—I wish I were the author.'

Manzoni visited him continuously in his last illness, and after his death the enthusiasms of youth came welling back, and he wrote of him in terms of affectionate admiration. This memorial to their friendship is preserved in every Italian anthology.

V

To the young Alessandro, thrown out into the world so young, experiments in friendship were essential for development. Don Pietro, looking on coldly and helplessly from Lecco, was not one who could help or influence him in any way. The youth had compensated by forming a series of friendships with men older than himself, such as Foscolo and Monti.

Among friends of his own age were a small group of ex-school-fellows from the Longone College. There was Gianbattista Pagani, 'the first and true friend of my Alessandro,' as Donna Giulia, who preferred her son's contemporaries, wrote from Paris in 1806. Pagani was described in the Austrian police reports after the abortive revolution at Brescia in 1831 as 'a rich landowner and freemason; unexceptionable as a gentleman; but the masonic writings he published in 1809 are permanent proof of his fanaticism for the French and open contempt for Austria. What is even more scandalous is that he still retains the same principles. Even in 1824 at the Ateneo of Brescia he professed himself an admirer of that worst of revolutionaries, the Abate Salfi.' [1] According to Manzoni himself, Pagani was responsible for his loss of religion, presumably at school. 'He was a boy of precocious capacity,' Manzoni's friend and biographer Fabris wrote of Pagani, 'and seduced many of his companions from the faith, among them Manzoni, who described himself as of an "incredulità ignorante." '

---

[1] An ex-priest, historian, and philosopher from Calabria, who took part in the Parthenopean Republic, opposed Napoleon, advised Murat in 1815, became a leading Freemason, and eventually withdrew to exile in Paris, when he became a friend of Claude Fauriel. In 1831 he helped to organize with Lafayette the abortive republican rising in Romagna. His frankness and warmth were much admired by Manzoni.

Another school contemporary was Luigi Arese, child of one of the great conservative patrician houses. Young Arese, as well as a rationalist and freethinker, was also a passionate bibliophile, and his and Manzoni's names figure among the first subscribers to the Milanese Typographical Society's edition of the Italian classics. His parents at one time forbade him to see Manzoni, considered then either as a bad influence or as socially dubious. But this, of course, if anything encouraged the intimacy between the two. This came partly from a common feeling of being victims of their times, of belonging to a generation which had missed the hopes and exaltations of the Revolution and seen only the disillusionment. 'Oh, Arese,' wrote Alessandro feelingly on his friend's early death in 1806, 'you good youth, you real friend of virtue and of your friends, who could have been perfect in better days but even in our ghastly corruption kept yourself uncontaminated, receive a farewell from those who loved you dearly in life.'

At intervals throughout life Manzoni was to go on seeing Pagani and another school contemporary, the 'golden, amiable, and respectable' Calderari. At school there had also been others, such as Federigo Confalonieri and Ermes Visconti, who became intimates only later. Another friend of Manzoni's own age in Milan, and later in Paris, was the Greek poet, Andrea Mustoxidi, whom he had met at Monti's lectures at Pavia. Mustoxidi, so Monti wrote, was 'the dearest thing I have in the world,' although he prevented the young Greek's marriage with his daughter.[1]

More important in their influence on the young Manzoni were a group of Neapolitan exiles, the intellectual flower of the defunct Parthenopean Republic. Though Manzoni never went to Naples, these friendships made him feel warmly for life towards that land which Gibbon had described as 'on the edge of Paradise and of hell-fire.' He seems to have been fascinated even by a Neapolitan like Signorelli, whom he rather despised as 'Bourbon at heart' and 'liberal only because of the blunders of a court.'

---

[1] After a spell in his native Corfu, where he became its official historian, Mustoxidi quarrelled with the British administrators of the island (politically he was always Russophile) and returned to Italy. He was to become the first Minister of Education of independent Greece.

Perhaps he felt the contrast between Signorelli's easy, open nature, with its vanity and facile courage, sometimes boldest when danger was passed, and his own closed character. Later, in Don Abbondio in *I Promessi Sposi*, he mingled some of Signorelli's weaknesses with, possibly, his own.

But there were Neapolitans in whom he found more than the attraction of opposites. Francesco Lomonaco and Vincenzo Cuoco, scholars and historians, dazzled him by their stories of the short-lived experiments of the Parthenopean Republic, in which they had both taken important parts. Lomonaco, a rationalist and anti-clerical historian, had achieved some fame with his *Report to Citizen Carnot* and his *Lives of Excellent Italians*. The attack in this book on the character of Cesare Beccaria does not seem to have disturbed Manzoni, who wrote for it in 1802 his first published work, a short *Sonnet to Dante*. The little poem, though still in the declamatory style of Monti, already showed signs of a warmer and more humane originality. In *Del Trionfo della Libertà* he mentioned Lomonaco's *energico e vesuviano rapporto* on the Neapolitan Revolution of 1799. This report, as well as the verbal descriptions of his friends, helped to crystallize the young man's political sympathies. Lomonaco's version, compared to more factual accounts, seems a series of warm-hearted and well-meaning generalizations, a tribute to his heart rather than his head. But, although the aureole of martyrdom from tyranny was bound to have a strong appeal to a youth of Alessandro's background and period, a year or two later, with developing balance and objectivity, he began to see defects in Lomonaco's mental attainments. Writing to Pagani from Paris in 1805 about a job which Pagani was trying to get Lomonaco, he showed that, though still full of admiration for Lomonaco's probity, he was dubious about his ability to fill a university chair. 'I am too ignorant of the subject which he wants to teach,' he wrote cautiously, 'and can make no prediction of the progress which it would make in his hands.' Lomonaco's tendency to wild exaggeration alarmed him; but when the emotional string snapped, and Lomonaco committed suicide in 1810, aged only thirty-three, Manzoni often recalled him with regret.

Vincenzo Cuoco was the Neapolitan who left the deepest and

most important intellectual mark. Cuoco was a more serious historian and a more balanced person than his friend Lomonaco, and after writing his *Saggio Storico sulla Rivoluzione di Napoli del 1799* was made editor of the Government paper *Giornale Italiana* by the vice-president, Melzi. Manzoni got from Cuoco a number of ideas which he was later to develop in his own way. They used to spend long evenings of discussion together, and become so absorbed, Cuoco in teaching and expounding, Manzoni in listening, that they would accompany each other back and forth between their respective front doors. To a Neapolitan friend, Masi, in 1861, Manzoni said that Cuoco had been his master in politics. He had been the first to arouse his interest in the possibilities of Italy as a nation; the first to write, in his study of the Neapolitan Revolution, that liberty was impossible in Italy without unity, and that the foreigner must be got out of the country before this unity could come about. Cuoco also made Manzoni think of the interacting problems of history. He would discourse on the philosophy of history of Gianbattista Vico, then and for many years afterwards known only to a very restricted circle outside Naples. Although it is doubtful if Manzoni ever understood or accepted Vico's concept of history as a continuous process as Cuoco did, Cuoco certainly developed his critical and empirical approach to historical studies, an attitude which was to be deepened a few years later by his friendship with the French historian, Fauriel. It may also have been due to Vico and Cuoco that Manzoni began to think about the social function of literature, years before he was to write: 'Belles-lettres will be treated correctly only when they are regarded as a branch of the moral sciences.'

Another social historian whom Manzoni saw in Milan and later in Paris was Carlo Botta, a Piedmontese revolutionary and opponent of Napoleon. Indeed Botta, according to his own account, began his most important work, *The History of the War of Independence of the United States of America*, after a party at Donna Giulia Beccaria's in Paris in 1806. There had been a discussion during the evening on modern themes suitable for epic poetry, and someone had suggested the American Revolution. The book is now almost forgotten, but its erudition, its lucid simplicity of style, its treatment of the revolution as

c

growing out of contemporary events and in turn influencing others, its objective—almost cynical—treatment of the motives of countries such as France, made it a classic on the subject not only in Europe, but in America itself; until it was supplanted sixty years later by a monumental work on the same subject by, oddly enough, another friend of Manzoni's, the American liberal, George Bancroft. As early as 1808, a year before Botta's book was published, Manzoni was writing to Pagani about it in terms which foreshadowed his own later view of history.

The subject, as you see, is most felicitous since it does not consist, as do the works of the majority of modern historians, in the narration of obscure diplomatic operations, intrigues, or the effects of the petty passions and private interests of princes. But the great actions which it presents, and the noble passion for the welfare and founding of a people, and I might almost say, the antique and classical characters of some of the heroes and of the entire American nation, give the book almost the poetic tempo that one finds in ancient historians, and permit the author to treat it in the same style, and without any affectation.

These friends scarcely justify the comments by one of Manzoni's biographers, Father Premoli: 'Lacking that religious sentiment which is the only thing, sometimes, that can absorb the more ardent spirits, Alessandro gave himself up to his school-fellows and new friends without caring about either their wild life or their subversive political doctrines.' A gay life and subversive political activity seldom, alas, combine even to-day. It is doubtful, indeed, if Manzoni was at any time either exuberantly gay or more than very moderately conspiratorial. Later, however, he was inclined, perhaps, to accept this version of his own youth.

VI

What may have suggested gaiety and corruption to Father Premoli was the short period in Venice that now followed. In the autumn of 1803, at the age of eighteen, Alessandro suddenly set off alone to spend the winter in Venice as the guest of an old cousin, Giovanni Manzoni, who had taken himself and his family off there to escape from the results of activities as a judge during

the Austro-Russian occupation of Lombardy.   Neither he nor
the other Milanese exiles in Venice could return to Milan for
fear of their lives.   Such hosts, even allowing for the strength
of Italian family ties, do not suggest any subversively political
reasons for Alessandro's visit; though it could not have taken
the liberal Venetians long to realize that they could say what they
liked to the young guest at the Casa Cromer.   It is more likely
that he was sent away to Venice to forget a youthful love-affair
in Milan.

'L'angélique Luigina' as he later called her, may have been
the sister of one of his school friends, Ermes Visconti di San
Vito.   Whether because they were both so young, or for some
other reason connected with his family scandals or his own private
life, Alessandro was forbidden to call by her parents, 'who
behaved very badly to me,' he wrote later, 'so that I had to stop
going to the house to preserve my dignity.'   It is odd that the
same thing should have happened, more or less at the same time,
with the family of his school friend Arese, who even had to
pretend to drop Alessandro to placate his parents.   But Luigina
seems to have thought that he had stopped calling from indifference.   For years he went on believing that he adored her,
though as time went on he realized that the failure had been due
partly to his own lack of resolution.   'What tortures me rather,'
he wrote three or four years later, 'is the idea that I lost her a
little through my fault and that she thought it was entirely my
fault.'   He seems instead to have sublimated his feelings in a
veneration lasting some years.   'And this sentiment,' as he
wrote when he and his mother made a special trip to Genoa in
1807 to look her over and find out if she was still eligible, 'was
not so strong as my aversion for marriage, an aversion born of
the ghastly spectacle of the corruption of my country, and which
the part I myself took in it (to my shame) has only increased.'
In Milan he had become such a bore talking about her and doing
nothing about it that it may have been the advice of his friends,
Foscolo, Monti, and Pagani, that finally took him to the other
side of the peninsula.   As he went he wrote her a poem describing himself as setting out on a hard road that was all the
finer for that.   In spite of these ineffective heroics he soon
seems to have settled down to the pleasures which Venice has

always provided for a young man of reasonable health and fortune.
At his cousin's in the Casa Cromer in the Piazza San Maurizio
(there is the inevitable plaque on the façade to commemorate
his visit), he met the beauties of the town, La Benzon, La
Tron, and many befurred senators, including the last doge,
Manin, an old beau whose snuff-box had been stolen four times
in the street that winter.

But in spite of his pleasures there is a sense of hurt pride and
bitterness in his writings of this period, an acrid air of solitude
which may have been due as much to adolescence and frustration
about Luigina, as to his feeling about the political and moral
situation of his country. He had tried to forget Luigina for a
time with a lady of *matura virginità* as he described her himself
(she was aged thirty), to whom he went so far as to offer his
hand in marriage. 'At your age one thinks of going to school
and not of making love,' was her crisp reply. He consoled
himself with easier game: 'mi giovin l'erbe dell' orto epicureo'
(let me enjoy the weeds of the epicurean garden), as he wrote in
one of his verse-letters, the *Sermoni*, to Gianbattista Pagani. The
'weeds,' there is a vague hint, may have left a slight but irritating indisposition which could not but have increased his sense of
isolation and frustration.

Looking back in old age, his chief memory of that winter was
the beauty of Venice; so freshly did he describe it at the very end
of his life that a Venetian lady who heard him asked in surprise
if he had recently visited her native city. 'About sixty-seven
years ago,' he answered, 'but I remember Venice and its story
very well; the impressions one receives in youth are never
cancelled from the mind.' In his memory Piazza San Marco
was still bounded at one end by the old church of San Gemig-
nano; the reverie drew him into one of the few remarks on art
or architecture recorded of him, though he soon passed on to
the Venetian language and literature. 'How often I return to
Venice in my mind's eye! Those palaces with their stupendous
variety of architecture! That dialect which is such a happy
mixture of cut-off phrases and slurs! And what a comic genius
Goldoni is; Molière makes one laugh at but sometimes hate his
characters, while Goldoni makes one smile and love them.'

The rippling lilt of the Venetian dialect may have had more

far-reaching effects than he realized at the time.   For the plays,
continuously staged at the local theatres, of the Venetian comedy
writers of the previous generation, particularly Goldoni, showed
him the possibilities of the direct application of popular speech,
as opposed to the artificial written Italian of the day which had
entangled even so sincere a poet as Parini.   His *Sermoni* or
verse-letters from Venice showed a break from the grandiose
models of Monti and Alfieri and an attempt at a more modest
and direct language.   There was still a preoccupation with the
antique world, but for different reasons: he could not, as he
wrote to Pagani in the third *Sermone*, think of the ancients without
making an immediate and sarcastic comparison with the moderns.
But he realized that the constant sharp acidity of these poems
might need some explanation.   'D' you want to know why I
write satires instead of epics celebrating heroes?' he wrote to
Pagani.   'It's because I can only present life in ways offered by
my experience, and all I see around me is unfaithful wives, en-
riched thieves, venal Brutuses, and bogus Catos!'   In his adoles-
cent despair the world seemed full of petty bureaucrats riding
high on the tide of incompetence, and becoming hopeless
ambassadors, inept judges, ignorant academicians.   Then there
were the 'newly arrived of the Revolution,' 'born of prostitutes
in taverns, enriching themselves, then selling themselves to
noblewomen as husbands'; and lastly—for his despair was all-
embracing—the corrupters of the people, the poets.   And again
and again, perhaps remembering Luigina, he attacked the ambition and 'financial interests' which presided over marriages,
an obsession that showed in advice to his friends.   'May heaven,'
he even wrote to Arese, 'keep you ever healthy and single.'

Some of these *Sermoni* contained such bitter satires on living
people (including friends), such attacks on the French occupation and Napoleon, that his mother, as he told the parish priest
of Brusuglio at the end of his life, thought it prudent to destroy
the more savage ones, and only four have been preserved.

VII

By March 1804 the Venetian experience was over and Alessandro was back in Milan.   The city was buzzing with preparations

for Napoleon's coronation in May with the Iron Crown of
Lombardy, and there were more French in Milan than ever—
'questi transalpini mercatanti,' as Calderari called them to Arese.
In spite of the obvious advantages to Milan, many of the Lombard
liberals had found the transformation of the North Italian republic
into a province or viceroyalty of the new empire a disillusioning
surprise. 'Once I was all for liberty, all for country, all for
public spirit; and now I've become perfectly apathetic. Explain
the phenomenon . . .' Calderari wrote dejectedly to Arese.
On the other hand, the French reoccupation of Naples had
brought new hope to the Neapolitan exiles in Milan, who were
slipping off southwards one by one.

It must have been rather a depressing summer for Alessandro.
Don Pietro was ill, and he went out dutifully to Lecco at intervals
to visit him. But some time in the late autumn of that year
fatherly letters of encouragement and advice began to arrive for
the first time from Carlo Imbonati in Paris, pressing him to come
and stay. Perhaps Donna Giulia, rather belatedly, felt her
mother's conscience calling; perhaps she remembered her advice
when Alessandro was in trouble over gambling, to visit France
as a salutary break. This time Alessandro accepted the invitation. But when the reply reached Paris Imbonati was dead.
The death was to cause Alessandro's transfer to France for five
years at the most impressionable moment of his career.

CHAPTER FOUR

Paris, the Idéologues, and Claude Fauriel

I

THROUGHOUT his life Manzoni was to love France, 'that land,' as Tommaseo wrote after twenty hours of apparently continuous conversation with him in 1825, 'which was always in his mind's eye as an example to follow and to flee—but even attempted flight was a kind of search.' And Manzoni, criticizing Alfieri's hatred of France, wrote at the end of his *Lettre à M. Chauvet* in 1823: 'Hatred of France! Of this France lit by so much genius and so many virtues! From which so many truths and so many examples have come! Of this France which one cannot see without feeling an affection which resembles the love of one's own country, and which one cannot leave without the memory of having lived there mingling with something deep and melancholy that almost feels like exile!'

He arrived under particularly fortunate auspices, for perhaps it was the best of contemporary France that was waiting to welcome him. The name of Beccaria which Donna Giulia bore (she had dropped the Manzoni on her first arrival in Paris, while her son added the name 'of which I boast' to his) was still venerated in Paris with the great names of eighteenth-century thought. With this advantage Donna Giulia combined a bright, intuitive intelligence, social gifts, a piquant beauty, a slightly hysterical sensibility, and a warmth for liberal ideas; ever since her arrival she and Imbonati had been welcome in the 'advanced' Parisian *salons*. She had struck up a particularly close friendship with Mme de Condorcet, the widow of the philosopher, a woman whose character and outlook, though she had had a considerably tougher life, were not unlike hers. She had also become the confidante of Claude Fauriel, the young man who lived with Mme de Condorcet, and who was to become one of the more distinguished of French historians, as well as Manzoni's most intimate friend for twenty years.

The group around Mme de Condorcet were the direct heirs of the Rationalists and Encyclopaedists who, half a century before, had prepared the way for the Revolution. The last of the old generation, the Marquis de Condorcet, had committed suicide during the Terror a few years before. Voltaire had died in 1778, d'Alembert in 1783, Diderot in 1784, Helvétius in 1771. The links with this vanished world were Mme Helvétius and Mme de Condorcet, and it was around them that the new generation of 'Idéologues,' as they had just taken to calling themselves, had gathered. The word 'idéologie' was a new one first suggested by Destutt de Tracy to the Institut de France in 1796 to describe the study of the origin and nature of ideas, particularly of the philosophy of mind started by Condillac which derived all knowledge from the senses, as opposed to that 'Science of Being,' metaphysics. The word was to become famous with Tracy's book, *Éléments d'Idéologie*, conceived in prison during the Terror and published in 1804. With the attacks of Napoleon and Chateaubriand a few years later, this ancestor of the word 'ideologist' was to acquire a new meaning of visionary, unpractical idealism, leading to its derogatory use to-day, far from that of analytical search for truth with which it started. The Idéologues, like the 'Bloomsbury Set' of the twenties, combined clear and unprejudiced minds, sensibility, and contempt of cant with a certain air of good manners and civilized living carried over from their roots in the *ancien régime*. For its leading members, like those of the 'Bloomsbury Set,' had good, solid, private incomes.

By the time Manzoni arrived the Idéologues were past their period of immediate influence on public affairs, which had been during the Directorate and the first part of the Consulate.

Old Mme Helvétius had died in 1800, after gathering round her in the quiet of Auteuil the remaining core of the *esprit logique* to which her husband had dedicated the latter half of his life. Helvétius, in his book *De l'Esprit*, had set out to prove that the only guides to men's actions were the principles of utility and self-interest. This had made him a subversive and controversial figure in pre-Revolutionary France, though some considered him 'the most generous of egoists and the most religious of atheists.' Stendhal's typical comment on him was: 'But as he had a cold

heart he never knew either love or friendship, or any other
living passions which create new and singular interests.' He
was the son of a farmer-general of the French State Finances, and
according to Stendhal the farmers-general were the leading
representatives of the new upper middle classes born of the
dissipations of the great nobles, and the first to support 'that
fatal public opinion which finished by ruining everything in
1789.' 'These received literary folk at their suppers and so
emerged a little themselves from the role of clowns, which they
had played at the tables of the real grandees.' Mme Helvétius
could remember these famous Tuesday dinners in the Rue
Sainte-Anne which had been frequented by Diderot and d'Alembert, Holbach and Condorcet, Galiani and Beccaria, Hume,
Marmontel, Morellet, and Chamfort: the 'États-généraux de
l'esprit humain,' as one of the guests had called them. Their
effect was not forgotten, for Helvétius had become posthumously
one of the heroes of the Revolution, and his daughters had been
protected during the Terror as 'daughters of the nation.'
Between 1792 and 1814 the Rue Sainte-Anne had even been re-
named the Rue Helvétius—expanded by the flair of cab-drivers
into the Rue Saint-Helvétius ('Voilà une singulière canonisation,'
murmured Helvétius's enemy, Mme de Genlis). After his death
Mme Helvétius had gone to live at a villa at Auteuil, which she
had filled with flowers, birds, and guests; and among the trees
at the end of the little park was a pavilion which she lent to the
needier philosophers and abbés of her new court.

Mme Helvétius was already an old woman—she was born in
1718—when she withdrew to this agreeable 'sanctuary,' as it
soon came to be known. 'Notre Dame d'Auteuil,' Benjamin
Franklin called her, and asked for her hand in marriage. Here
came Volney, the leading atheist in France, who to his own and
everyone else's surprise found himself an initiator of the Directorate; Garat, the physicist, who had read the death sentence to
Louis XVI; and Morellet, who had translated Beccaria's *Dei
Delitti e delle Pene*, a freethinker of whom Mme Necker said:
'He has just enough religion to suspect that there could be a
God, and sometimes admits it to his friends, when he knows
they are discreet and to be trusted.' The leading thinker of the
group, Destutt de Tracy, took a house near by. Twelve years

*c

before her death Mme Helvétius forged another link with the
past.　She adopted young Cabanis, who was the same age as her
only son, killed many years before.　'If the doctrine of the
transmigration of souls were true,' old Mme Helvétius would
say, straying slightly from her husband's strictly rationalist
principles, 'I should be tempted to believe that the soul of my
son had passed into the body of Cabanis.'

Pierre-Georges Cabanis, one of the liveliest minds of his time,
had started life as the kind of character which is recognizable in
many eighteenth-century memoirs.　As a restless and penniless
young literary adventurer, at the age of sixteen his charm and
looks had led to his being taken off to Poland by the Bishop of
Vilna as private secretary.　Like his friend Fauriel, Cabanis
had the gift of friendship; he was encouraged by Voltaire in his
translation of the *Iliad*, became an intimate of Mirabeau, and
even Benjamin Franklin left him in his will the unsuitable gift
of a ceremonial sword.　For on his return from Poland he
became a fervent supporter of the Enlightenment and then of the
Revolution.　When he was adopted by Mme Helvétius, he
decided, after much casting about, to become a doctor, a profession which he combined first with politics and then with
philosophic speculation, and as a doctor he was present at the
death of Mirabeau.　During the Terror his special poison recipe
was carried by many illustrious men and saved some of them,
including Condorcet, from the guillotine.　It is said that a phial
was even carried for life by Napoleon and nearly used after
Waterloo.　During the Directorate he reorganized the French
medical schools.　When Mme Helvétius died Cabanis married
another member of the Idéologues, Charlotte de Grouchy, sister
of Mme de Condorcet.　Practical politics, even medical
politics, were over for him when the Directorate ended, and he
and his wife settled down to a life of philosophic speculation and
literary composition in Mme Helvétius's old house in Auteuil—
a withdrawal which, wrote Charles James Fox, 'was a loss for
the whole of humanity.'　In time Cabanis, combining with a
brilliant mind deep qualities of honesty and sincerity (to Donna
Giulia he resembled her 'poor Carlo'), came to be one of the
pivots of the group.　As Ginguené wrote after visiting them in
1805, the conversations between Cabanis, Fauriel, Mme de

Claude Fauriel. From a portrait by Mme de Condorcet

Mme de Condorcet. From a portrait in the Château de Bignon, France

Condorcet, and Mme Cabanis 'formed a society full of interest and charm, of which Cabanis was the soul, ill as he was.' By his chief work, *Rapports du physique et du moral de l'Homme*, linking with a new breadth of scope the health of the body with that of the mind, he became a pioneer in a new science, and influenced later developments in psychology. In this book he treated the mind on the basis of Sensist philosophy, and dealt with both metaphysical and spiritual problems in materialist terms. The frequent contemporary references to Cabanis, by not only thinkers and philosophers, but novelists such as Stendhal—also by origin an Idéologue—show the influence of his thinking on his own time. He appears, too, under a pseudonym, in Balzac's *Peau de Chagrin*, where the hero, young Rafael, is also said to be engaged on a new epoch-making work of medical psychology, *The Theory of the Will*, in the manner of Cabanis.

'L'angélique Cabanis' had been a close friend of Condorcet's in his last years. When Sophie de Condorcet withdrew also to Auteuil to recover from the stormy years after her husband's death, it was Cabanis who helped her with her first essays in literature, to translate Adam Smith, and prepare a complete edition of her husband's works.

'La belle révolutionnaire' was still a young woman when she settled down to this new, calm life. She and her husband had been among the few members of the old nobility to side en- thusiastically from the first against the king, and Condorcet was not only the most prominent intellectual to support the Revolu- tion, but the only one of the great eighteenth-century philoso- phers to live to see an attempt at putting their theories into practice. From 1789 he had plunged actively into Revolutionary politics, until Robespierre denounced him for the constitution he produced at the Convention of 1793. Hiding in Paris, under an assumed name, he abandoned, on his wife's advice, work on a political justification, and immersed himself in the writing of *The Outline of a Table of Progress of the Human Spirit*, in which he summed up his knowledge and ideas, and elaborated for the first time his view of history as a progressive advance towards a future Utopia. Just as this last—and strangely optimistic— great work of his life was completed he was forced to leave his hiding-place and take to the woods. Arrested in a ditch, he committed suicide in a village jail under a false name. It was some time after his death before the philosopher was identified from a copy of Horace in his coat pocket.

Till then Sophie de Condorcet had considered herself as a gay, 'advanced,' and provocative young beauty with a famous old husband. Flung suddenly from a peak of power (in 1792 she had been offered the guardianship of the young dauphin), and with all property confiscated, she showed unexpected courage and energy. The eyes which had so often delighted visitors to her *salon* at the Hôtel des Monnaies, with their combination of the *air rêveur* of the age of Rousseau with the *air étincelle* of that of Voltaire, she now used to paint little pencil portraits for a living. She even penetrated, it is said, into the prisons of the Conciergerie to draw the condemned on the eve of execution. With her savings she bought a small lingerie shop, and so saw the Terror through. When Robespierre fell she not only recovered her husband's property under the Directorate, but had a sudden and surprising return to political power. The Condorcet constitution of 1793 was adopted, and from the group at Auteuil came some of the leading ideas, particularly on the reorganizing of education by the Institut de France, which distinguished that short and ill-managed regime. But more reverses were to come. From the first she had had her doubts of Bonaparte, as had old Mme Helvétius. He had visited the 'sanctuary' once or twice during this period, and some Idéologues like Volney had hoped much of him. But Mme de Condorcet's dislike of him was reciprocated, perhaps mingling in his mind with his feelings for that other brilliant and dominating woman, Mme de Staël. 'I don't like women who meddle in politics,' he said to Mme de Condorcet one day; and back had come the bright and irritating reply: 'How right you are, general, but in a country where their heads are cut off it's only natural for them to ask why!'

The Idéologues, who based their thought on developing the systems of logic and analysis which had been handed down by their predecessors, as opposed to that of 'force, egoism, and routine,' were bound to cut across the Napoleonic path at some stage. The liberal ideal of the individual's capacity for expansion, which left only the indispensable tasks of organizing to the State, was doomed to early disappointment. 'Days for ever celebrated and for ever to be regretted by us!' sighed Thiers of the Directorate years later.

The storms of the Revolution seemed calmed; the murmurs of the various parties were like the last sounds of the tempest; these remains of agitation were regarded as the very life of a free state. . . . A Government composed of bourgeois who were our equals ruled the Republic with moderation. . . . All voices were free. . . . All seemed great, pure, happy, full of the future! It was only a moment but in the lives of peoples as of individuals there are only moments. We were about to find opulence combined with repose; as for liberty and glory, we had them already.

Inflated dreams!

A year after Bonaparte broke the constitution in August 1802, he was talking of these philosophers of reason, in grimly familiar terms. 'There are ten or twelve metaphysicians who should be flung into the water. . . . They are a vermin I must shake off my clothes.' Perhaps, mingled with Napoleon's practical irritation, there was also resentment at watching those who were trying consistently to carry on the ideals of his own youth, 'revolutionary rubbish such as sovereign people and equal rights.' 'It is to the *idéologie*,' he pronounced in a speech in 1812 after the Foyot plot that might have been written by any member of the Holy Alliance,

to those shadowy metaphysics which search with subtlety for primary causes and want to found public legislation on them, rather than on a knowledge of the human heart and the lessons of history, that are to be blamed all the misfortunes through which our beautiful France has passed. Those errors were bound to lead, as indeed they did, to the rule of bloodshed. Who, in fact, proclaimed the principles of revolt as a duty? Who flattered the mob by calling it to a sovereignty which it was incapable of exercising? Who destroyed the sanctity and respect for the laws by making them depend, not on the principles of justice and on the nature of things, but solely on the will of an assembly composed of men who were totally without knowledge of the rules of civil, criminal, administrative, political, or military procedure?

Yet in spite of persecution the Idéologues, who had withdrawn from active politics ever since the trial of Moreau a few days before the Empire was proclaimed, were to support Napoleon as a last prop against the Bourbons during the Hundred Days.

II

Like the Società del Caffè the Idéologues formed in their retirement a defence against the world of closely knit personal relationships.   With greater French logic, however, they saw that these helped rather than hindered their work.   When Mme de Condorcet moved in 1802 from her first retreat at Auteuil after the death of Mme Helvétius, she took Claude Fauriel with her to La Maisonette at Meulan.   It was a simple house surrounded with great trees on the slopes above an old village, with a view from the terrace across the serene valley of the Seine to vast royal forests stretching to Versailles.   There they were to live and work happily together until her death in 1822.   Their reasons for never marrying may have various explanations.   Perhaps the Grouchys felt that one marriage in the family with a literary man, Cabanis, was enough; perhaps the Marquise de Condorcet felt her revolutionary principles quaver at the idea of becoming Mme Fauriel.

'Fauriel,' wrote Stendhal in a passage which has a strong flavour of envy,

was the handsomest man in Paris.   Mme de Condorcet, a great *connaisseuse*, snapped him up; the bourgeois Fauriel was foolish enough to fall in love with her.   When she died she left him an income of 1,200 francs a year, as if he had been a lackey; which humiliated him deeply. I said to him, when he gave me ten pages of Arab stories for *De l'Amour*, that in dealing with a woman who is either too rich or too grand, one must knock her about—or love vanishes; the suggestion filled him with horror.

Stendhal's other remarks on Fauriel were rather inclined to damn with faint praise.   Although he conceded that 'cet excellent Fauriel' was 'le seul savant non pedant de Paris,' he considered his style as an example of 'bassesse bourgeoise,' and went on to a patronizing reference to the works of 'ce bon bourgeois si conscientieux,' whose works would be forgotten by 1880 (as against, by implication, Stendhal's, which would only then be beginning to be read).   In spite of the justness of this pre-diction, it was possibly Fauriel's success in inspiring lasting devotion in a number of women that partly accounts for the touch of spite in all Stendhal's references to him.   'Tell me,' wrote Mary Clarke,[1] writing from Cold Overton Hall to Fauriel staying at Brusuglio in 1825, and asking his opinion of Thierry's books. 'Tell me, you whose wisdom is supreme and who are *nearly* always right (except when it's a question of women . . .).' For Mary Clarke had been deeply devoted to Fauriel and jealous of Sophie de Condorcet for years. Stendhal may have described such situations in wish-fulfilment, but it is very doubtful if they ever actually happened to him.

Claude Fauriel was the son of poor parents at St Etienne. As a very young man during the Revolution he had been an active Jacobin, and known as 'le démophile Fauriel,' even representing Robespierre at a local fête for *L'Être Suprème*; but he had also saved the libraries of the local suppressed monasteries. He was modest, hard-working, handsome, and reserved. In 1793, at the age of twenty-one, he became *secrétaire intime* of the Commander-in-Chief of the Army of Italy, who offered him, in a moment of euphoria, the ranks of Secretary of the General Staff and Captain of Grenadiers. Then for a time he had to go into hiding as a Jacobin. By 1799 we find him in the surprising position of private secretary to the much-feared Fouché, Minister of Police. There he seems to have been both tactful and pliant; he was in charge of some delicate tasks, such as the report on the political and sexual activities of the Marquis de Sade. For a time he was found both attractive and useful by the formidable Mme de Staël. But Fauriel was reluctant to fall into her net at Coppet. 'If you don't come,' she wrote in 1801 after awaiting him in vain, 'we shall never find that confidence in each other in the world of Paris which is inspired by solitude and the Alps.' Finally she rapped him impatiently over the knuckles: 'Your excuses are useless. They are more than sufficient for a certain degree of friendship; they are worthless for one degree more.' But Mme de Staël usually got what she wanted for a time, though her very persistence may have ruined the result. She still asked Fauriel to intervene in various matters at the Ministry for her, and in return had him to dinner and introduced

[1] Mary Clarke, later Mme Julius Mohl, was to be a lively figure in the intellectual life of Paris for nearly three generations. Thierry, Guizot, Lamartine, and Monckton Milnes were among her intimate friends. Her portrait by Downman in the Institut de France shows a piquant, inquiring face, bearing out Stendhal's description of 'la petite Mlle Clarke, faite comme un point d'intérrogation.'

him to people who might be useful in his career, such as Chateaubriand, then about to leap into fame with his *Génie du Christianisme*. By now, however, Fauriel had been taken to Auteuil by Cabanis, and met Mme de Condorcet, whose relations with Mme de Staël were and continued to be strained.[1] Mme de Condorcet, perhaps for more objective reasons, also disliked Chateaubriand, whose combination of romantic Catholicism and reactionary political views was particularly antipathetic to the group of the Idéologues.

It was probably Mme de Condorcet who first troubled Fauriel's conscience about the nature of his work, which he was finding more and more incompatible with his friendships and opinions. When Fauriel withdrew from active life in 1802 and settled down with her at Meulan, he wrote an account of the last public events he had watched as a close observer. *Les Derniers Jours du Consulat*, which was not published until after his death, gives a vivid and critical picture of the characters of his time, including his chief, the notorious Fouché,

the most striking example for posterity of the ease with which the ministers of a cruel and extravagant liberty can become the submissive and complaisant agents of a vile despotism. . . . Uniting falsity and indiscretion, wit and ignorance, he had contracted the habit, like those whose conduct throughout the Revolution was inspired only by personal interest, of considering absolute principles of justice and truth as absurdities which can only dupe fools. . . .

Renan once described Fauriel as 'an amiable and sensitive Stoic, a serious and curious investigator of all truth.' Like many imaginative people whose talents are critical rather than creative, he had great influence on all his friends. He used his honest diligence, his balanced critical sense and inquiring mind for an extraordinary range of studies. After an early start on Quakers' philosophy and botany, and a period with 'that mysterious Sanskrit which opened up an unknown world,' he

[1] Mme de Condorcet's open criticisms did not go much beyond hinting that Mme de Staël was too rich and smart to be a real liberal. But it seems likely that the reasons lay deeper and that Mme de Staël did not let go of Fauriel immediately. Most of the correspondence between Fauriel and Mme de Staël has been sealed up at the request of her descendants, the Ducs de Broglie, in the library of the Institut de France. There is no doubt that apart from any other relationship, Fauriel had a considerable influence on some of Mme de Staël's ideas.

settled for a time on the history of languages, particularly those of medieval France, with excursions into Provençal, Breton, and Basque. The list of his manuscript notes for unfinished works covers five pages of the catalogue of the library of the Institut de France, and ranges from Indian dialects to 'the least uncertain historical epochs of Greek primitive civilization'; from three note-books on Italian history to one on chivalry in England. He also wrote an elaborate history of Stoicism which literally never saw the light, as the manuscript was buried during the Hundred Days and never found again. The range of his interests, however few of them came to fruition, affected, as Sainte-Beuve said, the literary history of France. The friends he influenced ranged from Cabanis to Thierry and Cousin, from Stendhal to Guizot. He was one of the inspirers of Mme de Staël's ideas on romanticism and a devoted friend of Benjamin Constant; was consulted by Thierry for his studies on the Norman Conquest of England; collaborated with Schlegel in the first printing plant of Sanskrit in Europe; and was the first to hold a chair of foreign languages at the Sorbonne. This remarkable and agreeable person was for twenty years the intimate friend, correspondent, and counsellor of Manzoni.

The two young men were first thrown together by the close friendship between Donna Giulia and Mme de Condorcet. Soon Fauriel's combination of sincere encouragement, gentle humanity, and charm drew from Alessandro the warmest response, almost fascination. They had many traits of character in common. When Fauriel wrote later of Manzoni: 'He was incapable of accepting new ideas without first meditating and discussing them deeply,' he was perhaps thinking also of himself. They even had similar little quirks. When Fauriel, for instance, was visiting Manzoni in Italy in 1825, he could never sit down to work until he had caught and killed every fly in the room; Manzoni, elsewhere in the house, was ordering the servants to drive away the birds in the trees outside his study windows. But their affinity also went deep. Fauriel's firm aversion to superficiality or ambiguity; his determination to omit nothing relevant, and to exclude the irrelevant, in any subject he was studying; his refusal to fill gaps of facts with vague words or to build up theories by arbitrary or approximate suppositions; his lively sense of the complications to be observed when peering into the depths of history—touched some answering chord in the younger man and influenced him profoundly. Sainte-Beuve even went so far as to say that only through Fauriel can Manzoni be fully understood.

III

The death of Carlo Imbonati had been a stunning blow to Donna Giulia. Very little is known about him, and one has to look at the unstable Donna Giulia's reactions to realize that only a man of considerable character could have held her so deeply. But he is completely overshadowed by the great figures surrounding him from birth to death. On his eleventh birthday Parini had written one of his most famous odes, *Torna a fiorir la rosa* for his recovery from illness, while Manzoni was to sing his funeral ode. Stendhal, who may have met him in Paris, was firmly convinced that he had hidden talents of a high order. 'M. Imbonati was one of those rare geniuses,' he wrote when commenting on Manzoni's ode,

rarer perhaps in Italy than in all the other regions of our modern Europe, whose prudence allied to complete absence of vanity made him keep silent. It is the existence of men of the quality of M. Imbonati which has, I consider, made Italy into one of the first countries in the world. There were men of the strength of mind of M. Imbonati in Milan who dared to defy Napoleon at the height of his power. The practical virtues of Socrates and his school breathe from M. Manzoni's poem.

Imbonati, who still had a large fortune in spite of depletions due to abandoning his properties to agents, while he lived outside Italy, seems to have been a genuine practising Stoic. In 1797 he dropped his title and became citizen Imbonati, when he and Donna Giulia settled in a luxurious apartment in the Place Vendôme in Paris. According to friends who saw Donna Giulia at this period, she had never in her life been so happy. His death was to change her life completely.

It also, for the first time, made Donna Giulia and Alessandro independent financially. When the will came to be read it was found that Imbonati had left the whole of his fortune to Donna

Giulia for life, together with the property of Brusuglio near Milan, absolutely. In the preamble to this will, dated 1795, Imbonati had written that he was making Donna Giulia his universal heiress, 'as I desire to make public and solemn those pure, just feelings which I have for her; for not only have I had complete satisfaction from the years spent with her, but I am also deeply convinced that I owe to her virtue and true disinterested devotion that tranquillity of mind and happiness which will accompany me to the grave.'

When the will became known in Milan Donna Giulia was sharply criticized for having accepted the inheritance when many of Imbonati's sisters and nephews were almost in want. These, after abandoning the idea of contesting the will, showed themselves affectionate and loyal, waiting for a settlement, while the vice-president, Melzi, warned Donna Giulia not to show herself in Milan until she had made suitable arrangements for them. Partly because of this and partly on her own initiative, Donna Giulia provided for them generously, and confirmed the arrangements on a visit to Turin in 1806. But the scandal took some time to die down. Imbonati himself may have been partly the cause; for years his fellow citizens had been irritated at someone of Imbonati's distinction abandoning so chauvinist a place as Milan to go and live in splendour abroad. And then, though nothing could have been more easy going or indeed corrupt than Milanese society, it was shocked at seeing the laws of matrimony flouted quite so openly. And on top of it all both Imbonati and Donna Giulia—it was whispered—were intimate with Revolutionary circles in Paris.

When, in the summer of 1805, Donna Giulia bore the embalmed body of Imbonati from Paris to Brusuglio, she never appeared in Milan, and mother and son, after the burial, hurried straight off back to France. During their short visit she gave orders for an elaborate mausoleum to be constructed in the garden of Brusuglio. The porticoed tomb was reached by a staircase surmounted by a small temple adorned with medallions by Giuseppe Borri; to it, down the avenue with the double row of cypresses, 'the sorrowing heiress,' in the words of the family enemy, Custodi, 'would repair twice a day to pray for peace on her defunct companion.'

They arrived back in Paris in the middle of July 1805, and
took an apartment at 71 Rue Saint-Honoré ('Vis-à-vis les ci-
devant Jacobins,' Alessandro headed a letter in August), as
Donna Giulia could not face the memories of the Place Vendôme.
Alessandro's main preoccupation that autumn and winter was to
console his wretched mother. They had not seen each other
for years, and the discovery that they could be close companions
and give each other mutual support was a surprise to both. 'I
only live for my Giulia,' wrote Alessandro rather exaltedly to
Monti in August, 'and to adore and imitate that man who you
used to tell me was "virtue itself." ' 'Oh, my dear Monti,' ran a
postscript by Donna Giulia, '. . . you who love him, you who
really know him, so that you can suggest my adored Carlo as a
model, you can measure the immense love, the sacred unhealable
love which I feel for him. Oh! do not tell me to find distractions or consolations, do not imagine that I can find any
break in the eternity which has already begun for me.' The
years when the memory of Imbonati was to be forgotten, and
even rejected by at least one of them, did not weaken this re-
forged devotion of mother and son. In 1807 Alessandro was
writing to Pagani of 'the happiness of having as a mother and a
friend a woman speaking of whom I find more and more that
every expression is weak and inadequate.' His friend Calderari
was longing to meet this paragon, and to judge by his description
to Pagani, Donna Giulia's fascination seems to have worked.

During the journey my heart palpitated with longing to see such a
woman, whom I already revered as the person who formed the happiness of our Manzoni; and since I've seen her I must say that both seem
formed for each other's contentment: they both strive to foresee the
other's wishes and show how indivisible they are from each other.
You will find her a person who, without lacking any of the true graces
which adorn a woman, has a man's intelligence and an easy, sweet, and
affectionate way of speaking; and then her conversation is full of feeling.
. . . What a fine pair they are!

Arese, perhaps remembering conversations about her between
his parents, was inclined to be less effusive. 'Forgive me,
my dear Pagani,' he wrote in 1806 during the row about the
dedication of Imbonati's obituary ode, 'but that "incomparable
woman and friend" seems slightly mad to me.'

So closely did Alessandro identify himself with his mother that he was now on her suggestion writing this ode, almost as if to a mentor or father, although he had never met him. The *Carme in Morte di Carlo Imbonati* was published in a hundred copies by Didot in Paris in 1806. The poem is in the form of a dream in which Manzoni calls up Imbonati from the dead and holds conversation with him. 'The device of a dream,' commented Stendhal flippantly, 'has the immense advantage of popular belief, as in Naples or Turin visions are considered certain facts. A sure way to make a Frenchman laugh, and I suppose an Englishman, is to describe a vision to him . . . the chief works of Monti, Grossi, and Manzoni all have visions in them.' In this vision Imbonati is made to discuss a variety of subjects, such as the arts and the after-life, and gives Manzoni Stoic precepts for living:

> 'Sentir,' riprese, 'e meditar; di poco
> Esser contento; de la meta mai
> Non torcer gli occhi, conservar la mano
> Pura e la mente; de le umane cose
> Tanto sperimentar, quanto ti basti
> Per non curarle . . .'

(Feel, meditate, be happy with little; never take your eyes from your goal; keep your hand and mind pure; experience as much of human things as will lead you not to care for them.)

And the pessimistic attitude of the *Sermoni* comes up again:

> Dura è pel giusto solitario, il credi,
> Dura, e pur troppo disegual la guerra
> Contra i perversi affratellati e molti.

(Hard and solitary is it to believe; hard, and alas unequal is the struggle against evil-doers who are many and united.)

Throughout the poem Imbonati appears as a wise and beneficent sage, though a statement of the Stoic view of life as a battle with little hope of achievement is a curious memorial to offer one's mother for her lover.

According to Pagani and Arese, one of the reasons for the withdrawal of the dedication to Monti was that Donna Giulia did not want to share the verses with anyone. On the appearance of the poem in Milan, there were fresh batches of rumours: that it had only been written in gratitude for his mother's being

left the Imbonati property; even that Alessandro was really
Imbonati's son—which is chronologically very unlikely. The
poem became one of the many regrets of his after life, and he
even left it out of a later collected edition of his works.

As time went on his attitude to the memory of Imbonati
showed some curious workings of the mind. After Donna
Giulia's death Imbonati's name was not allowed to be mentioned
in the house. The coffin was even taken from the elaborate
mausoleum in the grounds and put into a graveyard on the
property, which during Manzoni's lifetime was turned into a
chicken-run. The temple and the cypresses were left to look
after themselves. But Brusuglio, the house Imbonati had left
his mother, remained his home for life.

IV

Perhaps it was as another partner in a free marriage that Donna
Giulia had first been drawn to Mme de Condorcet. For Donna
Giulia, as the years passed, La Maisonette of Meulan and its
châteleine were to become the nostalgic links with the last
period of her life when she had lived intensely: a world of past
love to which she would return in slightly hysterical reverie
even when she had taken to religion. While Imbonati was still
alive she had also struck up a warm friendship (a 'culto idola-
trico' her son called it) with Fauriel. This may have been due,
apart from Fauriel's charm, to a similarity of character and
tastes between the Stoic Fauriel and the Stoic Imbonati. 'I
long, my dear friend,' she wrote to him in 1803, 'for occasions
to show all the partiality of my feelings for you; and when I say
"my,"' she added, 'you must also, dear friend, understand
those of Imbonati.' When Donna Giulia, after Imbonati's
death, was so stunned by the sudden end of her happiness that
she could not even summon up strength to tell Imbonati's
relations in Milan, it was Mme de Condorcet and Fauriel who
had taken over the formalities for her. On their insistence the
embalmed body had been borne from the Place Vendôme to
La Maisonette, where it was laid for a time in a temple in the
gardens, a sort of classic shrine of grief, remaining there until
taken to Italy.

Henriette Blondel and Alessandro Manzoni at the time of their wedding.
From miniatures in the Braidense Library, Milan

When mother and son returned to Paris, links with the household of La Maisonette became closer than ever. With Donna Giulia's rapt approval, her Alessandro and Claude Fauriel quickly developed into intimate friends. The correspondence between them shows how close in character and interests were these 'amis de cœur,' as Fauriel's biographer called them.

Except for Alessandro's reconversion to the Catholic faith, which is only mentioned once, these letters follow the intellectual development of the friends (chiefly of Manzoni, for few of Fauriel's letters to him have been preserved) throughout the creative years of their lives. Already in February 1806 Alessandro was thanking Fauriel in particularly warm terms for his comments on the verses to Imbonati: 'After the satisfaction of having rendered homage to the memory of a man whose virtue I venerate, and to whom I am grateful as the guardian angel of my mother . . . after the satisfaction of having done for my mother and friend what she liked most, your letter is the greatest pleasure that those verses have procured for me. . . .' And here, in this very first letter to Fauriel, Manzoni set down for his new friend a view of literature whose essentials were to remain for the rest of his life: 'I think that the meditation over what is and what ought to be, and the bitter feeling which arises from this contrast—this meditation, this feeling are the springs of the best works either in verse or prose of our time.' Later, when the correspondence was established: 'Your letters give me the sweet illusion of a conversation; so that I will, if I may, continue to communicate to you the ideas which are stimulated in me by those scattered about your letters.' On Manzoni's side, there are, particularly in the earlier letters, expressions of the most extravagant devotion. 'I cannot but express,' he wrote during his visit to Genoa in 1807, 'the ever-strengthening hope that I will be your friend. This hope also makes my mother happy, for she is always repeating to me (as does my heart, though reason tells me it is a foolish pretension): "Oh, if you could only become necessary to that divine Fauriel"—don't be angry, the adjective slipped from me.' 'It's maddening to have to use to express the truest and deepest feelings of my being, expressions which everyone uses to feign them, but you, Fauriel, you read in my heart.'

My dear Fauriel, had I known that there existed a man who had your
kindness and purity of soul I would have searched out that man, and
having met him, I should only have been able to detach myself with
difficulty, and with very little hope of finding another similar; but
having met in you a combination of wit, talent, and knowledge with the
most amiable and virtuous heart, I cannot pass you by even if I be a
burden to you.   I long and hope to see you again soon, when my only
regret will be that I am not worthy of you.

On this trip to Italy Alessandro confided to his friend his
disgust at his native country, an attitude presumably acquired
from Donna Giulia, whose rancour against Italy for being the
scene of her wretched married life had stung even from the
gentle Arese a year before the protest: 'Oh, Giulia, Giulia,
virtue is not so rare in Italy as you think!'   'I'll tell you by word
of mouth,' wrote Alessandro, 'all the evil I think of this beautiful Italy, and the reason which makes me prefer France.   If
any of my fellow citizens heard this they would cry blasphemy;
but if they knew you and had a little common sense they would
realize that being near you should be reason enough to prefer
Paris; and I tell you sincerely to take what I say *à la lettre*.'
Fauriel was now studying Italian poetry (he later wrote a life of
Dante), and Alessandro wrote that he hoped this 'would be one
of the bonds—the smallest one—that will unite us for life.'   To
which Donna Giulia added a postscript in her rushed hand:
'Oh, this horrible Italy! . . .   How I'd like to see you and tell
you how thankful I am for your *union* with my Alessandro.'

CHAPTER FIVE

Marriage; the Jansenists, and Reconversion to Catholicism

I

But Donna Giulia, woman of the world that she was in spite of the gush, was looking for a more permanent and concrete union for her Alessandro. She was anxious, sensible mother, to see him married and settled; though she had no intention on her part of withdrawing. 'I am prepared,' she wrote to Pagani in May 1806, 'to consecrate my life to her who will be the companion of my Alessandro and the mother of his children.' Donna Giulia was used to acting on her ideas, however inopportune: it was on her insistence that she and her son suddenly set off for Genoa in February 1807, though the winter journey meant an alarming passage of Mont Cenis, to look up Alessandro's old love, 'l'angélique Luigina.' 'Donna Giulia,' wrote Manzoni to Fauriel, 'had founded the hopes of her whole life on our union; she did not know her personally, met her, and was much affected to find that she was married.' Though seeing Luigina again brought back memories of bitter humiliation, Alessandro was on the whole rather relieved; he had been docile about his mother's scheme, but rather unenthusiastic. The old love, if it had really existed, had flickered out. 'I must tell you,' he wrote to Fauriel a little ruefully in reply to a letter of sympathy, 'that all the fine consolations you give me about my passion are lost, for I do not feel any strong pain at being separated from Luigina. I have returned in her regard to those sentiments of veneration, of devotion, if I may so express myself, and this feeling is sweet rather than burning. I don't really know if it would be more honourable to suffer, but it would certainly be unworthy to impose on you.'

They were still in Genoa, intending to spend some weeks seeing lawyers in Turin before going back to Paris, when suddenly news came that old Don Pietro Manzoni was seriously ill.

Alessandro hurried to Lecco, to arrive after he had died, on 17 March 1807. In his letters immediately afterwards to Fauriel and Calderari the death got rather cursory mentions. With Calderari he passed quickly on to talk of mutual friends, and with Fauriel to encouragement about the lagging current work on the history of Stoicism. 'We shall see each other in a month,' went on Alessandro enthusiastically. 'It will be one of the happiest moments of my life; remember Paris is our homeland, that you are the first object in it, and that you must never leave me.' Don Pietro seemed already forgotten.

In spite of the past, Don Pietro had not harboured resentment in the end against either Donna Giulia or Alessandro. In a will made on the day of his death he made Alessandro his universal heir with an income, it is said, of about 3,000 crowns. Even Donna Giulia found that in a codicil added in the margin she had been left some diamond pendants 'in sign of my esteem and memory of her.' But his passing was unmourned, almost unnoticed, by his family. They stayed three days, never set foot in Milan, and within a month, in May 1807, were back in Paris, determined to establish themselves there for a long time.

Donna Giulia, disappointed in Luigina, was looking round for another candidate, feeling that a wife was absolutely necessary to her son. Fauriel had also made inquiries while they were away, and thought he had found just the right person, Mlle de Tracy, daughter of the leading 'Ideologist' philosopher, Destutt de Tracy. In spite of Alessandro's respect for Tracy as a thinker (a respect which, in spite of later divergence in ideas, he never lost—and was even annotating the third part, on logic, of Tracy's treatise L'Idéologie when writing I Promessi Sposi), he agreed rather rapidly to Fauriel's suggestion 'as I have for some time inclined to marriage,' but was afraid his 'supposed domicile in Italy might be a difficulty.' He had not met Mlle de Tracy, but his requirements in a wife, he wrote to Fauriel in June 1807, were 'a direct, gentle, and sensitive mind . . . a just and cultivated intelligence, simple habits, a calm, even character, no taste for burning pleasures, much taste for country life, a care and enjoyment of housekeeping, an interesting face, agreeable talents, and tender parents as estimable as they are esteemed,' and he added a 'good dose of goodness and tolerance.'

The only advantage he could think of for the girl in marrying him was 'the friendship and devotion of my mother, and I do not hesitate to say that that can compensate for some of my faults.' But, as he added to Fauriel, 'my fear of embarrassment, my complete isolation from society, my sullen glooms, and my invincible shyness (which sometimes leads me to seem very ridiculous) make me into rather an original being.' He knew nothing of his suggested bride, who turned out later to be quite an ordinary woman of the world. The idea of going to Auteuil to meet the Tracys alarmed him; it was only with 'a timid desire' that he awaited the day for Fauriel to take him along to be introduced.

Fauriel himself, who had promised to wait for their return from Italy, Alessandro was longing to see and in his eagerness was surprised at the time the other took to answer his letters or even to visit him; perhaps Fauriel was in difficulties as an intermediary, or he may have found Alessandro's warmth towards himself embarrassing. What happened to end this rather chilly suit of Mlle de Tracy is not known: apparently Alessandro did not find himself wanted. Years later, in 1821, the historian Thierry wrote to Fauriel to tell him that he was giving English lessons to the same lady, now Mme de Laubespin. Thierry had talked of Milan and Manzoni and she had listened with interest, as if some chord was touched—quoted Thierry in English—'as a tale of other days, of days for ever, ever gone. The poor woman,' he added, 'if she had been properly settled, might really have become something.'

II

So Donna Giulia returned to the search. Among her acquaint-ances in Paris were members of a family of Swiss merchants and bankers, the Blondels, to whom Imbonati had sold his house in the Piazza San Fedele in Milan when he went to settle abroad in 1796. The Blondel agents in Paris were now Donna Giulia's bankers. Mme Charlotte Blondel was probably the first to describe to Donna Giulia her young niece Henriette in Milan. The description so fired Donna Giulia that in September 1807, with Alessandro in tow, she threw up her plans anew and set

off back to Italy to meet her. The return was a sacrifice for
Donna Giulia, although they stayed some time on the lakes as
far as possible from Milan. From there Alessandro wrote a
little stiffly and correctly to Fauriel: 'Do please express to
M. de Tracy how sorry I am not to have seen him before my
departure, and assure him that my regrets will endure at not
having more sacred bonds both to his friendship and to all
surrounding him. . . .' Meanwhile the matter of Henriette
Blondel, in which no emotions other than mutual respect were
at first involved, was quickly coming to a head. 'I have a
confidence to make,' wrote Alessandro to Fauriel in October
1807 from the Beccarias' villa, Il Belvedere, on Lake Como.

I have seen the young person in Milan whom I mentioned to you
before; I found her very nice. My mother has seen her too and finds
even more than I do that she has an excellent heart; she only thinks
of household things and of the happiness of her parents whom she
adores; in fact, family feelings occupy her almost entirely (and I'll
add in your ear that she's perhaps the only one here). There is
another advantage which really is one in our country, and that is that
she is not noble, and you know Parini's poem by heart. What is
more, she is Protestant—enfin c'est un trésor; and it seems to me likely
that soon there'll be three of us longing to see you; so far the matter
is not quite decided and she knows nothing about it.

Mother and son then withdrew to Brusuglio to await developments. With Donna Giulia in control there never seems to
have been any intention of their living at Il Caleotto, the Manzoni
family house at Lecco which now belonged to Alessandro. At
Brusuglio he was learning about agriculture, buying a house
opposite the gates, redesigning the courtyard, planning to rebuild
the central block. 'But building it doesn't mean living in it
at once, and living in it one day doesn't mean we'll do so
exclusively.' Neither Alessandro nor Donna Giulia were yet
reconciled to the idea of living in Italy. 'There are so many
reasons, positive and negative, which make me prefer France,
that I always say to my mother—when we are at Brusuglio we'll
call it Montmorency or Auteuil.' The only person they saw
seems to have been Calderari. 'We live in the greatest solitude, trembling with fear every time we hear a carriage roll
into the court, for it might well be some importunate person

coming to steal our day so as to rid himself of his own.' The thought of going to Milan to arrange about furniture horrified him. He preferred soothing and classical pleasures, he wrote to Fauriel, such as watching a swarm of bees in the garden.

Verbal arrangements for the match were complete by 1st January 1808. The wedding took place in Milan on 6th February. Henriette was a small, fair girl of sixteen with large steady blue eyes, whose sweetness and gentleness hid, as events turned out, an unexpected strength of character. The Blondels were Swiss emigrants who had founded their fortunes on cotton mills near Bergamo and then, with their rapidly expanding capital, started a private bank in Milan. Both the Blondel parents were Calvinists: the mother strict and bigoted, the father tolerant and heterodox, influenced by the new currents of Socinianism in the Calvinist Church. Their religion did not worry the Manzonis. Donna Giulia had been rather drawn towards the Calvinists of late, and in 1805, in her despair after Imbonati's death, had even seriously considered withdrawing from the world to become a nurse in the Calvinist hospital in Geneva. But in Milan the mixed marriage caused another scandal. 'D'you know my fellow citizens are good enough to busy themselves with the marriage and make it the subject of a lot of talk? Ah! divine Paris!' wrote Alessandro to Fauriel. 'People who've never seen me take as much interest in my marriage as if they were relations.' What scandalized provincial and bigoted Milan even more than the bride's religion was that the marriage was not celebrated in a church. The civil ceremony was in the Town Hall, and the religious one in the Blondels' drawing-room in the Piazza San Fedele, officiated over by a Calvinist parson imported from Lugano. As Alessandro had not asked for a dispensation, whose essential would have been the promise to bring up the children as Catholics, the ecclesiastical authorities had refused to give permission for a mixed marriage in a Catholic church. And to make matters worse, one of the witnesses, the rumour went round, was a bad priest and 'natural philosopher,' Zinammi, Donna Giulia's agent in Milan. The young parson, Kaspar Orelli, had literary tastes and read the bridegroom's poems. 'This young Manzoni seems an interesting young man,' he wrote home to his parents from the Blondel house on the eve of the marriage. 'As inexperienced in the world as I am myself, but vigorous and innocent. He is hated by the priests and despises them. . . . I am sorry I only talked to him for half an hour. I really like him and feel that if I were at Bergamo instead of Lugano I would find in him, if not a friend (for the Italians only rarely know a real friendship), at least a good acquaintance.' 'The marriage,' he wrote again,

took place very quietly one Saturday evening at seven. As the bride-groom's mother, the Marchesa Beccaria, was ill, her son scarcely ever left her bedside except to visit his bride for an instant or two. . . . He's shy, as I am, and quite without pretensions. . . . There was no banquet. They gave me two pairs of silk stockings, a silk waistcoat, and two pairs of silk breeches. The Marchesa Beccaria must be a very sensitive woman. Her son once declared to her that he never wanted to marry. Then she made him read an idyll of Gessner's in which there is a vivid description, with an engraving, of a father surrounded by his family. This moved the young Manzoni, who guessed his mother's intention. One of his tears fell on the engraving, and his mother had the mark framed with a gold circle.

Two months of honeymoon passed, spent mainly at the Beccaria villa on Lake Como, 'between pain and pleasure' as Manzoni wrote to Fauriel in March 1808. 'My mother has had a terrible sore throat . . . in this interval I got married, which has perhaps contributed to improving my mother's health, filling, flooding her heart with happiness. We are all three very happy: this angelic creature seems made specially for us; she has all my tastes and I am sure there is not an important point on which we disagree.' Henriette, he added, was longing to meet Fauriel. Alessandro had now begun to think of settling at Brusuglio and asking Fauriel and Mme de Condorcet out to stay. But Donna Giulia's sore throat was turning into a melancholic yearning for France. 'This desire and her antipathy to staying in Italy are carried to such a point that she attaches to the execution of this project [another long stay in Paris] her perfect recovery, which she doesn't hope to obtain in any other way.' Would Fauriel and Mme de Con-dorcet be sure to wait for them in Paris, as Henriette was 'determined not to be deprived of the pleasure in meeting them'? So, in June 1808, abandoning the supervision of the new buildings at Brusuglio ('Ah, if you knew what pleasure there is in moving earth and stones!'), the newly married couple set off with Donna Giulia back to France.

III

One wonders how soon after marriage Henriette first made her influence felt.   A slight change of arrangements when they arrived in Paris at the end of June may have been significant or may have been purely accidental.   Mme de Condorcet had offered the family a home at La Maisonette until they got settled. Instead they put up, on arrival, at an *hôtel garni* in the Boulevard des Bains Chinois.   But they were soon seeing a lot of the *ménage* at La Maisonette, and part of the late summer of 1808 was spent there.

We have nothing but a hint or two of the attitude of Henriette to what she must have considered—with her strict upbringing —these loose friends of her husband's.   Donna Giulia noticed that she was sometimes *triste et chagrinée*, but put this down to home-sickness; while Alessandro, noticing nothing, wrote a nostalgic bread-and-butter letter after their return to Paris from Meulan: 'You cannot think how I regret the amiable company of La Maisonette, and our evenings, and the hillside and the thatched roofs.'   The interests Henriette was soon developing on her own were very different to those of La Maisonette. Not long after her return to Paris from Meulan she was drawn through a Swiss friend, Mme Anne-Marie Geymüller, into a new and absorbing inner life, which was finally to lead her, and the entire Manzoni family with her, into the Roman Catholic Church.

Gaetano Negri, a friend of Manzoni in the last years, wrote of his religious life:

No one will ever know the phases of the psychological drama by which Manzoni passed from scepticism to ardent faith, as he was a completely reserved person, one of those men who, entirely absorbed in the feeling of their own responsibility and held by a kind of intellectual shyness, know how to keep deliberately to themselves what they do not want to communicate to others. . . .   He was always on guard, and never allowed anyone to delve deeper into his conscience than he wanted. . . .

Interpretations on this mysterious subject are apt to vary according to the personal beliefs of his biographers, from the assumptions of orthodox Catholics to the remarks of a sympathetic and subtle Jewish sceptic, the late Professor Momigliano: 'His religious conversion took place at the sunset of the Revolution, under the influence of a moral weariness and an intellectual disillusion.'

Unexpectedly, one of the first to lead Manzoni into thinking of religion may have been Cabanis. Just before they started for Paris in June 1808, Alessandro had been shocked to hear the news of Cabanis's death. 'As for myself,' he wrote to Fauriel who, with Mme de Condorcet, had spent most of that last winter staying at the Cabanises', 'from the first moment I had the happiness of seeing him, I felt, instead of the kind of repugnance all new faces cause me, the pleasure of seeing a friend. . . . He was very good to me . . . and I cannot recall our walks together in Auteuil without suffering.' Certainly Manzoni had a deep respect for Cabanis's qualities. Was he the first to draw Manzoni into the beginnings of paths which are very difficult exactly to chart, towards a less severely rationalist view of the world? Although Cabanis had made it part of his life's work to explain the spiritual and metaphysical in material terms, there are, in his *Lettre à Fauriel sur les Causes Premières*,[1] written just before he died but first published in 1824, hints of doubt about the system he had put together, and mentions of a vague concept which he called 'Nature.' This concept, which was never elaborated, appears to have some parallels with Bernard Shaw's 'Life Force.' It could possibly, as Cabanis hinted, be made to lead by some processes of the mind to a reconsideration of the idea of Providence, which might in its turn draw the mind thinking along these lines into an acceptance of the whole system of religion.

Up to now, with Manzoni, the morality of 'liberty, equality, and fraternity' had taken the place of religion. But although they were principles he was never to abandon completely, he

---

[1] Sainte-Beuve considered that Cabanis wrote the letter after conversations with his intimate friend Fauriel, then deep in meditation for his history of Stoicism. 'Honneur à Fauriel pour avoir provoqué l'effort,' wrote Sainte-Beuve. But there is no sign that Fauriel ever followed up Cabanis's arguments.

was never active enough politically to try and weld them into a practical basis for life.

The death in Milan in 1806 of his school friend Luigi Arese, forced to die seeing, instead of his friends, 'l'orribile figura di un prete' (the horrible face of a priest), had jolted Manzoni into an expression of Stoic independence towards religion.

The illness of the dear and unhappy Arese, whom I always have before my eyes, draws me still further away from a country where one can neither live nor die as one pleases. I prefer the natural indifference of the French, who let one go about one's business, to the cruel zeal of us Italians, who take possession of one, want to care for one's soul, try to force their way of thinking into one's body; as if someone who has a heart, two legs, and a belly and walks by himself, cannot dispose of himself and of all that is in him at his own pleasure.

This precarious isolation had broken down on Arese's last letter from his death-bed with its moving exclamation: 'We shall see each other again!' and Alessandro had answered: 'Oh yes, we shall see each other again! If this hope did not sweeten the desire for good and the horror of evil, what would life be?'

In the adolescent's search for values at a period when all beliefs were in turmoil, he had erected for a time the shade of Imbonati as a kind of symbol of moral rectitude. It was Imbonati, he felt, who had first drawn him out of that habit of bitter negative railing against the world which had overshadowed his period in Venice and Milan. Imbonati had recalled him to the 'virile conscience of what he owed to himself and to other true poets.'

This may have been approaching a moral position, but it did not touch on any positive religious belief.

The vague pantheism hinted at by Cabanis could be no more than a phase to a mind in search of positive support. Marriage had gone far towards settling him physically for a time, and the key to the changes in his beliefs may also lie partly in his personal life. More than by any logical process they seem to have been encouraged, whatever the seeds originally present in his own background, through his growing devotion to his young wife. And she had been born with a strong religious temperament, fostered throughout her cloistered childhood by her bigoted Calvinist mother.

D

IV

Henriette's new friend, Mme Geymüller, was the widow of an officer of Louis XVI's Swiss Guard, and a member of a set which revolved partly round the Italian Embassy, where the envoy, Count Marescalchi, was an old friend of Donna Giulia's. Both Marescalchi and his friend Count Somis de Chavrie were Piedmontese who had supported the revolution at the time of the first French occupation of Northern Italy in 1796. They were now both members of the Imperial legislature, and Marescalchi, though resident in Paris, was in fact Foreign Minister of the new Viceroyalty of Italy. Both were fervent Catholics as well as liberals, and had adhered to the new Constitutional Church formed during the revolution, in opposition to the rigid and reactionary policy of the Vatican.

The leader, almost the creator, of the Constitutional Church in France was the Abbé Grégoire, who had been ordained Constitutional Bishop of Blois by Talleyrand when Bishop of Autun, and deposed as a result of Napoleon's Concordat with the Holy See in 1802. Grégoire, a battling cleric of saintly life and firm radical convictions, was the leading Jansenist and Church reformer of his day. He had been a prominent figure in the Revolutionary Convention, where he had voted for the abolition of the monarchy and the execution of the king. He had been such an active pioneer in the movement for the abolition of slavery that he is still a hero at Port-au-Prince. By 1808 his moral position was so strong that Napoleon, in an attempt to placate his opposition (for Grégoire not only remained a dogged republican but opposed the divorce from Josephine), nominated him Count of the Empire and Commander of the Legion of Honour. This had no effect on his opinions and he remained one of the most controversial figures in France; even his funeral in 1831, when students drew the hearse followed by twenty thousand people, nearly caused the fall of a Government.

Grégoire had been in touch for some time with the Jansenist and reforming trends within the Church in Italy, whose leader had been Bishop Ricci of Pistoia. The Italian delegate to the

Congress of the Constitutional Church, the Abate Eustachio
Dègola, had remained in France and become his great friend.
By 1808 Grégoire and Dègola together were the leading spirits
of the little group of French Jansenists who kept alive the
memory of the great shrine of the movement, the Abbey of
Port Royal. Dègola's speciality was leading prominent Calvinists into his section of the Catholic Church; among his recent
converts had been Mme Geymüller, whose spiritual adviser he
now was, and who had become a leading lay member of the
Jansenist group in Paris.

The Abate Dègola was now to play a decisive part in the lives
first of Henriette and then of Alessandro Manzoni. He was an
ardent, restless, and courageous character, rather rigid and
intolerant in his ideas on religion, but full of rectitude. His
pleasant manners and knowledge of the world (he belonged to
a prosperous Genoese family of Spanish origin) made him an
ideal confessor for some. 'Benevolent to everyone,' wrote a
friend, 'the only people who angered him were the perverters
of morality, and those who change their minds, thought, and
speech at every puff of contrary wind.' Such was his uncompromising ardour that two of his books were later put on the
Index. He had taken an active part in the new Ligurian
Republic founded by the French in 1796; after that he had been
the only Italian delegate to arrive (he was paying his own
expenses) at the Congress of the Constitutional Church in Paris
in 1801. When the Congress collapsed as a result of the
Concordat of 1802, he had stayed on to comfort Grégoire, and
together they had set off on a religious tour of Europe. In
Utrecht they were fêted by the German Jansenists, and from the
pulpit of the empty church at Wittenberg pronounced a private
anathema against Luther and Melanchthon. They even visited
England, 'in the hope,' wrote Dègola in his diary,

of finding some object of edification in spite of the crisis which
Catholicism has suffered in that island, once so illustrious in the annals
of the Church. . . . The British character, naturally reflective and
severe, made me hope that I should find on my journey the precious
remains of the old religion. To observe the customs of the islanders,
study their social habits, analyse the progress of public spirit, gather
outstanding examples of the advance of science and the arts, were

cares which I did not neglect, at least in so far as they could yield me a result analogous to religious spirit.

As Jansenists and reformers they both felt the need to draw religion more closely into social organization, and Grégoire was gathering material for a report on English agriculture for the Société d'Agriculture of Paris.   Dègola's political opinions were as advanced as those of Grégoire.   On his return to Genoa after this journey he found himself in difficulties with the Imperial police for denouncing, in a formal letter to the Genoa Town Hall, the end of Ligurian independence, and his right of confession was withdrawn.   But although two of Dègola's books were later put on the Index, no one could impugn either his or Grégoire's religious fervour.   On separating after their European tour, they had arranged that at seven in the morning on the last day of every month each would prostrate himself before God, wherever he were, and implore spiritual grace for the other.

It must have been a relief for Dègola to get away from Genoa and back to Paris in the autumn of 1809.   He was just in time to officiate at the centenary on 29th October of the destruction of the Abbey of Port Royal.   Sitting by the fountain of Mère Angélique with the faithful scattered around him among the ruins, he preached a panegyric on the story and doctrines of the Jansenists.

v

Since the suppression in 1709 of their headquarters at the Abbey of Port Royal just outside Paris, by order of Louis XIV, the Jansenists had been a persecuted minority.   Though the five propositions of Jansenius [1] had been condemned by the bulls

[1] The five condemned propositions all related to predestination:

1. Some of God's commandments are impossible to just men who wish and strive to keep them, considering the powers they actually have: the grace by which these precepts may become possible is also wanting.

2. In the state of fallen nature no one ever resists interior grace.

3. To merit, or not to merit, in the state of fallen nature we must be free from all external constraint, but not from interior necessity.

4. The Semipelagians admitted the necessity of interior grace, even for the beginning of faith: but they fell into heresy in pretending that his grace is such that any man may either follow or resist it.

5. To say that Christ died and shed his blood for all men is Semipelagianism.

Monsignor Luigi Tosi

Abate Eustachio Dègola

In Eminente of 1642, and *Cum Occasione* of 1653, and abandoned by his followers, they were still being persecuted for what Pascal had called 'une hérésie imperceptible'; 'a heresy so subtle,' said Cardinal Paolucci, the official Vatican investigator, in 1702, 'that when you think you've grasped it, it slips out of your hand.' But throughout the involved and complex controversy the Jansenists were constantly being saddled with opinions which they tenaciously refuted, while the debate whirled on in the evanescent, equivocal language of theology. One of Jansenius's main efforts had been to draw theology close to popular religion. The essence of his opinions and those of Arnauld of Port Royal, the pupil of Saint-Cyran who had been a friend of Jansenius, could be made to have various implications according to circumstances. No amount of church-going can save a man unless the love of God is in him, which cannot be acquired by will. Ignorance is the fruit of original sin, that sin which caused the decadence of man, as he was incapable of doing good by his efforts alone. 'The whole of religion consists in the recognition of the first and second Adam,' announced the decree of the Jansenist Synod of Pistoia in 1786. Only grace could save man from original sin, and God conceded this only to those predestined to be saved; so no action or act of will can save the soul not predestined.

Whether this rather forbidding insistence on the importance of grace was heretical or not, its implications for ecclesiastical authority were vast. Since, according to this theory, the individual soul was considered to be responsible directly to God, by inference it loosened the authority of the hierarchy. Without, perhaps, fully acknowledging these implications the Jansenists did come in time to stand for decentralization and the diminution of Vatican authority. They would have preferred to see the pope simply as chief bishop, rather than master of the Church. From this it followed that their main enemies, both in ecclesiastical politics and in theology, were the papal militia of the Counter-Reformation, the Company of Jesus. And the Jesuits, in their campaign to increase papal power, not only persecuted the leading Jansenists in France, such as Arnauld and Quesnel, but produced a rival theological system, based on the doctrines of Molina, which compromised between Divine Grace and a human liberty, which had, however, to bow to the authority of the Church.   And under these intricate controversies lay whole mine-fields of violent persecution and misery.

When eventually the followers of Saint-Cyran had been forced by disciplinary action, after numberless deputations and commissions, to agree that the five propositions of Jansenius were heretical, the next struggle which rent the Church concerned whether the propositions were, in fact, to be found in Jansenius's book at all.   The Jesuit-Jansenist struggle intensified. Pascal's *Lettres Provinciales*, published in 1656, had pilloried in brilliant and limpid style the political opportunism of the Jesuits, and brought great public sympathy for the Jansenists.   The Jesuits countered by getting the pope to reaffirm the Bull of Condemnation *Unigenitus* by the bold strategem, so rumour had it, of presenting a faked copy of Jansenius's book in which the five propositions were clearly to be discerned.   They followed this up by having an official questionnaire, the 'Formula,' sent out for all the French clergy to sign, confirming that the five propositions were in the book.   Such were the contradictory voices of the experts that Louis XIV in despair asked one of his courtiers, the Comte de Grammont, to look through Jansenius's book and report once and for all if he could see any sign of these subtle but explosive points.   Grammont's reply was a masterpiece of courtierly evasion: 'If the five propositions are in the book then they are there incognito.'   The king himself was wavering; behind the struggle now were looming the great political issues of Gallicanism and the independence of the French Church.   It was this 'Formula' from Rome, the signing of which admitted by implication a whole series of theological errors, that first brought the theologians of Port Royal into open conflict with the authorities.   Saint-Cyran had been the confessor of Mère Angélique Arnauld of Port Royal, and she and the Arnauld family had first brought Port Royal into the field on the side of the Jansenists.   Antoine Arnauld produced the most cogent statement in France of the Jansenist case in his book *On Frequent Communion* (so called because one of the Jansenist tenets, following on their doctrines on grace, was rare and long-prepared approach to the sacraments).   The reply to the 'Formula' by the rigorists of Port Royal was: 'It is better to expose oneself to the greatest sacrifices rather than to tell the smallest lie.' The expedient they found almost denied the doctrinal authority of the Church: they called it 'respectful silence' which did not need 'interior assent.' The use of this parallel to 'dumb insolence' in the army was a grave tactical error. The Jesuits at once exploited it to jockey the king into the decision to suppress the abbey and order its buildings to be pulled down. 'They are as pure as angels and as proud as demons,' said the Archbishop of Paris with grudging admiration. The arguments that finally convinced the king were that unless he repressed them he would not save his soul, and that they were dangerous republicans. Louis was worked into such a state that he is said to have been thrown into great alarm on hearing that one of his courtiers was a Jansenist, but reassured when told that he was 'only an atheist.'

Three years later the Jesuits scored another audacious triumph and stirred up new hatred against themselves by the papal condemnation of Quesnel as a Jansenist. From then on throughout the eighteenth century opposition to the Jesuits gradually urged the Jansenists into positions which were very far from their starting-point. From opposing papal infallibility, they became anti-absolutist, and some even anti-monarchist. Though not every opponent of Molina was a Jansenist, nor every rigorist against the papal authority, the name Jansenist became in the course of the eighteenth century a term of general abuse in the mouths of the orthodox. They were subversive, republican, almost fellow travellers of the Protestants. 'Jansenism,' says the *Catholic Encyclopaedia*, published in America in 1910, 'is distinguished by crafty proceedings, chicane, and lack of frankness on the part of its adherents; especially the pretence of remaining Catholics without renouncing their errors, of staying in the Church despite the Church itself, by skilfully avoiding or braving with impunity the decisions of the Supreme Authority.' The Jansenists replied, as their followers (now outside the Church) still do, that these were just fantasies, an 'inane spectrum,' as Arnauld of Port Royal had called the 'Formula' a century before.

By the end of the eighteenth century Jansenism had taken a variety of forms. The fanatical *convulsionnaires* thought by miracles to invoke the direct testimony of God himself on the Jansenist behalf. But so revolting were the scenes on the sites of miracles that they did much to discredit the movement, though providing the Encyclopaedists with useful examples of mass hysteria and apparent suspension of the laws of nature. In Italy the movement, under the influence of Joseph II and Leopold of Tuscany, had taken a more practical trend; it concentrated on Church reform and decentralization. In Germany it had been overcome by the *Aufklärung*. In Spain later it was centred on the mother of the Empress Eugénie, the Condesa de Montijo, who translated Jansenist books and corresponded with Grégoire. In France the *convulsionnaires* had been only an offshoot. In spite of Voltaire's 'fair and modest suggestion of strangling the last Jesuit with the innards of the last Jansenist' the main stream of the Jansenists became more and more political, so that from the middle of the eighteenth century until about 1830 it was a strong force on the side first of the Revolution and then of the more extreme liberals.

'Le Jansénisme des Chrétiens c'est le Stoicisme des païens,' said Chamfort. Jansenism with its vigorous ethic principles, its struggle against worldly and material interests in the Church, its austere conviction, its contempt for State favours, its disinterested devotion to public affairs, its insistence on first principles, in fact its dignity of life, was bound to coincide up to a point with the aims of the Revolution. But it is difficult to see how a doctrine which held that God had condemned most of the human race to damnation, that the predestined could do nothing to save themselves, and that children who died before they were baptized would go to Hell, could travel very far with the humanitarian aspirations of the revolutionaries. At bottom there was a deep conflict between the doctrine of original sin and the theory of the Enlightenment that all evil was based on social conditions. There was also a contradiction between liberal individualism and the Jansenist opinion that liberty is the liberty to do good, to live by the law ('the liberty of the angels and the holy,' as Professor Arturo Carlo Jemolo has called it). Yet although no school of modern Liberalism would now consider such a theory, if the basis of this idea were changed from theology to one of social co-operation, this conception of the liberty to do good has some parallels with the ethical theories of Marxism.

During the Revolution and the period immediately after, Jansenism reached the height of its importance in France. By the middle of the nineteenth century it was a spent force, though it has left scattered influences still on French religious life. Modernism was to take its place at the end of the century, with quite different theological doctrines, but with similar political aspirations.

VI

Henriette had been drawing closer to the Jansenist group in Paris, through her friendship with Mme Geymüller, during the autumn of 1808 and the early part of 1809. Somis de Chavrie had first caught her attention and respect when, during a lively discussion one evening among agnostics, he had jumped up from his chair and said firmly: 'And I believe.' Now, in the late summer of 1809, Mme Geymüller put Henriette into touch with the leading spirit of the group, the man who had converted her and whose spiritual disciple she was, the Abate Dègola.

The return of Dègola to Paris began a series of rapid moves in a process which must have been going on for some months. The birth of their first child, Giulietta, in December 1808, must have increased Henriette's influence over Alessandro. Did she impress a sense of conventional duty towards their child on her agnostic husband? Or was little Giulietta's baptism as a Catholic in the church of St Nicholas at Meulan on 23rd August 1809 a first result of the battering-ram of Dègola's tactics? There was an unusual gap between the birth and the baptism. 'It is from your opposition to orthodox doctrine,' Dègola wrote to Henriette almost in his first letter, 'from your zeal for Calvinist practices, from that will come a chagrin which will pierce your heart the day you present your child to a Catholic priest for baptism.' One step led logically to another. A month later Alessandro made a formal request to the Vatican through the Minister Marescalchi for his marriage to be recelebrated according to the Catholic rite, though Henriette was still technically a Calvinist, 'that, so as to render his conscience tranquil, and

* D

cancel every sinister idea among the Catholics among whom they both had to live, they may be reputed legally wed.'

How far Alessandro was being drawn along that summer in his wife's wake it is impossible to say. He seems to have taken little interest at first in Henriette's conversations with Dègola, whose attitude to much else he could not but have approved. Yet he seems to have helped, rather than hindered, Henriette's first moves towards the Catholic Church. 'Persons,' Dègola told her, 'who in other times would have distracted you from all idea of conversion, have been, in the hands of the Lord, instruments of mercy for you.' Whatever was germinating underneath, Alessandro's apparent preoccupations that year, if one can judge from his correspondence with Fauriel, were mainly with literature. A poem, *Urania*, of which Mme de Condorcet was the heroine, had been produced with some heart-burning that spring, and one on vaccination planned in the autumn. When he visited La Maisonette, where little Giulietta was left for part of the summer of 1809, he found Fauriel working away at his history of Stoicism, a subject near his own heart; he also met the Greek poet Mustoxidi in Paris again, and took him off to La Maisonette for literary discussions.

Events in the spiritual lives of both Alessandro and Henriette followed rapidly during the winter of 1809 and the following spring. Their Catholic remarriage by dispensation of the representative of the Apostolic Delegate (himself defying Napoleon from Rome) took place at the altar of the Italian Embassy in the Madeleine on 15th February 1810. On 22nd May Henriette formally abjured her Calvinism at a ceremony at the church of Saint-Séverin attended by all the chief Jansenists in Paris, including the owners of the ruins of Port Royal. Alessandro, having been baptized a Catholic, needed to make no formal renunciation, but from that date he can be considered as back in the Church.

The crisis seems to have come on the evening of 2nd April 1810, the day Napoleon was married to Marie-Louise.

That evening the centre of Paris was surging with crowds waiting for the celebrative fireworks. These began at the Étoile, and were taken up down the hill in sparkling waves of fire. Somewhere near the Place du Carrousel, as the *Moniteur* of the next day described (carefully hiding any mention of casualties), a rocket swerved into the crowd. Near the spot were standing Alessandro and Henriette, who had strolled out of their apartment in the Place Vendôme near by to watch the display. The crowd panicked. In the press Henriette, under Alessandro's horrified eyes, was swept away and apparently overwhelmed by the crush. Then there came on him the first of the nervous fits which were to attack him at intervals throughout his life. Near swooning and almost senseless himself, his nerves quite out of control at seeing, he thought, his wife crushed to death beneath his eyes he managed to drag himself out of the crowd, and stagger into the nearby church of Saint-Roch. The great baroque nave was dimly lit and almost empty, and a service was going on, probably Benediction. At that hour it would have been held in the first of the receding vistas of chapels behind the baldecchino, whose dark mass dims the music and the candlelight. The quiet, the singing, did something to him, for, according to one of the accounts which originated with him, he fell on his knees and cried: 'Oh, God, if You exist, restore my wife to me.' When he got up from his knees he felt strangely calm. Sure enough Henriette was waiting for him, safe and sound, at their apartment. A week later he formally began religious instruction with Dègola.

He would never talk about his conversion, either then or ever after. 'It was the Grace of God! It was the Grace of God!' he told his stepson, Stefano Stampa, fifty years later. His daughter Vittoria once asked him how it had come about, and he replied after a moment's pause: 'Thank the Lord who took pity on me, the Lord who appeared to St Paul on the road to Damascus,' and would add nothing more. The nearest we have to a description by Manzoni himself of the process and preparation of conversion is that of the 'Unnamed' in *I Promessi Sposi*, though that haughty nobleman's life and character were very far removed from Manzoni's own. Such crises usually come after long subconscious preparation, and were particularly prevalent among the Jansenists. Pascal, whose character and nervous disorders have close parallels to those of Manzoni, went through a similar experience on the bridge of Neuilly. Even Luther's decision to become a monk came during some illumination in a storm on the road to Erfurt. Manzoni himself, whose sceptical attitude

towards miracles in general is shown clearly in *I Promessi Sposi*,
considered as miraculous the lightning conversion from rationalism to fervent belief of a prominent Jewish banker called
Ratisbonne, in the church of St Andrea delle Fratte in Rome in
1842. This had been followed ten days later by the solemn
presentation in the church of the Jesù at the hands of the Papal
Vicar, Cardinal Patrizi, of the three sacraments of baptism, con-
firmation, and communion.

Whatever the preparation, there is a touch of paradox about
the actual crisis of conversion, a hint, possibly, of baroque emotion not very far removed, even, from that of the Catholic
writer particularly disliked by Manzoni, Chateaubriand, who in
his *Génie du Christianisme* had described approvingly the conversion of a Prince Carafa in Naples by the singing of a nun, and
the Jesuits' methods of conversion by music in Paraguay.
Usually Manzoni followed, as he wrote in *I Promessi Sposi*, 'the
method laid down for so long, of observing, listening, comparing,
and thinking before speaking.' Yet whatever the paradox in
method there is no doubt about the depth of his conversion.

VII

How Manzoni's talks with Dègola went we can only guess.
But we know it was a hard time for poor Henriette. Her doubts
and struggles with her Calvinist principles were long and the
discipline was severe. 'You have to fight with the flesh and
blood, my daughter,' repeated Dègola in innumerable interviews.
His notes on these conferences have been preserved. They
were the same, the famous 'Dègola method,' which he had used
to urge Mme Geymüller into the Church five years before, and
was to use with the same success on the mothers of both Mazzini
and Camillo di Cavour. In essence it was a series of discussions
by question and answer which drew the neophyte, through
criticism of the Pelagianism [1] of most of the Catholic Church,

---

[1] Pelagianism was so called after a Welsh theologian of the fifth century (Pelagius
is a translation of the Cymric name Morgan, which means 'the sea'). This heresy
denied both original sin and Divine Grace, holding that Adam's fall was not visited
on his descendants, and that the human will is capable of good by itself. The last
strongholds of this heresy were Wales and Ireland. Although officially refuted at
the Synod of Befry in 519, its influence has persisted throughout the centuries.
It was particularly strong in the High Tory Church in eighteenth-century England.

into his own special form of Jansenist Catholicism. To Henriette, too, Dègola's attacks on the Calvinism both of her lax
father and her bigoted mother were shattering, though she
seems to have shown considerable doctrinal knowledge herself.

Dègola's 'method' was based, possibly, on the instructions
given by Bossuet to the Duchesse de Duras nearly a century and
a half before. First came the teaching of catechism, in which
Dègola included the Jansenist conception of grace. The convert
then wrote these long conferences out from memory. Secondly
came the liturgical abjuration, pronounced according to an
agreed formula, and accompanied by a sermon from Dègola.
The third phase was spiritual direction. Henriette, and presumably Alessandro, were given instructions and rules to guide
them on their new religious road. These were extremely
severe. A copy of those given to Henriette may still be seen
in the chapel of Brusuglio. This 'Règlement de Vie,' as the
document is headed, contains instructions for prayers, litanies,
and the offering of every act to God. It also includes an intense
course of religious reading, most of it French and nearly all
Jansenist, such as Nicole, Arnauld, Le Tourneux, and Quesnel.
For some years Alessandro and Henriette were to find their
every act and thought surveyed by the benevolent but severe
eye of their spiritual adviser.

The news of Dègola's success with the Manzoni family soon
got around. What Fauriel and Mme de Condorcet thought we
can only guess; but by December 1810 the President Agier, one
of the most prominent lay Jansenists in Paris, was writing to
Dègola: 'What you tell me of the progress of the neophyte and
of her mother-in-law is very consoling and satisfactory.' (For
Donna Giulia, not to be left out of any family activity, had taken
to religion too, in her own way.) 'What you add about the
husband is wonderful. What a mercy to be called from so far
away!' And Constant, the former Constitutional Bishop of
Agen, added in the same letter: 'I profit by this little space to
congratulate you on what you tell me about the two Manzonis.
There is a glory in God for the wife and a crown of laurels for
you for your long conferences with the husband.'

The reasons for Dègola's influence over Alessandro are perhaps
summed up best by Francesco Ruffini, a liberal Catholic historian

who spent many years brooding over this problem, and wrote a long work on Manzoni's religious life to prove his Jansenist affiliations:

> Just as a Calvinist finds Jansenism a kind of comfortable theological passage to Catholicism, so a proud rationalist who is fervently converted to faith will not stop at forms and variations of Catholicism such as Molinism (and Socinianism in Protestantism), which concede a wide space to reason and the free human will. No, he will be carried to the exact opposite, that is to the currents like Jansenism which most mortify rationalist pride and denigrate free will, almost as a penance for past excesses of rationalism and as a fuller and more unconditional dedication to God. So Alessandro and Henriette, starting from opposite ends and moved by inverse spiritual impulses, met in Jansenism.

But though Manzoni had repudiated rationalism, he never ceased clinging to reason.

VIII

One result of these profound changes in Manzoni's inner life was a restlessness, a longing, for the first time, to leave France and return to Italy. 'It is only *you*,' he wrote to Fauriel at the end of May 1810, 'who still attach me to this Paris which I don't like at all now; and remember,' he went on, 'that in a short time you will leave me free to dislike it entirely'—he meant when Fauriel and Mme de Condorcet came to spend a long time with them in Italy.

During the early summer packets of plants, many selected by Fauriel, who was also a passionate botanist, were being sent from Paris to Brusuglio, and plants always heralded a move by the Manzoni family. On 2nd June, two weeks after Henriette's formal admission into the Church, the family, consisting of Donna Giulia, Alessandro, Henriette, and the little Giulietta, with numerous nurses and attendants, set off for Brusuglio, determined to try and settle there once and for all.

CHAPTER SIX

Italian Calm; the 'Inni Sacri'

I

THE Villa Manzoni at Brusuglio is a long low house with an enclosing forecourt, and a recessed pillared front in the Lombard Empire style. It lies in the plains some six miles to the west of Milan. Giving on to a large garden, full of rare plants and wooded walks, is a round hall flanked by a series of *salons* which still remain now much as they were in Manzoni's day. Most of the furniture is of the local Empire style, and was put there by Manzoni himself. The study in which *I Promessi Sposi* was written and rewritten overlooks the garden at one end of the house, and is exactly as it was when he died. It is a comfortable and roomy house, obviously built for considerable ease in living. Country houses in Lombardy and Northern Italy, unlike most of those in the rest of the peninsula, are often occupied for a large part of the year. And the house combines with an air of easy comfort which comes from continual occupation, a curious feeling of remoteness, even though it is so near Milan, like that of old houses in Ireland or Wales. But in the distance rise the filmy Alps and around it the poplars quiver in formal rows above the dusty plain.

The house was rather different when the Manzoni family arrived to settle down there in July 1810. The old central block, the villa of the Imbonatis, had been judged uninhabitable when Alessandro had come here with his mother in 1808. Considerable changes had then been begun, but building on the new villa was still in progress and was to continue until 1814. Meanwhile they moved into one of the old wings in the courtyard block. The house at Lecco, Il Caleotto, was in excellent order, and it is a tribute to the strength of Donna Giulia's will-power that this was only used, between 1808 and 1818, when it was sold, for a few short visits in spring and autumn. She never seems to have got over her repugnance to the parts where

97

she had spent her short, unhappy married life, and there is no hint that the thought of setting up house on her own even crossed her mind.   Henceforward she lived entirely with her son and his family, between her own property at Brusuglio and the house in Milan which Alessandro bought in 1813, No. 1 Via Morone on the corner of the Piazza Belgiojoso.

They had a very bad journey from Paris.   Donna Giulia was afflicted by a 'nervous cough.'   At Lyons they all fell ill and had to wait a fortnight to recover.   Bad family news awaited them at Turin.   Henriette received a severe letter of reprimand from her parents about her abjuring of Calvinism, which, they said, had even harmed her sisters' reputations.   Somis de Chavrie, reporting this unfortunate development to Dègola, suggested that Henriette's first reception of the sacraments should be hurried on, although the Jansenists made even greater preparation for this than was usual with a neophyte.   But he added rather despairingly: 'What is the point of making recommendations in something that concerns mother and daughter?'   Alessandro, seeing Henriette's distress, now wrote and asked an old acquaintance who had become Commissioner for Religious Affairs in the Viceregal Government 'to co-operate in tranquillizing a soul as innocent as it is torn and buffeted,' and intervene with the Blondels in their *smoderatissima colera*, their 'most immoderate rage.'   Henriette, in consternation, for she adored her parents, wrote to them protesting that she had not changed her religion just to please her husband (and indeed some would consider the opposite to be nearer the truth).   'If I have embraced the Catholic religion, it is in order to follow and practise what it teaches me; if I acted against my duty I would become contemptible to myself. . . .   I wanted to change my religion of my own free will, on my word of honour before God.'   She had been particularly disgusted, she added with spirit, by the sardonic comments of her uncle.

The correspondence continued when they reached home. Her mother replied that she had been 'betrayed,' would scarcely speak to Alessandro, and completely ignored Donna Giulia. 'She told me,' Henriette recounted to a cousin,

that I would be very silly to think that I had done anything fine or praiseworthy, and that on the contrary everybody despised and ridiculed

me for it; that all who changed their religion came to a bad end . . .
and that one day I would certainly regret the great folly I had committed; to which I replied that I was stricken at having lost her affection,
but as for regretting my change of religion, never! never!

For months the coldness of the Blondels persisted. 'Do not
think they persecute me, Father,' she wrote to Dègola, now
back in Genoa and keeping up an active correspondence with
his spiritual children. 'Oh, quite the contrary: there could not
be people colder or who care less what I do or whether things
go well or badly for me.' But in the end it was Henriette's
stubbornness that won the day. 'My reproaches are all made,'
Mme Blondel eventually wrote. 'You have no more to listen
to; may you be as happy as the tenderest of mothers desires.'
And soon the tables were so completely turned that the mother
was imploring the daughter to come to her, and, somewhat
illogically, blaming Alessandro for the delay. Relations of such
tension are always liable to sudden illogical changes, and when
Henriette did eventually call she found herself for a time being
abused all over again.

These complications had made Dègola realize that by remote
control he could not give his charges the guidance they needed,
and he now found a suitable confessor in Milan. But for some
years he kept an eye on them all by correspondence. Back in
Genoa he was busy on a diatribe against the Jesuits in the style of
Pascal, *Il Catechisimo dei Gesuiti*, and also continued to collaborate
with Grégoire from afar, a fact which was to be important for
Manzoni later on. The new confessor, Luigi Tosi, canon of the
Basilica of Sant' Ambrogio in Milan, was a more tempered Jansenist than his predecessor; for he was a disciple of the Italian
tradition of Bishop Ricci of Pistoia and the Grand Duke Leopold,
which was also considerably less radical in politics than their
French brethren with whom Dègola had identified himself.
Indeed, zealous though he was in religion, Monsignor Tosi was
far from holding any radical or republican opinions. The last
twenty years of his life were to be spent as Bishop of Pavia, an
office to which he was appointed by the Emperor Francis II in
1821. Some of his more saintly characteristics are said to
appear in the character of Cardinal Federigio in *I Promessi Sposi*.

The new confessor began his duties by soothing Henriette

about Dègola's *Règlement de Vie*, which 'tormented' her, as she felt incapable of following it completely.   Apparently when Donna Giulia suddenly presented Dègola's letter of introduction in the street, Tosi had heard nothing about the family conversion and only of the clamorous family scandals; so overcome had he been at the thought of a job which he considered beyond him, that for some time he had found no words to accept.   But once the first shock of the new mission was over, he was delighted with the Manzoni family, and soon reporting enthusiastically to Dègola.   'Not only Henriette, who is an angel of goodness and simplicity,' he wrote in August 1810, 'but also *madama* [Donna Giulia] and even the once-so-proud Alessandro are like little lambs, who receive the simplest instructions with the greatest avidity.'   'They are flowers to add to your crown,' another friend wrote to Dègola.

In Tosi's reports to Dègola life in the Manzoni household in those first years after the conversion appears as peaceful and pastoral as that of the Vicar of Wakefield.   Alessandro was spending his time between reading the New Testament and seventeenth-century French religious philosophers out loud, and experimenting with plants.

II

The interest in horticulture, together with so much else, had been instilled in him by his friends at La Maisonette.   Mme de Condorcet was a passionate gardener and Fauriel an enthusiastic botanist.   It was in fact in the Jardin des Plantes in Paris that the couple, like characters from Proust, had first met in 1801.

Manzoni's comments on gardening to Fauriel were sometimes almost sprightly.   'Come, do come,' he wrote to him on first arriving back at Brusuglio in 1810.   'We'll cultivate, you'll herbalize; ah, how happy I shall be.'   And in 1812, when redesigning the neglected park and garden at Brusuglio, after an aside about the progress of Fauriel's life of Dante he went on: 'You'll find quite a well-developed garden here . . . a mountain that's already about ten feet high, and which the geologists of posterity will affirm has been formed by the Severo, a torrent passing a short distance away.   You will also find some forests, but before they grow up you'll have to send me the seeds in the attached note.'

From 1810 onwards the latter half of most of his letters to Fauriel contained gardening notes or lists of plants. 'Come! Come! I've a thousand planting projects we can carry out together.' He was now experimenting with growing cotton, encouraged throughout Northern Italy by the Viceregal Government in competition with the English trade from Bengal; also with silk and coffee. He was in agricultural projects 'up to the neck,' he said. Requests went to Paris for seeds of flowers, bushes, even of trees such as cedar of Lebanon. He had rather a set-back with a date-palm, for he found after he had planted it six months that it was still only six inches high, and according to the *Dictionary of Agriculture* would take twenty years to grow two or three feet, 'C'est encourageant.' The attempts at cultivating cotton failed, though he reported: 'We've planted Liquidambas, Sopharas, Thuya, and Sapris, which will one day come peeping in at the window at us.' On his desk for consultation he always kept the copy of the *Almanach du Bon Jardinier*, given him with a dedicatory note by Mme de Condorcet; the volume can still be seen in his study at Brusuglio. He had always considered, even from the days of the *Sermoni* in Venice, that writing was not sufficient to occupy a man's life, and as time went on he became more and more immersed in agriculture, which was to be a constant resource in the long, empty periods of nervous prostration that lay ahead. He became an acknowledged expert, mingling the scientific interest of a child of the Enlightenment with the contemporary passion for embellishing parks and estates. Many of his experiments were of lasting value. A plant which he introduced into Italy, a kind of acacia, is now used particularly for binding loose earth together, and can still be seen growing on railway cuttings throughout the peninsula.

III

One enthusiasm which Fauriel did not encourage Manzoni to pursue in his letters was religion. As Sainte-Beuve remarked, this period after the conversion 'must have been a difficult and delicate time for their friendship.'   Only once did Alessandro, in his first golden glow of discovery, mention his religious feelings to the gentle Stoic with the critical mind.   'As for me I will always follow the pleasant habit of writing to you about every-thing that interests me, at the risk of boring you,' he introduced the subject rather diffidently on 21st September 1810, a few days after he, Henriette, and Donna Giulia had solemnly received the sacraments.

I'll tell you then that I am engaged in the most important of pursuits, following up the religious ideas which God sent me in Paris; and the more I have advanced in them the more my heart has been content and my mind satisfied.   Allow me, my dear Fauriel, to hope that you too will find an interest in them.   It is too true, alas, that I fear for you in these terrible words: 'Abscondisti haec a sapientibus et prudentibus, et revelasti ea parvulus'; but no, I don't really fear that at all, for the goodness and humility of your heart is not inferior to your mind and understanding;

then he added: 'Forgive this sermon which the *parvulus* takes the liberty of making to you,' and went on to the safer subject of agriculture.   Since Fauriel's reply is lost, we can only presume from Manzoni's subsequent silence on the matter that he received no encouragement to pursue it.

But the correspondence continued unabated and every letter from Fauriel was an excitement.   It is remarkable, indeed, that while Henrietta's letters to Dègola at this period were long, fervid, almost mystic, Alessandro's letters to Tosi, though full of filial submission and couched in the sincerest religious language, were very short indeed compared to the letters rippling with chatter of life, literature, and horticulture written to Fauriel. One explanation may be that the family were seeing a great deal of Monsignor Tosi during 1810 and 1811.   He would interrupt his heavy canonly duties to spend days, sometimes weeks, in spiritual conversation at Brusuglio and Il Caleotto.   'The Lord has given all three more simplicity and docility than I have ever found in twenty years of ministry among the roughest, lowest people,' he reported enthusiastically to Dègola in August 1810. 'Oh! what a miracle of divine mercy this is! . . .   Our city is highly edified by this prodigy of the Lord; all good people are touched, and foresee great advantage to the cause of religion from such an extraordinary and unexpected grace.' But by the beginning of the following year he was becoming rather less rhapsodical and more analytical about his charges. 'Mme Henriette could not conduct herself better,' he wrote in February 1811.

She has also acquired more frankness with her mother, while her timidity and tenderness used rather to alarm me. . . . Donna Giulia is becoming more and more tranquil; she is gradually detaching herself from the ideas—not wicked, but irregular—of which she was full; she is advancing in fervour and exactness and gives me better hope. . . . As for the good Alessandro, I confess I'm rather worried, as my fears about the waste that can come from so much expensive building at Brusuglio, the worries about his own affairs which he has quite properly begun to attend to, and his conversations with friends in Milan, have not been entirely vain. I should like to see him more seriously occupied, economizing his time more, and becoming more docile to the gentle hints of his wife and mother. . . . Pray much . . . that he may acquire all the grace he needs to respond properly to the very unusual favour which the Lord has granted to him and his family.

A few months after this letter Manzoni himself was writing to Dègola: 'Do pray that it may please the Lord to shake me out of my sluggishness in His service and withdraw from me a timidity which torments and humiliates me, a just punishment for one who not only forgot God but had the misfortune and daring to deny Him.' Meanwhile his friends in Milan were criticizing him from quite another angle. 'Alessandro is engrossed in domestic cares,' wrote the Greek poet Mustoxidi to Fauriel in December 1811. 'He seems to absent himself too often from the Muses, who were liberal in all their favours to him.'

Under the calm surface of the routine at Brusuglio the strains and stresses must have been intense, although family life there was also absorbing. Henriette, after a miscarriage in August 1810, was giving birth at regular intervals, and was to continue to do so until just before her death. The birth of their eldest son Pietro in July 1813 particularly pleased Donna Giulia, though her delight was expressed in rather a self-centred way. 'On the 21st,' she wrote, 'our dear Henriette presented me with a fine little boy, on the very anniversary of my birth and in the same house where I was born.'

Yet though he achieved very little between his twenty-fourth and thirtieth years, domestic cares had not distracted Alessandro entirely from the Muses. At intervals throughout those years he was at work on a series of religious poems, the *Inni Sacri*.

The first of these poems had been planned in Paris immediately after the conversion. But when, early in 1812, Dègola in his zeal began spreading the news that they were works of religious propaganda, Manzoni wrote to him: 'I feel obliged in conscience to disillusion you about something else, in which you show that you expect from me more than I think of doing. The little work which I had thought of in Paris, and which I am working at now, is not substantially religious, though religion is introduced with its precepts and rites; in fact the work is not apologetic as you seem to me to suppose.' Yet running throughout the poems there is, in fact, an oratorical tone which suggests a preoccupation with doctrine at the expense of artistry. Here and there, amid surprisingly florid exuberances, there are touches of the directness and sincerity which was to be his most marked characteristic as an artist. 'I agree with you more than ever about poetry,' he wrote to Fauriel when discussing the technical points of the *Inni Sacri*. 'It must be drawn from the depths of the heart. . . . One must feel, and know how to express one's feelings with sincerity.' Manzoni, like Goethe with his *Gefühl ist alles*, was not one to use such phrases without a deep conviction, and without realizing, too, the gap yawning between sincere feelings and sincere expression.

The *Inni Sacri* were intended to celebrate the various religious festivals of the year. He had planned twelve, but only five actually got written, the last after a long interval. 'The Resurrection,' 'The Name of Mary,' 'The Nativity,' 'The Passion' were written between April 1812 and October 1815. These were all published together in a privately printed edition which was almost completely unnoticed among the more exciting happenings of the year 1815. Even in 1819 G. B. de Cristoferis was writing in *Il Conciliatore* that no one had paid any attention to these poems, which seemed stupendous to him. 'I've tried to bring back to religion those great, noble, and human sentiments which flow naturally from it,' wrote Manzoni to Fauriel when sending him a copy of the verses. 'The Resurrection' was a hymn to truth and brotherly love, which, combined, were destined to regenerate the human family and change the future of the world. 'The truth shall make you free,' as St John had written. 'The Pentecost' foresaw the establishment of this renovated society and invoked various gifts of the Paraclete such as faith, hope, and modesty, all of which virtues were seen in a context of social reorganization.

Amid the general contemporary indifference to the poems [1] there was an unexpected enthusiasm from Goethe, the beginning of an interest which was to grow and be one of the first causes of Manzoni's European reputation. 'Let us accord with pleasure a truly poetic talent to Signor Manzoni,' was Goethe's accolade.

The subject and matter are old, but his manner of joining and treating them seems new and his own. . . . These *Inni* vary in expression and tone; the metres differ, the rhythms delight me. They are dominated by a simplicity of feeling; but their sure throb of talent, their metaphors and transitions make me want to compare them to others and to examine them more carefully. The author shows himself Christian without fanaticism, Roman Catholic without hypocrisy, devout without bigotry. . . . These poems prove that subjects treated in a language stilted for centuries appear fresh and new again as soon as a fresh and youthful talent grasps and uses them.

Stendhal, too, recognized their merits, though he had less sympathy than Goethe with their content; but he seems to have had a distorted idea of their author's fame at the time they were written. 'I have seen from afar M. Manzoni,' he wrote from Milan in 1816, 'a very devout young man who vies with Lord Byron for the honour of being the greatest living lyrical poet. He has written two or three odes which touch me deeply, and which never gave me the feeling of a M. de Fontanes rubbing his forehead in his efforts to be sublime while going off to the Minister to try and net a barony.'

These enthusiasms on the part of agnostics were not echoed in Rome. In an aside when reviewing in the Arcadians' paper a new translation of the odes of Pindar, the Abate Salvagnoli

---

[1] Nowadays, according to an assertion by a modern Italian critic which is difficult to check, 'very few are the nurseries that do not echo with these flowing verses in infantile prattle.'

Marchetti lashed out at 'the miserable, clumsy, and crude mode of versifying produced with so many other unpoetic, un-Italian things by Alessandro Manzoni.'

Sixty years later the founder of modern Italian literary criticism, Francesco de Sanctis, was writing of them in very different terms:

> Their basic ideal is substantially democratic. It is the idea of the century baptized as a Christian idea, of the equality of all men as brothers of Christ, of the reproach of oppression and the glorification of the oppressed. It is the famous trio of liberty, equality, fraternity, but in terms of the Gospels. It is Christianity led back to its ideal and harmonized with the modern spirit. This ideal contains in itself the moral world as modern thought has conceived it.

The implications of these profound and far-reaching generalizations were vast, so vast that it is doubtful how far Manzoni himself, if indeed he thought in such terms, faced up to them.

IV

The idea of Revelation as Revolution (if such a phrase is not drawing de Sanctis's interpretation too far) remained something around which Manzoni appears to have hovered for years. But thought, with men of his temperament, does not always lead to action. Not for him the excesses of the Abbé de Lamennais, who after leading with Joseph de Maistre the most reactionary wing of Catholic propaganda, suddenly took such a plunge to the left that he whirled right out of the Church itself, and finally appeared in the Constituent Assembly of 1848 sitting at the very top of the 'Mountain.' Manzoni, instead, like Don Abbondio in *I Promessi Sposi* (who seems drawn partly from ironical self-observation) felt himself to be 'an earthenware pot forced to travel among a number of iron ones' and took a great deal of trouble devising systems to avoid the impact of the world.

In the year 1812, with half Europe in turmoil and the French armies in Moscow, he preferred to shut himself up in Brusuglio, and write the small poem which he had planned in Paris on 'Vaccination,' modelled on the *Georgics*; 'Verbaque provisam rem non invita sequenter (Horace, Poetics, v. 311) I find is the only rule for style,' he wrote to Fauriel, adding: 'Don't you find it a little odd that in the middle of all this confusion I'm discussing my own affairs? But you know that one of the great merits of poets is that they can always find a moment to talk of their verses.' One effect of the 'confusion' outside was to be two long breaks in the correspondence between the two friends, the first time for a year and then for nearly two years. During these intervals the only news to come down to us from the closed family circle at Brusuglio is in the letters between relations. These give an occasional glimpse of Alessandro as the gay and tender father, couched in the style of eighteenth-century antithesis which was so ingrained in him. 'Giulietta spends as usual half her time laughing and the other half weeping.' 'Pietro vexes and charms us.'

The cares of his growing family, the study of history and the classics, the cultivation of his gardens, took Manzoni even through the dismal year of 1813 and part of 1814. 'Quant à moi,' he wrote to Fauriel after the first interruption of their correspondence at the beginning of 1814. 'Je suis entre la famille, les arbres, et les vers.'

CHAPTER SEVEN

THE END OF THE NAPOLEONIC REGIME; THE 'CONCILIATORE' GROUP; 'MORALE CATTOLICA'

I

THESE systems of defence against the outside world were not as watertight as they appeared. The European events of 1814 were to involve Manzoni in a nervous crisis whose effects were to run through many years. They were also to lead to one of the few direct political acts of his life.

Towards the end of 1813 the viceroyalty of Prince Eugène de Beauharnais in Northern Italy was already tottering. By the middle of December an Austrian army had occupied most of the Venetian territory on the mainland. In February 1814 Murat and the Neapolitan army reached Bologna. In March a force of English and Sicilians commanded by Lord William Bentinck landed at Leghorn. With an army of uncertain loyalty Prince Eugène was wavering in attitude to his stepfather Napoleon, and hoping that his charm and his wife's connections could still get him a throne somewhere. 'He seemed,' wrote Foscolo of him, 'born to reign only in quiet times. He had a strong common sense, but a perplexed heart. . . . He was loving but not liberal or confidential; not generous, except in things that could yield him a quick return; ready to be dominated by any mind superior to his own.' This was not the man to cope with one of the more confused situations of modern war.

In spite of the Holy Alliance none of the invading armies were in agreement. The commanders of every side issued proclamations to appeal to the better nature of the populace. 'You Piedmontese, you noble Tuscans, you subjects of the ancient house of Este,' went that of Marshal Bellegarde, the Austrian commander, 'will return to the happy condition you were in before. The capital of the Catholic world will cease to be the second city of a foreign state.' Murat meanwhile was making rousing promises about the unity and independence of Italy, which even led Manzoni in a moment of enthusiasm to compose *Il Proclama di Rimini*. Within the city of Milan, with the Austrians pressing from the east, the party of the liberal-pro-gressives, the Italici, was filled with ingenuous hopes of allied, particularly British, intentions. Manzoni's friend, Baron Sigis-mondo Trechi, went as emissary of the Italici to Bentinck, while two British officers were infiltrated into Milan and fêted there. Little did they realize that the proposed constitution, one of the more remarkable documents of its kind, put forward by the local British commander, was far too liberal to suit the Tory Cabinet in London; and the position of the two British officers in Milan was curiously like that of forward 'liberators' in the last war.

The situation crystallized quickly. On 8th February 1814, the day before Manzoni took up his pen to renew, after a year's pause, his correspondence with Fauriel, the Austrian army met the French-Italian forces under Prince Eugène on the Mincio. By mid April Prince Eugène was making for Germany with the viceregal treasure, and the Austrians were at the gates of Milan.

II

Now there took place in Milan one of those sudden outbursts of savagery which can sweep the mildest of crowds. The exactions of the last few years had caused a general exasperation in the city against the Viceregal Government. While Melzi, Prince Eugène's deputy, was lying seriously ill, popular hatred had fixed on the severe and unsympathetic figure of the Minister of Finance, General Prina. This feeling appears to have been partly canalized by the liberals of the Italici in the hope that opposition to the Napoleonic Government would encourage aspirations for independence, and so lead to the adoption of Ben-tinck's constitution. Manzoni signed with the Italici a petition to the Allies asking for the calling of electoral colleges, and also wrote to encourage his cousin, Giacomo Beccaria, who was leaving for Paris as secretary to the delegation bearing the petition to the allied powers.

On 19th April, just before this left, when the Austrians were outside the gates, General Prina was attacked in his official residence in the Piazza San Fedele, dragged out into the street, and literally torn to pieces by the mob.   Manzoni's house in the Via Morone was just round the corner from the Piazza San Fedele, and the balconies of the Blondel house in the piazza actually looked across at the house of the Minister of Finance.

The ever-malicious Baron Custodi was a colleague and admirer of Prina's, and went so far as to suggest in his memoirs that Manzoni, with other 'liberal nobles,' had, during the earlier part of the riot, applauded the crowds and urged them on, though they had been horrified later to see Prina, as a result, torn to pieces under their eyes.   It seems almost certain that Count Federigo Confalonieri, the future leader of the Lombard Carbonari, and later prisoner at the Spielberg, not only took part in the riot but led the crowds into the palace, and put his umbrella through the portraits of Napoleon and Prince Eugène in Prina's study.   It was raining hard and the number of umbrellas in the crowd was particularly noticeable—umbrellas were an expensive novelty and showed that progressively minded members of the upper classes were out in force.

Manzoni seems to have spent most of that ghastly day soothing his wife and mother as they listened to the howls of the mob 'in terrible agony and pain,' as Henriette herself wrote.   Four days later Manzoni recounted to Fauriel: 'Our house is situated very near the house where Prina lived [their garden abutted on a house where the wretched Minister escaped for a time until smoked out] so that for some hours we heard the cries of those looking for him, which kept my mother and wife in constant anguish, for they thought that the mob would not stop there. And in fact a few ill-intentioned people did try to profit by this moment of anarchy in order to prolong it, but the civil guards were able to stop them.'   This experience, whether or not it led, as Custodi wrote in an imaginative moment, to 'wild nightmares which threatened his health,' did confirm the nervous horror of crowds that had first gripped him during that firework display in Paris in 1810.   There is no hint from him that he actually went out and looked at the mob; but (a comment which Custodi did not fail to make) direct observation and not hearsay appears to lie behind the analysis of mob psychology in the description in I Promessi Sposi of the attack on the Commissioner

Manzoni at the period of
Il Conciliatore. From a
drawing by Gerosa in
the Casa del Manzoni,
Milan

The Villa Manzoni at Brusuglio. The entrance court
(By permission of Dott. Marino Parenti)

of Supply's house.   In the Prina riot the civil guards also halted
at the edge of the mob, just like that 'squad of Spanish soldiers'
whom Ferrer, in the book, saluted so ironically on his return.
But it is also possible that Federigo Confalonieri, an old school
friend, may have given details from his own direct participation.

In the same letter to Fauriel Manzoni made a balanced judgment on this assassination, and a premature assessment of the
situation:

> The revolution in Italy has been unanimous and I dare to call it wise
> and pure, although it has unfortunately been soiled by a murder.   For
> it is certain that those who made the revolution (and they are the
> biggest and best part of the city) have not been mistaken at all. . . .
> Some people profited by the popular movement to turn it against the
> man who was the butt of public hatred, the Minister of Finance, whom
> they massacred in spite of the efforts many people made to save him.
> Anyway you know that the people everywhere are a good jury and a
> bad tribunal.

This view of the Prina riot as a revolution was not borne out
by events, nor were the other Lombard hopes roused by the
first abdication of Napoleon; for the Austrians, when they
occupied the city two days later, soon acted in a way that the
Italici, but for the euphoria of the moment, should have
foreseen.

At the end of April 1814, before this was clear, Manzoni
congratulated Fauriel on this abdication ('What joy such a
happy denouement must cause you.') and on the draft for a
new French constitution supported by the Idéologues.   The
rejection of this by Louis XVIII was a first disillusion, soon
followed by the treatment of the Lombard deputation in Paris.
The Emperor Francis refused to see them; the Emperor Alexander received them for two minutes and kept the conversation
carefully to the subject of 'the beautiful Italian countryside and
sky'; while Castlereagh told them flatly that constitutions were
'expansive experiments.'   The first hints of allied policy made
most of the Idéologues veer back to Napoleon when he landed
for the Hundred Days, promising constitutions in all directions.
Manzoni too began to see Napoleon as a last prop against reaction,
and his defeat as a dimming of hopes for years ahead.   When he
was told the news of Waterloo he was sitting in a bookshop in

Milan. He collapsed into convulsions and had to be carried home.

Years later he looked back at the events of that year with an irony which seemed to hide, almost, a wry despair. 'When the revolution ended in 1814,' he told Cantù, 'it was found that the whole of Europe, exhausted, loved with a true love the representatives of despotism; first, because they seemed to be bringing back quiet; second, because very few can hate someone without loving that someone's enemy.'

III

One result, particularly nerve-racking for Manzoni, of the new Austrian occupation was that troops were quartered in every one of his homes. In the summer of 1814, with Donna Giulia, Henriette, and two sick children in the house, Il Caleotto was full of soldiers. At Brusuglio there were forty; even the new house in the Via Morone which they had bought the year before had troops in it 'like ants.' The family kept on moving from house to house to keep the best bedrooms from being requisitioned.

When the troops finally moved into barracks all three houses needed expensive repairs. Manzoni had been spending his own and his mother's money thoughtlessly for years. Even when it was first bought, at far too high a price, the Milan house (with which they were delighted 'for its really happy aspect both in winter and summer') had needed 'a great deal of repair.' Then huge sums had been spent on the building of the new central block at Brusuglio. Money was also flowing away alarmingly at Il Caleotto, where the estate was being maladministered by an agent. This sudden accumulation of debt brought home to Alessandro the fact that he was a disastrously incapable business man. A year or two later he handed over the whole administration of his property to his cousin, Giulio Beccaria.

Though the causes of his financial difficulties were various, it was more than a coincidence that these came to a head at this time of general nervous and emotional crisis, and that both happened just when the European situation was suddenly darkening.

Manzoni was not one of those neurasthenics who dwell on their ills, but in the letters of this period there are constant little mentions of them. The nervous attacks he had occasionally had in Paris, he wrote in March 1816, had been quite cured by his transfer to Italy; but they had started up again in the last months —ever since, apparently, that fit on the news of Waterloo. Restlessness, anxieties, strange discouragements, would dog him for days. 'Every time I feel I am without any help at hand I fear a collapse; and I find myself in such a state of unbearable agitation that the only remedy, long walks, becomes impractical.' This habit of long walks, unusual for Italians, was to last him all his life. 'When melancholy is gaining on me and I feel it getting me down I go for long walks. Sometimes I get discouraged and return; if I persevere I always feel better afterwards.' But he was never able to go out alone, for voids were apt to open up before him just as he was about to cross a street. These outings would last three or four hours, and he usually covered well over ten miles. Walks in Milan he found at first 'a cheerless distraction; streets seem to be one of the nastiest productions of man,' though later in life these afternoon perambulations round the city became a regular habit. In 1816 he would sometimes walk out from Milan to Brusuglio, spend three or four hours going round the gardens, and then walk back to the city, a round tour of nearly fifteen miles.

But these long tramps were palliatives and not cures. Henriette was getting very worried. 'The uncertain state of my Alessandro's health,' she wrote to her cousin and confidante Carlotta de' Blasco at the end of October 1816,

is another reason why I have so little time free, as his nervous pains do not allow him to be alone for an instant. I don't know what name to give to his illness other than the one I have given you, as, thanks be to God, his physical health is not bad. . . . You can imagine how worried we are about his condition, though he's usually so sweet and amiable that every time he mentions his ills the stranger they seem. He has tried to master them a number of times, but this effort does him more harm than ever. Once when he was alone in the garden he felt the pains seize him, tried to overcome them by forcing himself not to think of them, felt himself fainting, and then having nothing else to help him he nearly lost the sight of an eye by trying to breathe in some extremely

strong Lecco water [ammonia] which he had on him for such eventuali-
ties, and which in his distress he spilt into his eye. . . .   But happily,
thanks to prompt remedies and some days in bed, our blind man has
recovered all his sight. . . .   His health has not suffered, but un-
happily his apprehensions have only increased.

An uncontrolled imagination, he knew, played a great part,
'but that is not an enemy it's enough to know in order to defeat.'
And society could be quite other than a distraction.   As, with
his subtle novelist's observation, he wrote to Fauriel:

Many people, by recommending one to forget one's ailments, make
one think of them at the very moment one's thoughts are resting on
something far removed.   It's a strange sort of comfort to hear people
say ten times a day: be gay, there's nothing like it for your complaint.
Certainly it's an excellent remedy, but suggesting it is not putting it
into practice.   They don't realize that by saying 'be gay' they mean
'you're gloomy' and that nothing is less conducive to gaiety than that
idea.

Perhaps he could escape from himself by travel?   How green
seemed the far-off hills of France, and how he found himself
longing for his old friends!

'Neither a letter, nor two, nor a volume, can suffice for all I
want to say to you,' he wrote to Fauriel in February 1816, 'and
I must have the hope of seeing you again, of spending some time
with you, so that the memory of our friendship does not become
as sad and piercing as it is dear'; and a month later he repeated:
'I have never felt the prize of your friendship as I do at present,
never as at present have I so regretted your company.'   He was
filled with nostalgia for

that little room at La Maisonette which gives on to the garden, that
slope at St Avoie, that hillside from which one sees the course of the
Seine so clear; and that islet covered with willows and poplars, that
cool, calm valley, that is where my imagination is always roaming.
With what pleasure I recall the times we spent in those places with our
good friends; then a little bitterness was mingled with all my pleasure
—a poignant regret for Italy, a regret which I am sure of not feeling
now.   How often when I am meditating on something that interests
me, I imagine myself talking it over with you; how often I think, in the
middle of some tedious wrangle, that we would find ourselves agreeing
—you with whom one can never discuss grand and noble ideas without

learning something.   In my memory I go over our talks on literature.
It seems to me that the years that have passed since that time, and a little
solitude, have brought me very near your ideas, and that now I should
be much worthier of listening to you.

How were his old friends in Paris? he kept on asking, naming
a variety of people, most of whom were either rationalists or the
most active of radicals.   Was the long-promised visit of Mme de
Condorcet and Fauriel never to take place?   Then, he suddenly
thought, he would go to them.

IV

The idea of a visit to Paris horrified Monsignor Tosi and
worried Henriette.   'Pray that this plan may not be against
the will of God,' she wrote to Dègola in April 1817, 'that He
may deign to rectify our desires, and that all may be for His
glory.   It is certain that my husband only considers the journey
as a distraction . . . by which he hopes finally to vanquish, at
least in part, the nerves which make any sort of occupation
impossible for him.'   Then significantly she asked Dègola, on
her husband's behalf, for a letter of introduction to Grégoire.

It was a trying summer for poor Henriette.   Dry dusty winds
were blowing round the isolated house in the plain.   The silk
crop was destroyed, a storm had broken a number of acacias,
and the garden was like a devastated wood.   She could not even
take her sulphur baths because the weather was so bad.   And
on top of it all, 'Alessandro doesn't know how or is unable to
detach himself from his family, so we must all go with him.   It
seems rather a big enterprise and one which very much puts me
out, but it seems necessary for my poor husband's health.'   Her
worry was understandable as the youngest child, Sofia, was only
a few months old, and travelling in the unsettled Europe of the
time was difficult and sometimes dangerous.

Donna Giulia, however, was more than game.   At intervals
right up to the end of her life she would long for France and its
associations.   'When I remember Auteuil,' she wrote to Mme de
Condorcet, 'I can't bear to think of myself here.'   Donna
Giulia, ardent as her conversion had been, was also having
trouble with her religious life.   'So great has been the mercy of

E

God towards me,' she wrote to Dègola, 'that my humble love for Him should be as strong. Yet I find myself so negligent and so full of regard for my own person that I feel almost more blameworthy at present than during the life of iniquity which I lived in the past.' Alessandro's state of health clearly meant to her that they must all leave for Paris at once. 'Alessandro is permanently in the grip of convulsions,' she wrote, with her usual exaggeration, to her uncle de' Blasco in July 1816, 'and both he and us feel an urgent need [*bisognissimo*] of going to France.'

By the spring of 1817 Manzoni had reached the point of considering setting off alone, and built up an unlikely dream of himself travelling alone with a young couple, the Paravicinis, who were going to Paris on their honeymoon. On arrival, he wrote, he would go straight to La Maisonette; he added that he had been alarmed by the rumours of riots and white terrors after the trial of Marshal Ney, and would find out in Paris if it was safe to bring his family. 'Is there much police and diplomatic supervision?' he asked Fauriel. Family difficulties, however, finally made him 'hurriedly descend from the diligence when I was already sitting in it' in imagination.

Frustrating as all this was, it was nothing to the blow that was to fall a month later. In May 1817 Manzoni's passport, with medical and police certificates attached, was presented to the Austrian governor for counter-signature. This was refused.

Once more the walls enclosing the withdrawn household had not stood up to the impact of the outside world. Alessandro took the blow in silence. 'I don't like to dwell on this subject, which offers me nothing agreeable to say,' he wrote with careful understatement to Fauriel. It was Donna Giulia who had most difficulty in resigning herself, and showed 'haughty contempt' as Tosi wrote, while Henriette in the background was quietly relieved. Milan, they found, had become 'unbearable for all of us,' and the family withdrew to the solitude of Brusuglio. Manzoni was not to see Paris again until late in 1819.

V

The refusal of Manzoni's passport was due partly to his connection with the group of friends in Milan whose conversation and activities Monsignor Tosi was continuously deploring.

This group, most of whom had been members of the Italici party of 1814, were the direct heirs of the Società del Caffè of half a century before, and included the most intelligent and enlightened Milanese of the day. But these had quickly found the intentions of their Austrian masters very different from those of the early days of the benevolent monarchy of Joseph II and Leopold. This had already been foreseen by Foscolo from his exile in Switzerland in 1815:

Austria will give its laws, its criminal methods, the censorship of the press, the ecclesiastical inquisitors . . . not only will it return to its own institutions, but to straighten the tree bent to one side will pull very hard on the other, keeping for Germany the liberal reforms of Joseph II and sending to Milan a regency of priests, nobles, and Jesuit confessors . . . bitter opponents of every reform and of the very name of Joseph II.

The Emperor Francis I confirmed this judgment by announcing at the University of Pavia: 'I want faithful subjects, not enlightened citizens.' The new Austrian regime in Lombardy was in fact slow, ordered, and not at first particularly repressive: the Italian provinces of the empire were treated as conquests to be governed benevolently under bureaucratic and military centralization. Soon most of the higher posts of the administration were in the hands of Austrians.

Behind the enlightened nobles and liberal intelligentsia of the Italici was a new and as yet inarticulate power, that of the rising middle class which had been fostered and encouraged by the Napoleonic regime. This resented the return of aristocratic privilege and of clerical assertion, and was particularly hit by the condemnation of the Freemasons, of which the Viceroy Eugène had been Grand Master; more important still, it found that the new frontiers were paralysing trade.

Although the Italici were not to come out into the open until the Carbonari movements of 1821, already in 1815 the wily

Austrian governor, Marshal Bellegarde, was being as acute
though not so appreciative about them as the Abbé Galiani had
been of the Società del Caffè fifty years before.   'The men of spirit
and letters,' he reported to Metternich, 'are trying to write with
a common purpose, which under an academic form hides the
political aim of making Italy its own master, an idea that is
disturbing even as a Utopia.'   Even more alarming were the
reports from all over the peninsula that the liberal independents
were supported by English travellers, such as Byron and Lady
Morgan, and by Russian agents, representatives of the Emperor
Alexander's Messianic phase.

The activity of this Lombard group at first took forms which
did not appear on the surface to be subversive to the established order.   Federigo Confalonieri supported English methods
of education such as the Lancaster system, and helped to introduce
the new discoveries of the Industrial Revolution into Northern
Italy, particularly the spinning-jenny which started the vast
North Italian cotton industry.   He also built the first steamboat
to navigate the River Po, down which he and his friends slowly
chugged, discussing the relations of philosophy and industry.
The group also included men such as Romagnosi who was a
pioneer of Italian political economy, and Gaetano Cattaneo who
first tried to bring scientific methods into antiquarian research.
Closely linked to these reformers, whose practical trend followed
the traditions of Pietro Verri and his collaborators half a century
before, were writers such as Giovanni Berchet, the disciple of
the new romanticism, and the poet Silvio Pellico; these were
flanked by amateur and noble philosophers such as Ludovic de
Breme ('an open freethinker'), in whose box at the Scala in 1816
Stendhal met Byron, and the witty and erudite atheist, Ermes
Visconti di San Vito, who was one of Manzoni's greatest friends.
Round them, acting as a kind of international liaison officer,
fluttered the 'legendary baron' (as he was known in the Manzoni
household), Sigismondo Trechi, dandy, philosopher, and man
of the world, a remarkably efficacious and elegant conspirator,
well known in all the *salons* of Paris and London.

For years this group, who, as Marshal Bellegarde had admitted,
were the best minds in the North, refused to collaborate with
the official Government organ, the *Biblioteca Italiana*.   Monti

had at first accepted the editorship of this paper, but withdrew on finding that this effort at rehabilitation was as ineffective as the odes *Mystic Homage* and *Return of Austria*, with which he had greeted the new rulers. In August 1815 Manzoni also refused to collaborate. He had received the invitation 'with no less gratitude than amazement,' he wrote guardedly to the editor, Giuseppe Acerbi, but there were 'many reasons' why he had determined never to enter into any literary association. To a contributor to the paper he wrote in more open terms: 'I am ready to serve the Government in some decent enterprise which has a certain decorum, but not on something which announces itself in the first sheets as servile and entirely mercenary.' For five years Acerbi waited to get his own back, until the appearance of Manzoni's first tragedy in verse, *Il Conte di Carmagnola*.

In the autumn of 1817 the group managed to found their own organ, *Il Conciliatore*. It scarcely lasted a year. Silvio Pellico, then one of the most advanced radicals in the peninsula, was the chief editor, supported by Confalonieri, de Breme, Berchet, Visconti, and another poet and friend of Manzoni's, Torti.

Articles on literary polemics were mingled in *Il Conciliatore* with others on technical subjects, as they had been in *Il Caffè*. The ostensible aim of the new paper was a literary one: to reconcile, as the name suggested, the warring sides in the contemporary struggle between the classicists and the romantics, with the underlying aim of achieving some united front in ideas against the foreign occupier. 'We call it that,' wrote Silvio Pellico to Foscolo, 'because we propose to conciliate . . . not the true with the false but all the sincere lovers of truth. The public already realizes that this is not a publication of mercenary hacks but of literary men, who may have different views but are all joined together to sustain, as far as possible, the dignity of the Italian name.'

Most of the contributors were on the side of the romantics, a literary affiliation which then, unlike in France ten years later, almost inevitably meant also Liberalism in politics. But the repudiation of mythology and of all rules based on authority was linked in *Il Conciliatore* with the anti-academic, anti-rhetorical tradition of Parini. Manzoni, for instance, in 1818 wrote a short poem, *L'Ira di Apollo* (which he did not, however, publish in *Il Conciliatore*), ridiculing the use of classical mythology by poets such as Monti, and encouraging the romantic Berchet to find themes for poetry in the simple observation of life.   This direct and rooted sense of reality prevented the group of *Il Conciliatore* from falling into the exaggerations of contemporary European—particularly German—romanticism, with its love of the mysterious and the exotic.   The Lombard romantics declared in the announcement of *Il Conciliatore* that they wanted to be representatives of the party of reason, and affirmed that 'the imagination, if it is not based on the reality of people and things, is more an abuse than a release of the mind.'   They insisted on the study, through history and psychology, of man as an individual and as a social being.   Since political questions could not be openly discussed in the paper, these themes were put in literary guise, as in de Breme's review of the *History of the Inquisition* by Llorente, and Pellico's comments on the world in his dramatic criticism.

In spite of the editor's precautions, the anti-authoritarian trend of *Il Conciliatore*, with its insistence on logic and reason and its interest in practical innovations and reforms, was soon alarming the Austrians, who saw it as endangering their centralized administration and its rigid control from Vienna.[1]   Even in the first number of *Il Conciliatore*, published in September 1817, the aims of the paper were clear to an observant eye.   It opened with a long and apparently innocuously literary review by Pellico of a new edition of Camoens's *Lusiads*.   The article went on to recall the days of Portuguese prosperity and ended with a picture of the great Portuguese of the past calling to the living: 'We are still alive.'   Articles followed on law, economics, and science by names soon to be famous all over the peninsula. The Geneva correspondents were Pellegrino Rossi, the future Prime Minister of Pius IX in his liberal phase, and Simonde di Sismondi, the historian and intimate of Mme de Staël.   The

---

[1] In the words of De Sanctis, the Austrian Empire and the papacy were then becoming the champions of 'a new philosophy, a new literary and political vocabulary.   Scepticism and materialism were the two enemies now, and against them rose spirituality taken even to mysticism and idealism.   Divine rights were opposed to the rights of nature, legitimacy to the sovereignty of the people, authority, and order to liberty.   The Middle Ages came to the surface again, glorified as the cradle of the modern spirit.   The first words of the new century were religion, faith, Christianity, the ideal, and the infinite.'

sales, as is apt to happen with this type of magazine, were badly organized, particularly abroad.   Sismondi, for instance, asked Pellico why no canvassing had been done in England, where the paper would have aroused particular interest.   In Germany Goethe, on his own initiative, got the support of the Grand Duke of Weimar.   In each successive new issue the character of the paper became clearer, and the censorship grew heavier, until it was tapping, either as contributors or subscribers, all the chief currents of opposition to the Austrians in Northern Italy.   Soon the editorial committee meetings of *Il Conciliatore* (at one of which Byron's *Childe Harold* was read to enthusiastic applause) [1] were being considered as subversive plots.   On 17th October 1819 Silvio Pellico was called by the Austrian police and warned that the paper was to avoid any reference to politics.   Five days later the group of founders spontaneously decided to cease publication.

Il Conciliatore, like *Il Caffè*, was a landmark in the long Italian journey towards national self-respect.   Like *Il Caffè* it prepared the way for the great movements and struggles whose aims, both in the next fifty years and in modern times, went and still go far beyond national independence.

VI

Manzoni in these years must have found the attitude towards the Austrians of his confessor, Monsignor Tosi, increasingly irritating.   Tosi was more and more inclined to accept the Austrian occupation and all its implications, and evidently had no hesitation in showing what he felt about his spiritual charge's rationalist and agnostic friends of *Il Conciliatore*.

The relations with Monsignor Tosi seem to have reached some sort of crisis in 1817, after the refusal of the passports for Paris. Donna Giulia, writing to Mme de Condorcet, attributed her

---

[1] Byron's association with *Il Conciliatore* first aroused the suspicions of the Papal Secretary of State, Cardinal Consalvi.   'At Milan a so-called romantic society has been formed with the aim of teaching that man is not subject to any principle of religion or morality; many gentlemen are inscribed in it, particularly the celebrated Pellegrino Rossi, who is in touch with Lord Byron.   This Byron went to Bologna to form the sect there. . . .'   The cardinal's information was typical of inaccurate agents' reports.

son's abnormal state that summer to 'des causes morales,' as well
as to a number of physical disturbances.   Manzoni's inner life,
as Ruffini, the biographer of his religious life, wrote, was rather
like the water on the high seas, which is less liable to choppy
waves than the shallower water nearer the shore, but hides
inscrutable depths.   There are hints that he was profoundly
restive during that spring and summer of 1817.   Tosi, who had
been so delighted at the refusal of the passports that one biographer has even suggested that he had a hand in the refusal
himself, after commenting exultantly to Dègola in June: 'It was
the Grace of God!' went on to write of his penitent in terms
which show how restive, for a time, had become the once quiet
'little lamb' of 1810:

Henriette has written to you about the projected journey, and how
Alessandro took the reverse in good part.   I must add that after the
Grace received in Paris, of which you were the principal instrument,
this was the greatest that could be obtained from the Lord.   The
excellent young man has very much changed.   Reflections on the
grievous error he was about to commit have recalled him to his good
sentiments.   He has put himself in the hands of the Lord, and received
Holy Communion twice since that period.   He has returned to the
confidence he first had in me, which had rather cooled, as I had declared
myself too openly.   He scarcely talks politics any more, or talks of
them with moderation.   He attends to his Christian duties to the real
edification of his family.   Though he has not yet taken up serious study
again because of the time wasted in preparations for the journey . . .
and partly because of nerves, he is quiet in the house, sparing in his
food and drink, modified in his projects for spending—in fact he has
received great benefits from the Lord.

This mysterious crisis was not so safely overcome as Tosi
considered.   A rather false calm was reigning at Brusuglio.
'May God preserve the tranquillity which reigns among us now,'
Henriette wrote to Dègola three days after Tosi's letter, in what
seems to have been a breathing-space between difficult moments.
'I hope you understand of what tranquillity I am talking, for it
is only in appearance, and though God be thanked for that, it is
not the one which we desire.'
Tosi, as he had mentioned in his letter to Dègola, was expecting Manzoni to get down to some serious work which would

mark the end of this limited phase of independence.   By this
Tosi did not mean the verse-tragedy of *Carmagnola*, begun in
January 1816, which he considered as a frivolous deviation of
his talented charge's creative energies.   The serious work
advised by Tosi, which held up the completion of *Carmagnola*
for two years, was a detailed apologia for Catholicism, *Osserva-
zioni sulla Morale Cattolica*.   This was based on a refutation of
Volume XVI, Chapter 127 of Sismondi's *History of the Italian
Republics*, which contained an attack on the abuses of the Catholic
Church.

At times during the composition of this work Manzoni seems
to have had recalcitrant moments, for Tosi reported rather
proudly to Dègola that his charge was apt to deviate on to more
enthralling subjects, and had to be locked up sometimes in the
study at Brusuglio until he had composed a certain number of
pages of *Morale Cattolica*.   The group of friends in Milan were
surprised that the 'once so proud Alessandro' accepted these
methods of coercion, and objected to the way he allowed himself
to be turned from poetry to theology.   The antiquarian Gaetano
Cattaneo, when sending Goethe the copy of *Inni Sacri* which the
sage was to greet so enthusiastically, added that they were by
'the same person who is working on the tragedy of *Carmagnola*;
but the devil has interfered to distract him from this enterprise,
which looked like being original, and to plunge him into theological works.   He is a Newton who begins his Apocalypse too
early.'   Such strictures could not but irritate their object,
however he may have acknowledged their truth in his inmost
heart.   'It is understandable that Alessandro should prefer
living in Paris to living in Milan,' wrote Donna Giulia rather
disingenuously to Tosi, 'as he gets so disgusted with that blessed
mania they have here of talking over other people's affairs.'

Ruefully, as he laid aside the manuscript of *Carmagnola*,
Manzoni wrote to Fauriel, that it was 'rather like the building
of the Louvre, which had been begun in the Middle Ages and is
not finished at the time I write,' and later: 'One of my friends
says he'll have to get a machine for me so that I can compose
tragedies!'

He was plunging into a whole new cycle of reading and study
for *Osservazioni sulla Morale Cattolica*, which was absorbing him

* E

more and more deeply, and left him little time for other work. *Morale Cattolica*, paradoxical and contradictory as it sometimes is in detail, turned out to be a reasoned statement of its author's beliefs, many of them fundamental to his later work. It was conceived as a counter-attack to Sismondi's, not as a creative expression of Catholicism in the grand manner such as the books of Chateaubriand and Lamennais, and it has no notable place in religious literature. Although its style, dry, reasoned, concentrated, does not make for easy reading, it is an index of the religious thought that he was to express later, in poetic and imaginative terms, in *I Promessi Sposi*.

Sismondi had tried to show that Catholic morality was a 'reason for the corruption of Italy,' and Manzoni began firmly: 'I am convinced that it is the only morality that is holy and also reasoned at every point; that every corruption comes not so much from transgressing it, as from not knowing it, and from misinterpreting it.' He then went on to discuss the indivisibility of faith and morals from logic, and showed his constant preoccupation to identify truth and goodness. In any system of morals which was absolutely distinct from theology Manzoni found two faults, lack of beauty, or rather lack of completeness, and lack of motives. 'No system of morals apart from the Catholic can at the same time suggest the most beautiful feelings and actions, and give motives for preferring them.' And yet he put in one or two remarks which showed no great reverence for the superstructure of the Church, and expressed a lifelong attitude towards the Vatican. 'I may be deceiving myself, but I believe that when religion was despoiled in France of external splendour, when it had no other strength than that of Jesus Christ, it could talk louder and was heard more.' He made a closely reasoned attack, on the other hand, on Utilitarian philosophy. 'This system puts forward that the true utility of the individual always accords with general utility'; but the Utilitarians, in taking over the words of the Gospels, 'love your neighbour as yourself,' interpreted the morality of an action in proportion to its usefulness for the greatest number; which, Manzoni went on, is to say 'that there are people of whom one need take no account whatsoever as they are the smallest number, and still operate morally.' Implicit in this attack on the Benthamites was Manzoni's belief that there is no logical or moral truth which is not accessible to all, as it has its roots in a quality which belongs to all. This intuitive quality he called 'good sense' or the 'intimate sense,' and made it into a criterion that could distinguish the true from the false, the good from the evil, and so the beautiful from the ugly. 'The interior modesty of the ordinary man deepens his intelligence, and carries him straight to the point which the greatest thinkers reach after having travelled through a vast cycle of sublime thoughts.' This concept is not original, nor indeed is anything in *Morale Cattolica*. It may have come from Vico and was certainly developed later by Rosmini; but it is constantly present in Manzoni's thought, and permeates *I Promessi Sposi*.

Manzoni left logic for faith when he attempted to put forward a positive philosophic system based on religion. As Sismondi wrote about *Morale Cattolica* to a friend: 'We [i.e. Manzoni and Sismondi] are like two fencers trying to fight on a dark night without seeing each other. When he thinks he has got in some blows at me in one corner of the room I am in the other, and we never get to grips. We do not attach the same sense to words, we have not the same ideas in view.' Manzoni, for instance, after establishing by a series of logical moves that there is no identity but a concord between what is useful and what is just, concluded: 'This concord has been explained by Revelation, which has shown how, by means of this justice, one can arrive at perfect happiness.' And once Revelation was reached no more logical discussion was possible.

Here and there in his analysis of the processes of faith we catch sight of the subtle observer in a moment of detached penetration. After attacking Voltaire's statement that belief is not in itself a virtue, he went on: 'The truths of faith are opposed in so many ways to pride and the sensual appetites that the mind feels a certain aversion and fear, and tries to avoid concentrating on them'; for 'whether one likes or dislikes a thing that is put forward for belief has a potent influence on the way such a thing is examined, in admitting or rejecting its proofs.' But faith 'depends on the act of will, which decides the mind to examine' and on 'the disposition of the heart.' So everyone can believe, it is just a question of being well disposed; in fact it is a moral duty to believe. But, as the agnostic Professor Momigliano remarked, the will can modify the feelings but not bring faith to birth; and Manzoni forgot that his own first impulse to faith lay in a complex and mysterious state of mind, without which the serene grandeur of his attitude to religion would vanish altogether. The application of logic to faith, in fact, the attempt to unify all truth in a logical religious system, could scarcely succeed, as such a system was based on a truth or a feeling which was itself not logical. But once this was accepted, and the starting-point admitted, the rest was difficult to refute.

Manzoni himself was very humble about the book when he sent a copy to Fauriel: 'I feel the title, if you just heard that alone, is of a nature to arouse cheerless forebodings. It is a *refutation*, that is a kind of work none of which, I think, live long, and where the lowest passions of literature (and that's saying a lot) have been exercised.' Underlying the religious explanation in the book is a curiously cheerless note, a sense of the inadequacy of every human joy. It was an attitude Manzoni was to give to a number of his characters in various works at this period of his life: to Ermengarda in *Adelchi*, Napoleon in *Il Cinque Maggio*, and the 'Unnamed' in *I Promessi Sposi*. There was a revealing phrase, perhaps, about his attitude to religion in the fragmentary second part of *Morale Cattolica*, which was never finished. 'Religion only wishes to lead us to wisdom and moderation without unnecessary pain, only to take us by tranquil reflection to that reasonableness which we reach by weariness or by a kind of desperation.'

The reception of the book naturally varied according to the belief of the reader. To Rosmini it expressed the moderating force of intellect applied to religion, as opposed to the inflated morbid sentimentality of Chateaubriand with his exaltation of passion and of the dark instinctive forces of man; while Sismondi commented: 'Signor Manzoni describes Catholic morality as it ought to be, I describe abuses as they are.' The opinion of the group of *Il Conciliatore* was reflected in remarks by Giusti, the poet and friend of Manzoni, who told Sismondi that the Italians had never applauded the book much, 'and without in any way lacking in respect to Manzoni it was judged an error, or at least a work suggested with other aims by someone near him.' Ruggero

Bonghi's opinion was that 'even those who do not like the doctrine of the book must admit that it shows a rare force and a subtle and perspicacious argument,' while modern agnostics such as Benedetto Croce have dismissed it as 'illogical' and 'anachronistic.'

Morale Cattolica took a year to write, and was published in 1819. Some biographers consider that by this more or less formal submission to his confessor, the breach between Manzoni and Tosi was healed. But with Manzoni's hidden nature, much prouder, more stubborn and independent than ever appeared on the submissive surface, it may be doubted whether the flowing trust and confidence of the period immediately after the conversion was ever fully re-established. A passage which he wrote for *Morale Cattolica* and then cut out before publication may be significant of his attitude towards his confessor:

There is perhaps no discovery which so much affects a man's pride as that of finding himself in intellectual dependence, of discovering that he has been, without knowing it, the instrument of an astute domination, of having done on another's impulse what he had thought he had done voluntarily and mainly on his own judgment. At this idea all the passions rise as at a usurpation of their rights, and with all the more cause as they find a support in reason.

For, like his fellow scholar Don Ferrante, whose portrait he painted in *I Promessi Sposi*, Manzoni 'wanted neither to command nor to obey.'

In 1819 Monsignor Tosi sent a copy of *Morale Cattolica* to the Abbé de Lamennais, whom he admired at this time, with the remarks: 'It's by one of my spiritual children, who after deplorable straying during his long period in Paris, when he knew the most celebrated thinkers, consented to use his rare philosophical talents in the service of religion. . . . He undertook the work at my suggestion.' But the quiet stubbornness of Manzoni's technique in resisting Tosi's 'suggestions' may be gauged by the way he treated a new task now imposed on him by his confessor, the translation of Lamennais's *Essay on Religious Indifference*. Although it was never directly stated, and no translator's name appeared on the title-page of the Italian edition (an omission which may in itself be indicative of Manzoni's attitude), it seems almost certain that the translator, 'the young fervent convert' mentioned by Tosi in his letters to Lamennais, was Manzoni himself.

The Italian edition comprised, however, only the first and strictly religious part of this essay. Try as he might, Tosi was unable to get his 'young man of most cultivated mind' to translate the second, political part, a plea for the divine right of kings and for the reactionary Jesuit politics which took the traditionalism of de Maistre and Bonald to extreme consequences. 'Some chapters of this work,' wrote Silvio Pellico of the second volume of the *Essay* in *Il Conciliatore* of 24th June 1819, 'breathe an intolerance which is very contrary to the pacific spirit of the Gospels.' Another review in the same number of *Il Conciliatore* warmly commended Grégoire's and Lanjuinais's *Chronique Religieuse*, 'the reading of which we cannot recommend warmly enough to those who are capable of seeing religion, philosophy, and liberty united in a holy and indissoluble alliance.' When Manzoni finally got to Paris in 1819 he avoided Lamennais. Tosi, anxious to arrange a meeting, had to make lame excuses to Lamennais, such as that Manzoni was very shy and bad at meeting new people, and that only old and intimate friends brought him out of his reserve. Eventually Tosi was forced to admit that Manzoni was unlikely to visit Lamennais as in spite of his admiration for the French abbé's writings on religion, he disagreed profoundly with the other's absolutist ideas. 'He [Manzoni] wants everyone to have a constitution which removes rules and absolute powers, and prevents abuses.' Instead, on arrival in Paris, Manzoni was to make straight for the Abbé Grégoire, whose group Lamennais had attacked as 'anarchists.'

It is an ironic comment on the changes brought about by time that forty years later, when Lamennais was condemned for his extreme radical views and had left the Church, Manzoni criticized the ardour with which the old abbé was then battling against Catholic abuses. Lamennais's move to extreme democratic fervour, his opposition of 'the Christianity of the human race' to 'the Christianity of the papacy' shocked the old Manzoni. 'Too much pride! The pride of doubt! . . . His pride precipitated him into incredulity. He didn't die in the Church.' And when Mme Louise Colet, who has described this conversation, interjected that Lamennais's death showed a simple and

Stoic firmness and a detachment from the world (he even asked to be buried in a pauper's grave), Manzoni replied: 'Stoicism is not religion; one must die a Christian.'

Yet there is much in Lamennais's later work, with its influence on Gioberti, Mazzini, and even the Christian Socialists at the end of the century, that would have appealed to the Manzoni of this second Paris period.

VII

The feeling that he must get away and the recurrent nostalgia for Paris, had been growing on him ever since the sale of the Caleotto property in November 1818. This proof of his own incompetence, for Donna Giulia now took over the management of Brusuglio and her brother that of the rest of Manzoni's property, seems to have been one cause of the nervous attacks which seized him again at the end of 1818. Losing Il Caleotto was a wrench for him, though not apparently for Donna Giulia, who could obviously have prevented the sale: presumably she was only too glad to see the last of the house. It was sold with all its contents, and with fourteen properties of varying size—farms, fields, and vineyards—around it. At the sale, which was very carelessly conducted, valuable furniture and pictures sold for a fraction of their value, such as a collection of thirty-two Piranesi prints covering an entire *salon* which went for 200 lire. It is significant, when one considers the cult of parent worship in Italy, that the grave of Don Pietro was left in the grounds, where it may still be seen to-day.

If Manzoni was an inefficient landlord he was a kindly one; on completion of the sale he struck off all the debts owed him by his peasantry and tenants. Leaving the scenes of his youth affected him more than he showed at the time. 'Don't talk to me about Il Caleotto,' he said years later when the son of the purchaser, Scola, invited him to revisit his old home. 'I would only go back to weep.' The famous invocation to his native mountains at the end of Chapter VIII of *I Promessi Sposi*, which most Italian children have at some time been made to learn by heart, is obviously based on nostalgia for that overwhelmingly lovely scenery. 'Farewell, mountains springing from the waters and rising to the sky; rugged peaks, familiar to any man who has grown up in your midst, and impressed upon his mind as clearly as the features of his nearest and dearest; torrents whose varying tones he can pick out as easily as the voices of his family; villages scattered white over the slopes like herds of grazing sheep; farewell!'

By the spring of 1819 he was feeling an almost unbearable ache for Paris. Donna Giulia was suffering from it too. 'My dear, my only friend,' she wrote to Mme de Condorcet, adding that Alessandro had woken up one April morning and told her: 'This morning I had a group of trees from Meulan on my heart, they were suffocating me.' In July 1819 Henriette, who had just been delivered of her fifth child, was loyally telling her confidante Carlotta de' Blasco that the journey to Paris was absolutely essential to her husband's health. She did not mention that at one moment, apparently, the possibility was even being considered, by Alessandro and Donna Giulia, of a permanent move to France. Before they left, Giulio Beccaria was told to look for a good purchaser both for Brusuglio and for the house in Milan; these sales were prevented by the bad condition of the Brusuglio crops and the high price asked—to cover the high price paid—for the house in the Piazza Belgiojoso.

The passports were signed. Acidly Tosi commented on 'la tanta a me disgustosa da lui andata a Parigi con la famiglia' (this very displeasing journey that he and his family are making to Paris); and he was not assuaged by Manzoni's dropping the second part of *Morale Cattolica* unfinished into his confessor's hands before he went. When from afar Tosi wrote imploring him to complete it for the good of his soul, all Manzoni produced in reply was a vague (and unfulfilled) promise to 'scribble the second part . . . in a shorter time.' Tosi knew, too, that before leaving for Paris Manzoni had finished the play *Il Conte di Carmagnola*, which he had left untouched for over a year.

VIII

The party that finally set off for Paris in the middle of September 1819 consisted, apart from the servants, of Alessandro, Donna Giulia, Henriette, and five children, the last of whom was just two months old. 'We'll get on as best we can,' he wrote gaily to Fauriel before he started, 'but since one sees the English travelling round taking a complete Noah's Ark with them, one is no longer frightened of journeys with a large family group.' One wonders whether Henriette, who was feeling so feeble from her last confinement that even her sight was affected, took it quite so light-heartedly.

On the way to Paris the convoy stopped for some days at the Château de Mongox near Chambéry with Somis de Chavrie, now the Intendant for the Kingdom of Sardinia in Savoy. There were long disputations with a young priest staying in the house about the problem of grace, when Manzoni evidently sustained the Jansenist view. This young priest, who afterwards became Cardinal Billet, used to remember how Manzoni always had an empty chair set beside him at table, to soothe his constant fear of falling into an abyss.

They reached Paris on 1st October 1819 and took an apartment at 66 Rue Neuve de Seine (the inevitable plaque now hangs somewhat incongruously above one of the livelier corners of Saint-Germain-des-Prés). Mme de Condorcet and Fauriel welcomed them with open arms. There was plenty of room at La Maisonette, she wrote, as her daughter Mme O'Connor had just left with her three children, a tutor, and two servants. 'After nine years I can breathe again because I breathe near you,' replied Donna Giulia, but she pointed out that with nurses and servants their party numbered ten, and insisted on paying something towards the expenses of such a huge consignment of guests; they also, she added in parenthesis, would all be needing fish on Fridays. By now, it seems, Donna Giulia had taken over all the family arrangements. When her brother Giulio Beccaria wrote to Alessandro to say that he could not find a purchaser for the Brusuglio property, as the vineyards and mulberries were in such a bad state due to storms, he prefaced this information with the remark: 'Now let us talk a little about business, and if you don't want to read this part of the letter, hand this sheet straight over to your mother.'

Down at La Maisonette they found Fauriel happily immersed in his *History of Southern Gaul*. This included a great deal of painstaking research on the early formation of the French language. When Manzoni had first heard of this project he had written in vague terms to encourage the friend who, like himself, found it so difficult to finish a book: 'Some works recently have made me feel that the history of literature is no longer a frivolous subject and that it could even be linked to the most serious ideas.' Now he himself found, in conversation with Fauriel, an increasing interest in the problems of the origins and development of language.

These absorbing literary subjects at La Maisonette contrasted with his interests in Paris, where he was spending a good deal of time with the Jansenists. Indeed Donna Giulia, loyally following in her son's footsteps, was finding the Rue de Seine too far from the Jansenist church of St Severin, particularly as the streets between were infested with *piqueurs* who attacked women with variously bladed instruments. The family often saw Mme Gey-müller; they dined at her house on Easter Sunday 1820 and admired her model of the Abbey of Port Royal.

Grégoire had received him most cordially and written a long article on *Morale Cattolica*, and it was probably this new intimacy which made one of his priestly biographers write that Manzoni's friendships then 'gave a heretical colour to this visit to Paris.' Grégoire was then in the middle of one of his biggest political storms. Although since the Restoration he had been forbidden to take part in any political activity, that autumn he had been elected to the Chamber of Deputies. This had focused on him the fury of the monarchists, who could not forgive him for being the first to ask for the trial of Louis XVI, and for having called Marie Antoinette 'la femme Jézébel.' Manzoni sprang (privately) to his defence; he said he would read Grégoire's election manifesto to all his friends, and wrote to Tosi of 'the scandalous persecution by his [Grégoire's] enemies, and the harm it does to his reputation and tranquillity.' For a time Grégoire seems to have become for Manzoni almost a symbol of rectitude, a kind of Imbonati who had advanced from Stoicism, and allied liberal opinions with genuine piety.[1] The treatment

[1] When a society was founded after the Restoration for the abolition of slavery it was decided to offer the presidency to Grégoire, who had been working for abolition for nearly twenty years. At the first meeting of the society, however, the intended election was reversed by a prominent Catholic getting up and saying: 'Had I to appear before God to-morrow I should prefer to present myself with the conscience of M. Grégoire rather than my own; but under the government of the Bourbons it is impossible for us to associate with him.' This was just the sort of incident to increase enormously Manzoni's admiration for Grégoire.

of him helped to disillusion Manzoni with contemporary France. It was largely from Grégoire that he got the reflections about the contemporary French Church which he wrote to Tosi in December 1819:

The sorrow which a Catholic feels on seeing that respect for religion is diminishing day by day in such a glorious and important part of the Church is all the more bitter, as many circumstances made one hope that religion here could not only enjoy a profound peace, but also increase its conquests. The savage and jeering spirit of irreligion had, if not vanished altogether, at least been almost reduced to nothing. A large part of those who had not the happiness of faith were disposed not only to tolerate it, but to respect it as an opinion which was harmless, useful, and beautiful. But in spite of the efforts of some good and enlightened Catholics (i.e. Grègoire) to separate religion from the interests and passions of the century, in spite of the disposition even of many without faith to recognize this separation and at least to leave religion in peace, it seems that the efforts have prevailed of others who insist on linking it to articles of political faith. . . . When religion is presented to the people thus accompanied, how can we ever hope that they will be able to distinguish what comes from God and what comes from men's imaginations? The solitaries of Port Royal did so; but there were few of them, they were learned, segregated from the world, and helped by that grace which they never ceased to implore.

On 2nd April he returned to the subject in such clear terms that Tosi must have been alarmed for the censorship. 'Finally, due to the forces of the Revolution religious liberty was proclaimed; but then not only did the clergy avoid publicly abjuring the principles of coercion, not only did they never show disapproval of the conduct of the clergy before the Revolution: they did nothing but exalt and yearn after those times and hold them out as an example.' Particularly after the recent restoration of eighty Jesuit houses, 'all the efforts of the enemies of religion and now of the agnostics tend to discredit religious ideas, because by doing so they hope to destroy the foundation on which the clergy can establish their edifice.'

In contrast both to the Church and to the general political situation in France, Manzoni began to see in disproportionately bright colours the practical reforms and innovations of his group of friends in Milan. He hoped that there they were well free of those impediments that come in France from a hostile, senseless, and systematic opposition, and from a reaction which is rarely wise and moderate and which this opposition provokes and irritates. To do good without discouragement and without passion, to resist obstacles without anger or malice, one would have to be an angel; there aren't any of these in any part of this planet, and if there were any in France I don't know how they could avoid becoming somewhat devilish, when they see themselves provoked, insulted, and threatened at every step;

and he went on to one of his typical involved generalizations: 'When the intention to do good mingles with a taste for anger, the good is spoilt; and this temptation is very strong in a country where so many are inimical both to good and to common sense, that to succeed in enraging them seems a real victory for common sense.'

In spite of the comparatively retired life which he continued to live in Paris, and which shows in the detached style of some of these observations, in the archives of the Milan police are copies of reports sent to Metternich about the subversive activities in France of Manzoni and his old school friend Calderari, both 'ex-collaborators of *Il Conciliatore*' and 'known for their liberal opinions.' Calderari was on a short visit to Paris at the time, and he and Manzoni went for long walks together. Apart from this and those long hobnobs with Grégoire and his friends, Manzoni seldom went out, though very occasionally he would appear at a musical party given by some member of the Condorcet set, and chat to some literary man in a corner—he had little interest in music. In the first months in Paris his nerves had been improved by the movement and the change. In February 1820 he wrote to a friend in Milan: 'I find myself in a state of calm of mind and sometimes I'd say almost of contentment, for which I could not myself give a reason.' At the same time Donna Giulia reported to Tosi that 'Alessandro is well because he sees very few people. He alternates between a hearty appetite and having none; he is a slave to his monastic system, getting up before daybreak, going to mass every day, then writing, reading, and walking out'; after Calderari left, most walks were with Donna Giulia, for Henriette was usually left behind to look after the children. He was working hard at a new tragedy in verse, *Adelchi*, based on the relations between the native Italians and their Lombard conquerors in the eighth century. And he was writing a long, closely reasoned essay on morals and aesthetics, *Lettre à M. Chauvet*, which was not to be published until 1823. Giulio Beccaria was even writing to his sister from Milan that Alessandro should amuse himself more and not work so hard, and added a comment which probably Donna Guilia was too tactful to pass on: 'What does it matter to him if he finishes a tragedy in one year rather than in two?'

For apparently he did not consider he was working hard enough, or was finding his work unsatisfactory. By April 1820 he was writing to a neighbour at Brusuglio that he had decided to return somewhat earlier, as he found it very difficult to occupy himself seriously in Paris with so many distractions, and the enforced idleness made it impossible for him to settle down. And from afar the life of his friends in Milan sounded more and more stimulating. Ermes Visconti's letters were full of local literary gossip, of Berchet's latest work, of Pellico's new tragedy, of Cattaneo's two volumes on antiquities, of Confalonieri's and Porro's newly opened Lancaster school. Rossini was in Milan, 'fat . . . mad as usual . . . moving towards immortality, laughing, love-making, always getting richer, and sometimes getting drunk.' There was a chance that Rossini might put the chorus of *Carmagnola* to music; Visconti had recited part of it and Rossini had said that a great deal of it could be sung. But the composer had whirled on his way and nothing came of this. And then Manzoni wanted to discuss Visconti's ideas on the origins of poetry, for a correspondence on this subject was now going on between Visconti and Fauriel. Visconti had begun by describing how Vico had shown the origins of poetry in half-savage customs, where poetry had also acted as the first popular encyclopaedia of science, theology, morals, laws, and economics as well as grammar and vocabulary. Fauriel was now trying to develop this idea and distinguish between what in poetry we take from habit and what we take from 'the intimate dictation of our way of feeling.' Could all the conventions of the learned be abolished, and ideas, style, and expression drawn from our own depths to form a popular poetry based on immediate reality?

By early summer Manzoni's nerves were becoming worse

again.   As soon, Henriette wrote to her family, as Alessandro 'could get into a carriage without imprudence' they would all leave for Milan.   But 'the only flaw in the joy Alessandro has at the idea of seeing his friends . . .' she wrote to Tosi in June, 'is the idea that those friends judge, as it were, not only his actions but his intentions.   It is a feeling which often torments him. I would like to see him humbler, and often try to persuade him, but he replies that: "A man face to face with other men, having nothing to reproach himself with in their regard, can well expect of them an interest exempt from continual censorship."'   The generalization may have contained a hint, at some removes, for Tosi himself to loosen up the controls on their return.

Early in August, 'in the blazing heat,' wrote Henriette, 'but putting up with every discomfort at the pleasure of the idea of being once more quietly in our own home,' the family set off back to Italy.   Alessandro was so weak after bleedings in Paris that they had to travel by very short stages.   They reached Brusuglio on 8th August 1820.   He was never to leave Italy again.

CHAPTER EIGHT

I

They returned to troubled times in the peninsula.   1820 was a
critical year for post-Napoleonic Europe.   In France the triumph
of the 'Ultras' after the murder of the Duc de Berry was the first
step in a series of moves and counter-moves that was to lead to
the final dislodgment of the Bourbons.   As Stendhal wrote in
that 'breviary of the romantics,' *Racine et Shakespeare*, ten years
later: 'In the eyes of Louis XIV, Henry IV, and Louis XVIII there
are only two classes of persons in France: the nobles who must
be governed by *honour* and rewarded with the *Cordon Bleu*; the
canaille, to which sausages and hams must be thrown on great
occasions, but who must be taken and massacred pitilessly if
they dare to raise their voices.'

Unexpectedly the precursors of change came from the deep
South.   In July 1820 official Europe was thrown into alarm by
one of the odder events of the century, whose repercussions
were to spread far beyond the confines of the peninsula, the
Carbonaro revolution in Naples.   One result of this movement
as it reached Lombardy was to be the imprisonment or exile of
many of Manzoni's group of intimate friends, the only people he
saw outside the family circle.

The Carbonari, or 'Charcoal-burners,' were originally an
offshoot of the Freemasons.   They had probably been imported
into Southern Italy and grafted on to existing traditions in the
early 1800s by French soldiers, members of the old secret
societies of 'Charbonniers' in the Jura, which were linked both
to the Freemasons and to the earliest forms of trade unions or
guilds.   The Carbonari statutes and ceremonies hid a rather
engaging form of early Christian Socialism cloaked in portentous
symbols.   The groups went under various high-sounding and
hopeful names, such as Republican Protectors, Hope, the
Brothers,   the   Shirtless   Ones,   the   Philanthropists,   the

Hermits, and the Faithful. Their form of address at meetings, the equivalent of 'comrade,' was 'good cousin.' Sitting on tree-trunks in dark Calabrian barns they pronounced discourses on brotherhood and freedom in vague and elevated language which hid a nucleus of common sense:

> Nature when she created man meant him to be free. At first the strong usurped the rights of the weak. Then violence was superseded by cunning. Hence arose intrigue, hatred, treason, imposture, superstition. . . . Yet reason, sovereign of the human mind, enlightened some wiser individuals as to the real nature of things. She preserved them from the general corruption, and they endeavoured to bring back their wandering fellow mortals to the neglected paths of virtue. But, deaf to the voice of reason, men rejected these precepts. It was then that, indefatigable, these benevolent sages conceived the idea of secret societies which, assiduously labouring to give a better education to mankind, might be the means of exciting them to virtue; and these societies were called the Carbonari.

This was a concept of reason which could only too easily be twisted to fit the files of secret police.

As the tone of this speech shows, there was a strong religious and moral side to the movement. In theory drunkards, blasphemers, and slanderers were not admitted, though as activity increased a number of murderers were included. Christ, 'the first victim of tyrants,' was the first of the 'good cousins,' and reunions ended with the formula: 'To the glory of our Good Cousin, the Grand Master of the Universe, and to Christ His Regent on earth, to establish the rule of philosophy, liberty, and equality.' The colours of the societies were black (or charcoal) for charity, blue (or smoke) for hope, and red (or fire) for faith. Red, white, and green, the colours of the Italian flag to-day, were also based on other colour symbols used by the Carbonari, with green for hope and white for charity. Mutual recognition signals between 'cousins' included a particular way of handling wineglasses and also, according to Saint-Edmé, some odd survivals from the past such as a toast to Francis I of France, considered as the founder of the Charbonniers. But by far the most important symbol of all was the cross. New members were elected with ceremonies taken from the trial of Christ. The Grand Master played temporarily the role of Pilate and the new member announced on his election: 'I am the Son of God.' He then swore to 'devote every moment of my existence to bringing about the triumph of those principles of liberty, equality, and hatred of tyranny, which are the soul of the secret and public actions of the Carbonari.' The Sacred Drama was in fact adapted so that its popular impact could be as immediate and general as the mass had been on the early Christians. Once in 1806 the entire population of a Calabrian village sacked by royalist troops greeted King Joseph Bonaparte kneeling in the ashes of their houses, all crowned with thorns.

There was a strain of cloudy Utopianism in the movement which was apt to divorce it from practical facts. One of the original aims of the Neapolitan Carbonari had been to found the state of Ausonia. This was to include all Italy from the islands to the Alps, and to be a federal republic headed by two elected kings, 'The King of the Land' and 'The King of the Sea,' with all appointments elective, equal rights for all citizens, and religious toleration. There seems to have been no attempt to face economic facts, and there were certainly no provisions for any transfer of property. This constitution laid down, however, that the army uniform was to be like that of Roman soldiers with the addition of rifles, bayonets, and two pistols, while the navy was to wear green tunics, wide pantaloons, tricolour sashes, small turbans, and green socks.

By 1812 the movement had spread throughout Southern Italy, and embraced almost every class except the feudal peasantry and the *lazzaroni*, Bourbon-subsidized, in the towns. Although with a movement whose organization was so loose there was bound to be some diversity of aims, these soon crystallized into a demand for a constitution as a first step towards them, particularly as the news spread of the liberal one granted by the British commissioner in Sicily, Lord William Bentinck, in the teeth of Bourbon opposition. In Naples itself, meanwhile, when the king, Joachim Murat, was away in Russia with the Grande Armée, the Napoleonic Minister of Police tried to reach a compromise with the Carbonari, particularly with the Grand Lodge run by Gabriele Rossetti. Although the result of this minister's efforts was recall to Paris and arrest, such was the growth of popular pressure on the side of the Carbonari that

two years later, when King Joachim landed at Pizzo, he carried
a copy of the Spanish constitution, which was based on Bentinck's, in his pocket.   Murat's failure did not affect the
movement, for soon the British minister to Naples was writing
home that the number of Carbonari all over the kingdom '. . .
may at any time be made into the instrument of revolution.'
By now they were so numerous that there were three hundred
and forty lodges in Naples alone, and no less than three on a
Bourbon man-of-war anchored at Capri.   It was the attempt by
the Bourbon Minister of Police, the Prince of Canossa, to found
a rival organization, the *Sanfedisti*, based on the *lazzaroni* and the
peasants, which brought things to a head.   Without any
violence, 'not a handkerchief has been stolen, not a knife drawn
from first to last,' reported the British minister, the Carbonari
occupied Naples and forced King Ferdinand to swear loyalty at
the altar to the Spanish constitution.[1]

The news was greeted with great alarm in Vienna.   'The
high character of the Carbonari is what causes anxiety,' wrote
Metternich as he hurriedly summoned the Council of Leibach.
For the democratic ideals of the Carbonari, their high aims of
purifying society, inspired partly by Christianity and partly by
eighteenth-century Enlightenment, were now sweeping in
converts of every kind all over the peninsula.   So certain, indeed,
seemed this new dawn seen from Southern Italy, so sure the
Carbonari faith in the pervading justice of their cause, that
everyone was accepted in the movement with open arms.   It
was even considered that the pope himself, in spite of his
condemnation of both the Carbonari and the Freemasons, could
not fail to see the fundamental truths they put forward.   The
Carbonari Parliament which opened in Naples in 1821 started
right from fundamentals with a heated discussion on whether
God the Father, the Son, or the Holy Ghost was the legislator
as well as the author of the universe.   The Deity won by a
narrow majority.

As the movement spread northwards, canalizing all discon-
tents, it took in more and more members of the middle and
upper classes.   So loose was the organization that it began to

---

[1] 'Although,' commented the British minister, 'of all the grave counsellors who
advised him to accept the constitution, there was not one who had read it.'

mean different things in different parts of Italy.   The 'Guelf
Knights,' the 'Adelfi' of Piedmont, the 'Federali' of Lombardy
were formed.   In Piedmont the new trends were used by the
liberal constitutionalists struggling against the old-world absolutism of the returned Savoys.   In Lombardy the movement was
directed towards the unification of Italy rather than to any
fundamental social change.   Its leader in Milan was now Count
Federigo Confalonieri, an aristocratic sceptic who had little in
common with the new religious liberalism.   During the previous
few years he had travelled round much of the peninsula and,
while making scientific and educational inquiries, had also
contacted most of the Carbonari movements he could find.
But, as he had already shown when he instigated the mob to
attack the house of General Prina in 1814, he was too head-
strong and irresponsible to make a good leader.   It was in
October 1819, when the Austrian police 'smelt the charcoal of
the Carbonari' in *Il Conciliatore*, that Confalonieri and many of
his chief supporters decided to pass into open conspiracy.

Their plan, which was very carelessly thought out, was to
drive the Austrians out of Italy by concerted action with
the Piedmontese constitutionalists.   The rising was disastrously
timed.   It broke out in Piedmont three days after the Austrian
troops, on 28th March 1821, had entered Naples and suppressed
the Carbonari Government.[1]   Confalonieri hoped, he said, to
cut off the Austrian retreat.   But the Piedmontese revolt was a
dismal failure due to the last-minute volte-face of Charles-
Albert, Prince of Carignano,'[2] the heir to the throne, an

---

[1] A sad little mocking song to Pulcinella—as a Carbonaro soldier—was sung in
Naples at the collapse:

> 'Pulcinella malcontenta
> Disertò del reggimento,
> Scrisse a mamma a Benevento
> Della patria il triste evento
> Movimento, parlamento,
> Giuramento, pentimento,
> Gran fermento e poco argento
> Armamento e nel cimento,
> Tra spavento e tradimento
> Siam fuggiti com il vento.
> Me ne pento, me ne pento,
> Mamma cara, mamma bella
> Prega dio per Pulcinella.'

[2] One of Manzoni's friends, the Marchese di Collegno, with whom he often stayed

unfortunate man almost forced into a split mind by his position.
The defection of Charles-Albert and Confalonieri's own am-
biguous and irresolute behaviour precipitated disaster.   At a
battle outside Novara on 8th April 1821 the constitutionalists
were routed before the Lombard Carbonari could bring them
any effective help.

The collapse of the revolt was followed by the arrest of Confalonieri, Maroncelli, Silvio Pellico, and others, and their trial
and confinement in the remote Bohemian fortress of the Spielberg.   There they were to become the first symbolic martyrs
of the new Italy.

II

There is a story that Manzoni was nearly involved in their fate
by attempting to draw into the conspiracy a Lombard prelate,
Monsignor Sozzi.   For a moment his enthusiasm had almost run
away with him.   He had also composed an ode, *Marzo 1821*,
when the Piedmontese constitutionalists seemed about to cross
the Ticino to join up with the Lombard Carbonari and march
together against Austria.   Whether because the river was never
crossed, or because of other fears, this ode only saw the light
in 1848 during the 'Five Days' fighting in Milan, when hopes
of liberation were again high.   The poem was dedicated to
Teodor Koerner, 'poet and soldier of German independence,'
killed fighting Napoleon in 1813, and was a rousing, almost
bouncing hymn of exaltation:

> . . . Non fia che quest' onda
> Scorra più tra due rive straniere:
> Non fia loco ove sorgan barriere
> Tra l'Italia e l'Italia, mai più!

(Let this wave flow between foreign banks no more, let there no more
be a place where barriers rise between Italy and Italy.)

Prematurely he announced that the days were over of:

> . . . quel volto sfidato e dimesso,
> . . . quel guardo atterato ed incerto,

(Gloomy discouraged faces, hangdog and uncertain glances.)

---

in after life, was Charles-Albert's aide-de-camp at the time.   Collegno, at the
news of the volte-face, slapped the prince's face, then broke his sword at his feet
and went into exile.

where for the Lombard:

> L'altrui voglia era legge per lui;
> Il suo fato, un segreto d'altrui;
> La sua parte, servire e tacer.

(Others' wishes were his laws, his actions other's secrets, his part to serve in silence.)

Though the image throughout the poem is of a mother who has suffered enough, it made Carducci think of Fra Cristoforo of *I Promessi Sposi* giving a homily to the Austrian emperor on his duty as a Christian to leave Italy.

This was the only part Manzoni had taken in the conspiracy, yet its failure gave him one of his nervous collapses. 'I'm all right when I can work,' he wrote to Fauriel in the summer of 1821. 'That makes four or five hours pass and gives me a lassitude for the rest of the day which dispenses me from thinking. . . . Often now there are days when I just have to idle as there's no way of getting my head to work.' 'One must bow one's head and let the clouds pass. It's true we sometimes find ourselves passing before the clouds do. In these *ghastly* days [dans ces jours néfastes—he underlined the last word] I take up a book, I read two pages of it and put it down, to take up another which does the same round; it's just like a presentation at court.' This unexpected simile of a bored royalty repeating automatic phrases as he goes the rounds of guests is curiously reminiscent of Stendhal. But Manzoni's attitude to court life was very unlike Stendhal's, and in the phrase he hid a sigh almost of nervous despair, a despair caused by his sense, at the time, of awful inevitability in the march of events and of his own impotence before them:

> . . . Una feroce
> Forza il mondo possiede e fa nomarsi
> Dritto; la man degli avi insanguinata
> Seminò l'ingiustizia; i padri l'hanno
> Coltivata col sangue; e omai la terra
> Altra messe non dà. . . .
>
> *Adelchi*, Act V, Sc. VIII.

(The world has a ferocious strength, which it calls right; the blood-stained hands of ancestors sowed injustice; our fathers fertilized it with their blood; and now the earth has no other harvest.)

The lines foreshadowed Verga's sombre view of everyday life in Sicily eighty years later.

Apart from *La Proclama di Rimini* and *Marzo 1821* Manzoni's work seldom showed any direct impact of events. There are very few references to politics in his letters to Fauriel, an omission which may be due, partly, to fear of the censorship. But although Manzoni's detachment from the activities of the Carbonari did not go without criticism at the time, in his new play, *Adelchi*, sombre gloom alternated with choruses that, as de Sanctis wrote fifty years later, 'produced a great impression on Italy: when everything appeared lost, they were the first tolling of the awakening.' In 1848 the volunteers sang them as they marched through the streets, while the ode *Marzo 1821* was greeted as a revelation.

With temperaments such as that of Manzoni, events, even if apocalyptic, have to be absorbed into a vaster background before they find expression. The composition of *Adelchi* was to lead directly to that of *I Promessi Sposi*. And the first idea of the novel came to him, as he told his stepson Stefano Stampa years later, when he retired to Brusuglio in April 1821, after the first news of the collapse of the Carbonari.

III

This last return to Italy from Paris marked the end of Manzoni's attempts to escape from his internal contradictions by flight. To sell Brusuglio, to establish himself with his growing family and large household in permanent exile, was a fading dream. He was now thirty-five. The trip to Paris had at least proved that escape was no solution to his problem, which always travelled with him. 'At his return,' wrote his watchful friend Ermes Visconti to Fauriel in October 1820, 'he still felt the weakness of convalescence, which caused some increase of his usual nervous fantasies; but he was not altogether discontented.' At Brusuglio he gradually improved, but for some time the condition of his nerves was such that he could never be left alone, even in the house. He was much better, added Visconti, since he had been to Milan. 'Our friend needs distraction and movement, living in the city can provide him with both'—though

Paris had apparently provided too much.   And once Italy, once Milan was faced, and Manzoni settled into a routine of work, he entered on the most productive period of his life.   Within seven years he was to be acknowledged as the leading writer in the peninsula.

This creative energy was canalized at the price of an increasing withdrawal from any activity but gardening and producing children.   The family letters of this period show a closed, intimate, apparently monotonous family life, with Alessandro, Henriette, and Donna Giulia each nursing the other's ills.   But Donna Giulia, in spite of her growing religious preoccupations, was never to rid herself of that nostalgia for the great Parisian world in which she had been so happy.   She even complained, as time went on, of the dullness of the plain in which Brusuglio was set: 'There's always something very glum about flat country.' In the resigned melancholy atmosphere of the silent house, broken only by occasional visitors, Alessandro gradually plunged deeper and deeper into his literary studies.

The verse-tragedy *Il Conte di Carmagnola* had been his first important contribution to Italian romantic literature.   He had sketched out the first draft of this during that cheerless winter of 1815–16, when he was continually starting work and then laying it aside, and gardening had been his principal solace.

He had worked on this play off and on for years, including the long break for *Morale Cattolica*.   'I'm almost ashamed of writing to you about literary projects when I have carried out so few,' he wrote to Fauriel in March 1816,

but this time I hope to finish a tragedy which I have begun with much ardour and the hope of doing something new in Italy.   I have my plan, I've divided up the action, I've put a few scenes into verse, and I've even prepared in my head a dedication to my best friend: do you think he'll accept it?   The subject is the death of Francesco Carmagnola; if you want to remind yourself of his story in detail look at the end of the eighth volume of Sismondi's *Italian Republics*.   The action begins with a declaration of war on the Duke of Milan by the Venetians, and ends with the death of Carmagnola, which is described at the end of the volume.   It carries over six years; this is a strong blow at the unity of time, but you are not the man to be shocked by that.

He was trying to do something entirely new in Italian literature, by breaking away from the classical rules of the unities, until then accepted without question, even in the plays of Monti and Alfieri. 'After reading Shakespeare thoroughly,' he went on to Fauriel,

and some of the things recently written about the theatre, and having thought them over well, my ideas have considerably changed on certain reputations. I do not dare say more, for all I want to do is to compose a tragedy, and nothing would be so ridiculous as to criticize those who have already done so and who pass for masters in the art. But what a lot of trouble people often take to do badly! To avoid the great and beautiful things which present themselves naturally and whose only fault is that they do not conform to the narrow and artificial system of the author! How much labour to make men talk neither as they do talk ordinarily nor as they could talk, to set aside prose and poetry and to substitute for it the rhetorical language which is the coldest and the least adapted to produce any sympathetic reaction.

In July 1816 he returned to the subject: 'Do not believe that I have been making war on the rules just for the pleasure of struggling against them unnecessarily; all I do is to avoid them when I find them on my route, and when they seem to prevent me from arriving or even walking.'

The year 1816 had been a period of intense reading. Long lists of French works on history, religion, and philosophy were sent to Fauriel, who was now acting as a kind of agent for him in France. He also asked for many dramatists' works, including those of Corneille and Racine, and the French translation of Shakespeare by Le Tourneur. By late in 1816 he had reached, by fits and starts, the middle of the second Act of *Carmagnola*. He had even been stimulated to starting an essay on the three unities, writing to Fauriel as he did so: 'I'm still on the morality of tragedy. Well! I've come to think there are difficulties in Bossuet, Nicole, and Rousseau which no one has resolved, which can be resolved and which I have resolved.' This statement— unusually confident for him—foreshadowed a deepening interest in the connection between morals and aesthetics. It was a subject he was to concentrate on almost exclusively some years later.

Carmagnola finally appeared in Milan in January 1820, three months after its author had left for Paris. It was dedicated to

Fauriel, who was later to translate it into French. There were five Acts, with a chorus between the second and third, and it was almost unstageable, being acted only once, with no success, in Florence in 1828.

Manzoni's thesis, one sustained by no other historians except Pietro Verri, was that Carmagnola was innocent of treachery, and that a simple straightforward man had been betrayed to death by the machinations of his adversaries, particularly of the subtle, twisted Venetian, Marino. This theme gave Manzoni a chance of developing the moral and religious issues that interested him.

The play was heavily criticized both in Italy and abroad, particularly in the *Biblioteca Italiana*, whose editor Acerbi had not forgotten Manzoni's refusal to collaborate five years before. 'We have hundreds of tragedies like this, everyone knows those of Goldoni and Ringhieri; the only new thing about them is the name: they are called "romantic."' The London *Quarterly Review* found it 'lacking in poetry,' and the English reviewer went on to advise Manzoni 'to gratify the public in future with fine odes rather than disgust it with feeble tragedies,' although he praised the chorus as 'the noblest lyric piece that modern Italian poetry has produced.' Even Silvio Pellico found the play's character too starkly real. 'Poetry is avowed more beautiful than reality. The inhabitants of that world should be a rung above us in love, in feeling, in political virtue, etc. . . . .' Goethe again came to the rescue. He agreed with Manzoni, he began, that a work of art should be judged as a healthy product of nature. He then picked out for praise various parts such as the monologue of Marco in the fourth Act, which he called 'a perfect picture of the doubts and torments of a delicate conscience,' and ending by lauding the author for proceeding calmly and firmly on his own path and against the rules. 'We have not been able to find a poor expression or a redundant word.' The encouragement of Goethe, who had been in touch with Italian literary developments for years and was an assiduous reader of *Il Conciliatore*, helped Manzoni over the harsh criticisms of *Carmagnola*, criticisms which were to be taken up later by Foscolo in the *Westminster Review*. 'Goethe deigned to consider me worth something,' Manzoni told Frederick von Müller in

F

1839.   'It is his merit if they applaud me; before him I had a bad
time from the critics.'   'I must admit,' he wrote to Fauriel
when he first read Goethe's praise, 'that I am agreeably surprised
to find such a man has had the patience to examine my intentions
and has judged them so kindly.'

Manzoni and Goethe never met.   In the only letter Manzoni
wrote to him, in January 1821, he confessed: 'Had I ever thought
when I was working on *Carmagnola* that it would be read by
Goethe it would have given me great encouragement and been
an unexpected prize,' and he went on:

> Without mentioning those who have treated my work with open
> derision, those very critics who judged it most favourably saw
> everything in quite a different aspect from what I had imagined.   They
> praised things to which I had given little importance and criticized as
> carelessness and ignorance of the best-known rules of drama, those
> parts which were the fruit of my most sincere and persevering poetic
> meditations.

He had come to wonder finally, he went on, whether his
intentions were illusions or whether he had been completely
incapable of carrying them into effect.

> In this irritating and numbing uncertainty what could be more of an
> encouragement and surprise than to hear the voice of the master, to
> realize that he had not found my intentions unworthy of being pene-
> trated by him, and to find in his pure and splendid words the simple
> expression of my concepts?   This voice encourages me to proceed in
> these studies with a lighter heart, and confirms me in the idea that the
> best way to produce a work of art is to contemplate calmly the subject
> one wants to treat, without taking any notice of the conventional rules
> and of the wishes, most of which are temporary, of the majority of
> readers.

IV

A personal link between Goethe and Manzoni resulted from
the arrival at Brusuglio in the winter of 1820, with a letter of
introduction from Fauriel, of the liberal philosopher Victor
Cousin, who had been deprived of his chair at the Sorbonne as
a result of the triumph of the 'Ultras' in France.   Cousin then
seemed far from the brilliant success he was to be at the end of
the decade, when his lectures at the Sorbonne were to echo all

over France and draw crowds such as had never been seen at lectures since the great days of medieval scholasticism. Cousin, although now ill and in difficulties, was a stimulating companion. 'Tell him,' Manzoni wrote to Fauriel in January 1821 after Cousin had left, 'that I so much regret those moments when, seated on my sofa, he, Visconti, and myself, we used to have heated disputes, interrupting each other, shouting like blind men—or like deputies.' For 'notre spirituel sophiste Cousin,' as Auguste Comte was to call him, was not one with whom Manzoni could agree beyond a certain point, though Cousin himself seems to have hoped at one moment that his 'eclectic and sceptical' system would be accepted by the Church. 'After your short stay in this country,' Manzoni wrote to him in February 1821, 'you have left friends who never concealed their disagreements with your points of view, and who did not let you perceive a quarter of the esteem they have conceived for your intelligence and your heart. You see,' he went on slyly, 'how much deceit there is in this Italy which your novelists call the homeland of deceit.'

Cousin was to remain a friend whom Manzoni seldom saw but often asked after and discussed, particularly with Arconati, Visconti, and Fauriel, the three friends whose own ideas were nearest to Cousin's. They still corresponded occasionally, and Manzoni wrote a long essay on his philosophy, in the form of an unfinished letter, in 1829–30. As time went on Manzoni was to disagree more and more with what he called Cousin's 'unreasonable reasoning.' 'Like all constructors of systems he had two voices prepared in advance, the vague and the contradictory.' This attack on the fine-drawn 'spiritualist' and metaphysical philosophy of Cousin foreshadowed remarks on philosophers in general in *I Promessi Sposi*.

Cousin was to become a practical philosopher when he reorganized the school and university education in France under Louis Philippe. Busy though he was, he kept his links with Italy, and became a lifelong friend of Massimo d'Azeglio, Manzoni's son-in-law, and of the Piedmontese patriot, Santorre di Santarosa. Some years after this first stay in Italy, during a journey in Germany in 1825, he was even arrested as a Carbonaro conspirator.

A conversation he had with Goethe about Manzoni during

this journey showed how warm, in spite of the differences of philosophic opinion, were his memories of that visit to Brusuglio. Goethe, as Sainte-Beuve noted, had *l'amour du génie*, and would study new talents as different as Byron's and Manzoni's with extreme interest and no personal feelings. He questioned Cousin, wrote Sainte-Beuve, with insatiable curiosity 'until he could get a real concrete idea of this object, this being, this new production, which was called Manzoni, absolutely as he, a botanist, would have done with a plant.'

'Ah, Manzoni,' said Goethe to Cousin in the latter's account of the conversation in the *Globe*.

'He's a dear and worthy young man. He has begun to emancipate himself from the rules of convention, especially from those of the unity of place. But *les anciennistes*,' he added, smiling to himself at the word, 'do not want to allow it. Yes, they have certainly got furious with him, although he has set to work with much discretion, for which I can only praise him. . . . I have received a copy of *Adelchi*, in fact I have written a short analysis of it, which perhaps I shall print some day. I have studied this tragedy: there are some very beautiful things in it. . . . I have not paused very much over details: I think one must always look at the whole. . . . But tell me, do you remember that Lombard soldier, at whose home the conspirators collect, and who thinks of nothing but his own advancement? How clever that man is at arranging things for his own advantage!'

And here poor Goethe was shaken by coughing and weakness, and had to help his words out with looks and gestures, although he was obviously enjoying himself.

'How that man makes use,' he managed to continue, 'of the designs of others for his own ends. . . . And then at Charlemagne's court, how he gives the impression of protecting the very people he has betrayed! Of course Manzoni keeps closely to history and to the real characters in it. But'—and here he gave a charming smile—'he brings them nearer to us by the way he treats them, by the human, even liberal sentiments which he lends them; and he's right. We can only be interested in people who resemble ourselves a little and not in Lombards and Longobards and the court of Charlemagne, which are all rather rusty to us now. Look at Adelchi himself, he's a character entirely invented by Manzoni.'

At these words I added, rather moved:

'The sentiments of the dying Adelchi are those of Manzoni himself. Manzoni, although he is a lyric poet, has drawn himself in Adelchi.'

'Of course, of course,' replied Goethe. 'Some time ago I saw his soul in his *Inni*. He is a simple and virtuous Catholic. . . .'

I thanked him, as a friend of Manzoni's, for the kindness with which he had, without knowing him, defended him against the criticism of the *Quarterly Review*. He replied in a tone which showed inner conviction: 'I have a very high opinion of *Carmagnola*, a very high opinion. *Adelchi* is bigger in subject, but *Carmagnola* is very notable for depth. The lyrical part is so beautiful that even that malicious critic praised and translated it.'

I told him that Manzoni was now writing a novel, in which he would be more faithful to history than Sir Walter Scott . . . a novel in which he would put his historical system rigidly into practice. 'The subject?' he asked. 'Milan in the seventeenth century.' 'Manzoni is a Milanese, he'll have studied that century well. . . .   Oh, if you see him, tell him how much I love and esteem him.'

When Goethe died in 1832, entwined in Manzoni's wreath was a flower from the garden at Brusuglio.

v

With the publication of *Il Conte di Carmagnola* and of his preface attacking the rules of unity of time and place, Manzoni found himself considered a leader of the romantic school in Italy, and a controversial figure, which was the last thing he relished. The *Gazzetta di Milano* wrote that the author of the preface 'could be a better writer, but not a more mediocre logician.' Now, although he always loathed literary polemics and kept out of them as far as he could, the attacks on *Carmagnola* produced one of his few efforts in this style, *Lettre à M. Chauvet sur l'Unité du Temps et du Lieu*, written during his stay in Paris.

Manzoni, because he stood out against the classical rules, now found himself considered as the heir to Foscolo. Yet he was scarcely representative of romanticism at all, certainly not of Nordic romanticism, which he castigated as 'a mixture of witches, ghosts, and systematic disorder, a search for the bizarre, a renunciation of common sense.' For Novalis life was a dream, to be contemplated with voluptuous fantasy. For Manzoni, in the famous words about Cardinal Federigo in *I Promessi Sposi*, it was 'a responsibility for all, for which each one will have to render an account.' Linked perhaps to this moral aspect, Italian romanticism had preserved the practical trend which it inherited from the rationalist reformers of half a century before. *Il Conciliatore*, as we have seen, tended to avoid the gloomy medieval subjects of recent German and French literature and to stress useful, definite, and limited aims.   So Giovanni Berchet wrote in his *Lettera Semiseria* of 1816 that the romantics were to base their work on modern life and so renew their inspiration, and went on to affirm that in art every content created its own rules of construction.   Manzoni now asked: was it not the duty of the poet 'to give expression to the desires, the sufferings, and convictions of society'? [1]

M. Chauvet was a French literary critic who, in an article in the *Lycée Française*, had supported the classical school of drama, and deplored in general the modern tendency to break the classical rules.   Manzoni's reply was the most acute of the defences of the Italian romantic attitude to the unities, and took the argument much further.   In *Lettre à M. Chauvet* he explained in greater detail than he had in the preface to *Carmagnola* his reasons for abandoning the unities.   He was more preoccupied in defending these reasons than in justifying his own work.   'To want to prove,' he wrote with humility, 'that one has written a good tragedy in every way is always an unsustainable thesis, which would be ridiculous here [he was writing in Paris] with a tragedy written in Italian by a man whose first effort this is, and who cannot, consequently, attract any attention in France.'

Manzoni's objection to the unities went far deeper than most contemporary arguments on the subject.   They prevented, he considered, a real and solid presentation of reality and historical truth.   This is a concept fundamental to his whole attitude towards both morals and art.   In *Racine et Shakespeare* Stendhal, also a pupil of the Idéologues and of Destutt de Tracy, put

[1] This was a milder adaptation of the theories popularized over Europe by Mme de Staël in her book *De l'Allemagne*, and which were said to have been influenced by Fauriel.   Quickly translated into Italian, *De l'Allemagne* was soon being read all over the peninsula, most of all in Milan, where the controversy it aroused drew Monti to take the side of the classicists with his *Sermone sulla Mitologia* in 1825.   Manzoni admired Mme de Staël and wrote about her in a tone of unqualified praise, unusual to him, as 'one of the most splendid intellects who have at any period occupied themselves in the contemplation of mankind, who has carried into her writings the most intimate, most subtle, most spiritual part of her thoughts.'

forward a similar view in his very different way, for his standard was pleasure, not morals. 'Romanticism,' he started his definition, 'is the art of giving people literary productions which, in the present state of their habits and beliefs, are capable of giving them the greatest possible pleasure. Classicism, on the contrary, presents them with the literature which gave the greatest possible pleasure to their great-grandfathers.' And Stendhal went on to denounce the Alexandrian couplet as a *cache-sottise*. 'I raise my voice because I see clearly that the knell of classicism has sounded. The courtiers have disappeared, the pedants are falling away and becoming police-inspectors.' Somewhat less crisply expressed, Manzoni's opinion was based firmly on a moral urge and was drawn to closely reasoned conclusions. So reasoned, in fact, were his conclusions as to the place of truth in art, and his insistence that the poet should 'strive for the perfectioning of society,' that in the end they were to draw him away from artistic creation altogether.

Historical truth, he wrote, is an incomparable source of observation, and no poetry can equal close study of and meditation on, the thoughts, passions, and contrasts of interests and wills that are shown by history. The cult of truth (*il vero*) was more essential in Manzoni's attitude to life than in that of any other romantic. Being incapable, by nature or conditioning, of facing and acting up to contemporary truth as he saw it, he was inclined to express his experience through the parallel contrasts and motives he saw in the past. So in *Adelchi* he wrote of the hopes of native Italians oppressed by Lombards in the Dark Ages, and in *I Promessi Sposi* of the trials of Italian peasants under Spanish rule in the seventeenth century.

Such aims were far from the 'romanticomania' of which he was accused by the *Giornale Letterario* of Florence in 1816. The short poem, *L'Ira di Apollo* (Anger of Apollo), written in 1816, had shown Manzoni's new attitude towards both classical mythology and the mirages of romanticism. This poem's mock-grandiloquent language is reminiscent of the bogus baroque opening paragraph of the 'Anonymous Chronicler's' introduction in *I Promessi Sposi*. In rotund language he makes Apollo condemn Berchet for wanting to abolish mythology from poetry, and as a punishment tells him to release the reins of the charger of classicism; which then goes soaring up into the realms of mythology, while Berchet himself is left walking on the hard earth of simple truth.

In Manzoni's conception, as in Shelley's, truth and poetry were very near. 'To anyone who says that poetry is founded on imagination and feeling and that reflection cools it, one can reply that the more one penetrates in the heart of a man to discover the truth, the more one finds real poetry.' He developed this argument in his *Lettera sul Romanticismo*, written in 1823 to a friend, Cesare d'Azeglio. The Marchese d'Azeglio had published the year before a reprint of one of the *Inni Sacri*, *La Pentacoste*, in the Turin paper *Amici d'Italia*, and sent Manzoni the reprint with a note regretting that such a great poet should adhere to the romantic school, which to the *marchese* appeared to mean something both unconventional and subtly subversive. Manzoni replied, in spite of his dislike of polemics, because d'Azeglio was not a literary man but an ardent Catholic, who was trying to spread ideas which he obviously thought morally useful. In this reply (which was originally private until in 1846 Cristina di Belgiojoso published it in her paper *L'Ausonio* in Paris) Manzoni started by explaining that he was in favour of romanticism as he considered it contained a Christian tendency; and the whole letter is an explanation of Christian liberalism rather than of any text-book romanticisms. Romanticism for him, he said, meant the search for truth, the repudiation of mythology, of laws in art founded on 'rhetoric, authority, and the limitation (not the study) of the classics.' He went on to sketch an idea which was to be particularly dear to him and fundamental also to his later studies in philology—that the language of poetry should be intelligible to the man in the street, and its subjects well based on human reality. Historical truth, Christian inspiration, simple popular form: such was his idea of what romantic literature should be. 'Art should have truth as its object and the interesting as its means.'

The German romantics were trying to attach both religion and old legends to a national cause, and ended by creating the disastrous legend of the divine function of Germany. But for Manzoni: 'Religion is belief. Belief is beautiful and reasonable when it lends itself to truth. It can be blameworthy, it is

certainly deplorable and wretched when it lends itself to error
mistaken for truth. . . .'

VI

In October 1820 Ermes Visconti had written to Fauriel about
Manzoni's plans for *Adelchi*:

> It will be useful to him to compose another tragedy, which he began
> to rewrite all over again towards the end of spring; the prospect of this
> work animates and excites him.   Also when Manzoni worked resolutely
> at *Carmagnola* he seemed to become a different man. . . .   It [*Adelchi*]
> will be more generally moving, more popular, and in spite of that it will
> be planned on new, more deeply historic, lines, and deal with little-
> known facts about the relationship of the Lombard Government with
> the Italian population; and with the intimate reasons for the weakness
> of that Government, when Charlemagne conquered King Desiderio.

At the end of the same month Manzoni wrote to Fauriel on
this subject:

> I have a tragedy in hand which I am going to work at and finish this
> winter if I can; for *Adolphe*,[1] which you suggested to me, I have had to
> put off, as I can only treat it in a way to which the public would be too
> little accustomed, and against which it would have too many pre-
> judices.   The one I want to do now is much more popular: it is about
> the fall of the kingdom of the Lombards, or rather of the Lombard
> dynasty, and its extinction in the persons of Adelgise the last king,
> with his father Didie.

Although the plot of *Adelchi* is historical, and placed between
the years 772 and 774 during the Lombard conquest of Northern
Italy, some characters and incidents, as Manzoni admitted, were
'invented altogether and infiltrated among the historical per-
sonages.'   Adelchi himself was the mouthpiece for the author's
moral, religious, and political ideas.   His character, as Goethe
and Cousin had noted, was close to the author's own, but
elevated into a kind of Italian Hamlet.   Charlemagne was the
conqueror, the deceiver, the shrewd politician, who used other
people's principles and beliefs as stepping-stones; the chivalrous

---

[1] This may have been about Adolf of Nassau, the German conqueror at the end of
the thirteenth century, who tried in vain to halt the expansion of the Austrians, and
was killed in battle by his rival and supplanter, Albert of Hapsburg.

Charlemagne of legend has gone, and the model is evidently Napoleon. The world of the play is that of the oppressed and the oppressors of *I Promessi Sposi*, though most of the protagonists here are princely. Happiness is impossible for Adelchi, torn from Ermengarda, who awaits him only when the storms of earthly life are over. Is Providence the only hope? The punishment of God, not of man, will fall on the Lombard conquerors for their oppression of the native Italians and for their occupation of papal land. This last was an unexpected theme for Manzoni, all his life an opponent of the Temporal Power; but it showed the logical working of his mind, for he saw the papacy of the ninth century as the only bulwark in Italy against a foreign aggressor. This role he was firmly to deny to the papacy of his own day.

There is a sadness, almost a gloom and discouragement over the whole of *Adelchi*, which must come partly from the time in which it was written. There were circumstances then affecting him even more closely than the Carbonari disaster. In the autumn of 1821 Henriette had fallen so seriously ill at her seventh confinement that at one moment her life was despaired of. The play was dedicated to her, and one of the famous choruses at the end of Act IV about the dying Ermengarda breathes so direct a warmth that it was obviously written with Henriette in mind. 'I have never felt as in those moments,' he wrote after her recovery, 'how much uncertainty, danger, I might almost say terror, there is in even the calmest happiness.' This sadness is emphasized rather than dispelled by the Christianity of the play. It has a sense of bitter desolation, a lack of confidence in human nature. The only secure refuge against the intolerable iniquity of the social struggle, Manzoni seems to be saying in parenthesis, is death and the hope of a better life hereafter. The horror of universal injustice, the hatred of triumphant evil are not, as in *I Promessi Sposi*, tempered by either irony or the alternating and intermingling of hope and resignation, astringent satire and rationalism, which give the novel its bitter-sweet flavour.

His studies for *Adelchi* were deep. As he plunged into them he found that he was making new discoveries about historians in general. So inaccurate and arbitrary were their statements about that period of the Dark Ages that the play, he said, was taking on in spite of himself a *couleur romanesque.* 'Searching around everywhere for observations on this period,' he wrote to Fauriel in October 1820,

I have seen, or thought I have seen, that it has not been understood at all by those who have written of it.   As for contemporary chroniclers, you know they are usually just very arid narrators, who are very far from having divined the things in their period which would most interest posterity.   Later scholars, while amassing many facts and sometimes making ingenious and difficult deductions about some customs of the Middle Ages, have never seen what was important and true in these institutions, and in the character of the period.   As for the historians we call philosophers, they are much worse, as they have seen what wasn't there at all.   For instance, to show you their way of treating just one point, I find that from Machiavelli to Denina and afterwards, all agree in regarding the Lombards as Italians, and that for the excellent reason that they were established in Italy for two centuries. By that count the Turks must be real Greeks by now.   You see that, by starting off with this supposition, they came to false judgments on facts, laws, persons, etc.   To try and get the most complete idea as possible on this point, I plunged into the collection of chronicles called *Rerum Italicarum* and even, I boast, some of the nineteen thick volumes of M. Thierry, not only for the immediate relations of Charlemagne with the Lombards, but also for some indication about the methods of the barbarian conquerors, which all have a strong resemblance to each other.

Thierry saw history as a succession of conquerors and conquered, the conquerors eventually becoming the new upper class in the countries they had occupied. What surprised Manzoni in his study of history was the way the vast masses of the population (the 'conquered' of Thierry's theory) were ignored.   In October 1820 Manzoni asked Fauriel to suggest some modern work which had 'tried, successfully or not, to pierce through the mists surrounding the barbarous invasions of Italy in the Middle Ages, and which had above all mentioned the condition of the native people, subjugated and *possessed*, the point on which history is poorest.   One scarcely finds a mention of the Italians in Lombard history, which was, after all, made in Italy.'   He returned to the subject in November 1821.   'You still find in your chronicles and in Frankish laws things from which the situation of the Romans under the Franks can be guessed;

but what can we say or suppose about the state of the native population of Italy in those two centuries to which we have almost attached a Latin name?'

These theories and observations were developed in the remarkable notes attached to *Adelchi*, which he called 'A Discourse on some Points of the History of the Lombards in Italy,' and which are almost longer than the play itself. He wrote these, he told Fauriel, because

you complain of the uncertainty of your history and of the arbitrariness of your modern historians. But that is nothing in comparison with some parts of our history, such as, for example, the period of the Lombards. As for modern history, I vow that I can scarcely understand how they have passed the most important problems by without perceiving them; or believing they have resolved them by vague and cowardly formulas which have no application, however stretched, to the facts they are trying to characterize, and the only clear thing about which is the need to uncover their serious errors.

He did not claim, he said, that the 'Discourse' would clarify the history of the Middle Ages: 'I only wanted to make its obscurity visible, and to show that what had been taken for light was not light at all.' The relations he examined in detail between the conquerors and the conquered in the time of Charlemagne bore many parallels—unstated but implied in the 'Discourse'—to those of the Lombards with their Austrian masters after the fall of Napoleon.

The conquering Lombards of the ninth century, he was convinced, left their laws to the defeated Italians not out of clemency, as the eighteenth-century historians had stated, but out of convenience and self-interest, a comment which obviously applied to the pseudo-paternalism of Austrian rule in his own day. He had had plenty of opportunity during the previous twenty years for observing many varieties of relations between conquerors and conquered; and finding the parallels in history caused one of his most striking and significant observations: 'An immense multitude passing on the face of the earth, passing on its own native piece of earth, without leaving a trace in history, is a sad phenomenon the importance of which cannot be overlooked: and searching for the causes of this silence may give rise to even more important discoveries.' This was a line of thought which

Romantic conceptions of
Manzoni:

From a widely diffused
print, based on a drawing,
probably not from life, by
Pietro Ermini

From a portrait of uncer-
tain history, said to be by
an English painter, and now
in the Casa del Manzoni,
Milan

had brought Saint-Simon in his chief work *The New Christianity*
almost to announce a new religion: 'The whole of society ought
to strive towards the amelioration of the moral and physical
existence of the poorest classes; society ought to organize itself
for this aim.' But such extreme conclusions were not for
Manzoni, who had too many tensions inside him. Mingled with
his rationalist approach to the problem of poverty was a touch of
pity, of passive compassion, a hint that the masses should remain
content in their role of oppressed majority, for so it was determined by God, whose ways of rewarding suffering are inscrutable.

Life on earth, he wrote sombrely in these dense notes, is
'that state which is so natural for man and yet so violent and so
full of pain, which creates so many aims whose fulfilment it
prevents, which endures every evil and every remedy rather than
stop for just a moment.' It is 'a mystery of contradiction in
which the mind is lost unless it is considered as a state of trial
and preparation for another existence.' How far then, he
implied, was it worth while trying to change anything in this
world?

VII

Ambivalent temperaments are always subject to sudden fits of
enthusiasm, often misplaced and afterwards regretted.

On 17th May 1821 Manzoni was in his garden at Brusuglio
when he was brought the Milan *Gazzetino* announcing the death
of Napoleon at St Helena ten days before. 'The news shook me
as if something essential was now lacking from the world,' he
wrote to Fauriel. 'I was seized with an urge to write about
him and had to throw off that ode.' For almost the only time
in his life rapid direct inspiration seems to have seized him.
'I could feel the verses grow up under my feet,' he told Fabris.
Hurrying into his study he sat down at his desk, while Henriette,
abandoning her family duties, was kept continually playing
military marches in the next room. In three days he produced
the finished ode on the death of Napoleon, *Il Cinque Maggio*.

Manzoni had doubts as to whether the ode would see the
light of day at all. Guessing that the Austrian censors could do
nothing but refuse a poem in honour of their dead enemy, the
spread of whose cult was being anxiously watched not only in

France, Manzoni enclosed two manuscript copies with his application, in the hope that the other copy might find a limited circulation among the censors themselves. Only one was in fact returned, while the other was not only copied out by one of the censors, but was soon circulating in other manuscripts in Milan, and then throughout Europe.

The poem appeared just when many were feeling an unspoken sympathy for Napoleon, partly for positive reasons and partly from reaction to what came after, and it took Italy and Europe almost by storm.

Goethe was one of the first to translate it. Although this was a poor translation (as Goethe himself acknowledged, adding that he had done it to encourage others to do a better one), he read it out to the court at Weimar so effectively that it made an immense impression. 'Isn't it true,' exclaimed Goethe into the deep hush he had created in the Grand-ducal drawing-room, 'isn't it true that Manzoni is a great poet?' Soon Longfellow, Lord Derby, and later Mr Gladstone put their hands to versions in English. The Emperor of Brazil, Don Pedro II, translated it into Portuguese. Twenty-seven translations were collected in a volume published at the inauguration of Manzoni's monument in Milan in 1883. It outdid in popularity all the other odes on Napoleon, by Lamartine, Béranger, Wordsworth, and Byron.

Manzoni's own opinion of the poem was not high, after the first enthusiasm was over. 'Seeking for the reasons for its extraordinary reception,' he wrote to his old school friend Gianbattista Pagani, who had been a high official of the Napoleonic Kingdom of Italy, 'I feel two very potent ones to be: its subject and its clandestine publication. A third reason, perhaps, is a certain obscurity suited to giving an impression of recondite and profound thought where there was nothing but a deficiency of perspicuity.' With this last remark the contemporary critic Giordani was inclined to agree. 'I don't question the subject, everyone says what they want. But as to the phraseology, it seems to me that sometimes he has not been able to say what he wanted, and sometimes I don't know what he wanted to say.' Richard Garnett at the end of the century pronounced it superficial: 'The note of personal compassion which pervades it was then in place, but now that Napoleon's exploits and disasters are ancient history, and he is chiefly regarded as a world-shaker and incarnate elemental force, we feel the need of a deeper insight and a wider sweep.'

With this judgment on Napoleon, quite apart from that on the poem, Manzoni would not have entirely agreed, nor would many enlightened Italians even to-day. The laws and institutions of the Napoleonic Kingdom of Italy continued to have a profound effect on Italian life, long after the 'elemental force' of his conquests was spent. The old Italy of the princes, even though temporarily restored, was shaken to its foundations by the Napoleonic administration, by the laws for the abolition or curtailment of feudalism, the opening of new careers for talent, the stimulation of industry, the revolutionizing of the land system and of education; a minor sign of this democratic trend still visible to-day was the number of public gardens, such as that of Venice, which were opened during the Napoleonic period. This sympathy for Napoleon in Italy ('Moi, j'ai une grande faiblesse pour Napoléon,' said one of the most distinguished Italian liberal historians at an international congress recently) has another reason: Italy was the only place in the empire where Napoleon, either because he was an Italian himself or because he thought the unification of the peninsula inevitable, encouraged the spirit of nationality: he was almost as much responsible for the Risorgimento as Cavour.

'Anyway,' Manzoni wrote to Cantù later, 'he was a man whom one had to admire, without being able to love him: the greatest of tacticians, the most tireless of conquerors; with the highest qualities of the statesman, knowing how to anticipate and knowing how to act.' There is a hint here of an approach that was particularly personal, of the neurotic's wonder at 'that fateful phenomenon,' the man of action. Years later he decided, when reading Napoleon's letters to his family, that he was a man without a heart.

Since that memorable evening in 1801 when he had sat under the gaze of the conqueror's eyes in the box of the Contessa Cicognara at the Scala, Manzoni had only seen Napoleon once— in Paris in 1805, crossing the Place du Carrousel in state after attending a Te Deum for the victory of Austerlitz: 'In the full flower of pride and haughtiness, with the air of a tragedian, as if he were distributing blandishments to trick his enemies and brutalities to overwhelm them,' an observation which shows clearly the influence of the friends whom Napoleon called 'the grumblers of Auteuil.' Soon Manzoni was going further. For already at the period of *Il Cinque Maggio* he was beginning to doubt the role of the hero in history.

VIII

Il Cinque Maggio was an emotional interlude in the considered preoccupations of those years. But it marked the point at which he abandoned the representation of the heroic and the great, in favour of poetry made from 'the memories and daily impressions of life.' Carmagnola was a famous *condottiere*. Adelchi was a king's son, although the play had no hero of legend as its protagonist, unlike the tragedies of Alfieri and of Schiller, by whose *Egmont* it was partly influenced.

In 1822 Manzoni started a tragedy, *Spartaco*, based on the story of the slaves' revolt in the first century of the Roman Empire. Spartaco, the leader of the slaves, was another protagonist of the 'gente di nessuno' (nobody's people), Manzoni's equivalent to Hugo's *Les Misérables*. This play was later abandoned as he became increasingly absorbed in that vaster saga of the oppressed, *I Promessi Sposi*. But he did a good deal of research for it and sketched out a number of Acts. With the help of the librarian of the Braidense, his old friend Cattaneo, he immersed himself in the details of Roman life. He had always felt strongly about slavery (and was to praise warmly *Uncle Tom's Cabin* for having had more influence on the abolishing of slavery in America than any other book). In one of the books he studied for *Spartaco*, Rollin's *Roman History*, he found a description, in approving terms, of Cato punching on the mouth a slave who had refused to give him his arms, and noted on the margin: 'And the slave's blood on the hand, M. le Professeur?' When in Crevier's history he found Augustus praised for his humane treatment of slaves, he noted: 'The great indignity was that there should be slaves at all.'

The plans for *Spartaco* that he jotted down show touches of his paradoxical spirit. The play was to put the opposite case, under the influence of Thierry, to Rollin's view of Brutus as 'ce héros du Stoicisme.' Brutus, Manzoni considered, was just an ambitious man who represented the interests of a privileged few, and lacked the real fundamental virtue—that directed towards universal justice and charity.

All that has remained of these studies for *Spartaco* is a curious and unexpected comparison between Brutus and Philip II of Spain, which he put into the first draft of *I Promessi Sposi* and cut from the finished version of the novel:

Both Brutus and Philip II were grave and rigid preachers, the one of philosophy, the other of religion; both of them committed without remorse . . . actions which are abominated by the normal morality and universal sense of humanity; both of them believed that in their case a profound reason, an intention of perfection, made virtuous that which is commonly criminal. Both of them, by their active and ardent opposition, reinforced and extended the things they had at first tried to prevent and exterminate; and both had partisans in life and after death who approved their conduct and who praised them for having taken endless risks to obtain the contrary of their aims. . . .

From this paradoxical view of the effects of personality on history he went on to brood over the anti-heroic. He was becoming now more and more interested, as he had written in the notes to *Adelchi*, in the abysmal lack of information about the conditions and feelings of 'the vast number of men and women who had played no active part' in history, but had felt its effects. This again showed the influence of Thierry,[1] who wrote in *Lettre sur l'Enfranchisement des Communes*:

The obstinacy of historians in not attributing any spontaneity, any ideas to the masses, is a very singular thing. If an entire people emigrates

---

[1] The conversion of Thierry to Catholicism is a curious pendant to that of Manzoni. In 1848, blind, paralysed, and disillusioned by events, the former Carbonaro, now hoping only for a temperate monarchy, gradual reforms, and a progressive evolution of the Third Estate, wrote to Princess Belgiojoso: 'If God gives me the Grace I'll become a believer and a Catholic. What rationalism there is in the Reformed Church does not please me at all. I've always had more of that in me than I want. But I am not tempted in becoming a Christian to become a revolutionary Christian: I've enough revolution around me. . . .' And to the Abbé Carron: 'I want to have the faith of the simple. I'm not a philosopher, I'm a historian. I don't try to delve into the metaphysic of Christianity. I can't explain it to myself. I take the Church as a fact which imposes itself on my attention, and which I am not able either to eliminate or to elude.'

and makes itself a new home, it is, according to the essayists and poets, some hero or other who has the idea of founding an empire; if new customs are established, it is some legislator who imagines and imposes them; if a community organizes itself, it is some prince who gives it light to do so; people and citizens are always the material for the thought of one man.

This, for Manzoni too, was a myth, created perhaps for the advantage of the rulers. But from another side of his contradictory nature he could still, with a resigned sigh, see in history an illustration of the 'many different ways in which human nature bows down and adapts itself to society.'

As the inner experience of that fateful year sank in, Manzoni moved on from the tortured doubts of Prince Adelchi, whose despair could only find hope in another life, towards what seems at first a serene and balanced view of the troubles of the two unknown peasants, achieving their aims, apparently, amid universal upheaval. The beliefs, the doubts, the self-torture, the humanity, and the ambivalence were to find a fusion of artistic expression in the limpid whole of *I Promessi Sposi*.

CHAPTER NINE

'I PROMESSI SPOSI'

I

'AFTER having satiated you with chatter and details of all kinds of different literary productions,' wrote Manzoni to Fauriel on 29th May 1822, after elaborate instructions about the French translation of *Adelchi* and the publication of *Lettre à M. Chauvet*,

I scarcely dare to add yet another few words on literary projects. To do so shows a real longing to be a substantial author (*une envie d'auteur gros*), which is what I have. You must know then that I am immersed in my novel, the subject of which is placed in Lombardy, in the period between 1628 and 1631.

The memoirs that have come down to us from that period give a picture of a very extraordinary state of society: the most arbitrary government combined with feudal and popular anarchy; legislation that is astounding, both in its aims and its results; a profound, ferocious, pretentious ignorance; classes with opposed interests and maxims; some little-known anecdotes preserved in trustworthy documents, which develop all this very much; finally a plague which gives rein to the most consummate and shameless excesses, to the most absurd prejudices, and to the most touching virtues, etc. etc. . . . That's the stuff to fill a canvas, or rather that's the stuff that may only show up the incapacity of the person who sets to work on it. But let us perish if we must. I dare to flatter myself [J'ose me flatter]—a phrase I learnt from my tailor in Paris—I dare to flatter myself that I shall at least avoid the reproach of imitation. To this end I am soaking myself as far as I can in the spirit of the times which I have to describe, so as to live in them; so original was this spirit that it will be entirely my fault if I do not communicate this quality in the description of it. I think the best way not to do the same as others with the sequence of events and the plot is to set myself to consider the way men behave in reality, above all in everything which reality opposes to *l'esprit romanesque*. In all the novels I have read I seem to see an effort to establish interesting and unexpected links between the various characters, to bring them on to the scene with others, to find events which at some time influence them all, and so in different ways all their destinies, to discover in fact an artificial unity which is not to be found in real life. I know that this unity gives the reader pleasure, but I think that this is due to ingrained habit. I know that it passes for a merit in some works which have real quality, but I consider that it will one day be an object of criticism, and that this way of linking events will be cited as an example of the sway which custom exercises even on the freest and most refined spirits, and of the sacrifices which are made to established taste.

And he told Tommaseo later that when writing the novel he was *sliricato* (delyricized).[1]

In the preface to the first version of the novel, originally called *Gli Sposi Promessi* (at the last moment, when the title-page was set up in print, the name was changed to improve the sound), he noted with mock horror that he had been accused of writing a romance. 'A romance? This is a species outlawed in modern Italian literature, which vaunts the glory of having none or very few. And although that is not the only negative glory of our literature, yet it must jealously be preserved intact, and this is seen to by those thousands of readers and listeners who enjoy foreign novels.' With an involved and introspective irony he kept up the wry pretence of historical truth even in the invented parts. 'If I were inventing a story,' he wrote commenting on a criticism of repetitions in Renzo's two entries into Milan, both of which were of course fiction,

I would be very careful not to deserve an accusation of sterility of invention, one of the most terrible in the republic of letters. But I am transcribing a story which really happened; and true events . . . proceed with quite other rules to those laid down by imagination; they do not bother about satisfying people of good taste. If it were possible to subject these rules to the course desired by poetic spirits, the world would become even more delightful than it is; but that is not a thing that can be hoped. And it is through the fault of this wasteful and material procedure of facts,

concluded Manzoni, 'that Renzo twice arrives in Milan, stays

[1] In this, as in much else, Wordsworth's attitude has some parallels with Manzoni's. In the preface to the 1798 edition of the *Lyrical Ballads* he wrote: 'It is desirable that . . . readers for their own sakes should not suffer the solitary word poetry to stand in the way of their gratification; but while they are perusing this book they should ask themselves if it contains a natural delineation of human passions, human characters, and human incidents; and if the answer be favourable to the author's wishes, that they should consent to be pleased in spite of that most dreadful enemy to our pleasures, our pre-established codes of decision.'

Manzoni at the time of the publication of *I Promessi Sposi*. From a portrait
by Molteni, the background by Massimo d'Azeglio, now in the Braidense
Library, Milan

there, and leaves it, all in rather similar ways.' To bridge the gap between reality and invention he used the device of an 'Anonymous Chronicler,' in whose 'scratched and faded manuscript' he pretended he had found his story. This device, of course, was in no way original, and an English critic of *I Promessi Sposi* in the *Monthly Review* in 1827 even found the 'Anonymous Chronicler' a hackneyed idea, too reminiscent of Walpole and Sterne. Its most notable use, where it also served to ridicule the pompositities of the past, was in *Don Quixote*; and perhaps that gave Manzoni the idea, although there it was hinged on a much looser plot.

The original plot of *I Promessi Sposi* was indeed suggested by a genuine historical document. 'One day,' wrote Manzoni's stepson, Stefano Stampa, many years later,

when I happened to be in his study on the ground floor and he was standing at his desk turning over his manuscripts, he suddenly said: 'Do you know what it was that gave me the idea of *I Promessi Sposi*? It was that edict which I happened to see by chance, the one I made Doctor Quibble-weaver read out to Renzo, the one with the three penalties against a parish priest who doesn't carry out a marriage, etc. And I thought that this (a hindered marriage) would be a good subject for a novel, with as a grandiose finale the plague which sets everything to rights.'

This edict he found in one of the books he took with him on his retirement to Brusuglio in the spring of 1821, *Economia e Statistica*, by that Encyclopaedic revolutionary Melchiorre Gioia, who had reprinted it from Muratori's great collection of historical documents, *Annali d'Italia*. Gioia, incidentally, also brought home to Manzoni the uselessness of laws which were not in harmony with the customs of a country, particularly when the legislators were foreigners. In Ripamonte's *Milanese Chronicles* Manzoni found the originals of the wretched Signora of Monza, Suor Virginia de Leyva, of the 'Unnamed,' Bernardino Visconti, and of Cardinal Federigo Borromeo. There also were the bare accounts of the famine, the riots, the plague, and the passage of Wallenstein's army, which he amplified from innumerable other sources. From this he went on to study the history of the period in detail: he read books on seventeenth-century economics, laws, and medical theories; he brooded over ecclesiastical and civic

archives, and military manuals.   A stream of demands for the
most abstruse works of the period went to his friend Cattaneo
at the Braidense library in Milan; and at the end of one of these
lists he added: 'You'll learn to choose your friends more carefully in future.'

He set out to describe the historical facts with what he thought
scrupulous honesty.   'To show you briefly what my chief idea
about historical novels is,' he wrote to Fauriel when he was well
on with the first draft, 'I will tell you that I conceive them as
representing a state of society by means of actions and characters
so similar to reality that they could be believed to be true history
which has just been discovered.   When historical events and
characters are mingled with this I think they should be represented in the most strictly historical manner; in this, for instance,
Richard Cœur-de-Lion in *Ivanhoe* seems deficient.'   In the
event, his choice was biased by moral purpose or artistic pattern
—sometimes perhaps, unlike Scott in *Ivanhoe*, by a combination
of both; for he saw history, not with the objective eye of an
historian, but with that of an artist, a humanist, an ironist, or a
moralist.   Possibly, too, as the modern critic Fausto Nicolini
has pointed out, he was inclined to judge Italy of the seventeenth
century by the anti-absolutist standards of the nineteenth; while
Spanish absolutism, which was anyway milder in Milan than in
Naples, could be considered from one view as an advance on
the feudal regime before it.[1]   In January 1821, some months
before starting on the novel, Manzoni had written to Fauriel,
about his friend Tomasso Grossi's projected narrative poem *I
Lombardi alla Prima Crociata*, in terms which obviously applied
to the ideas germinating in his own mind.   'His [Grossi's]
intention is to illustrate a period by means of a fable of his own
invention, more or less as in *Ivanhoe*.   To collect the characteristic traits of a period of society and develop them in action,
and profit by history without trying to rival it, without pretending to do what it can do better—that, it seems, is something
that can still be accorded to poetry, and what it alone can do.'

[1] Nicolini also quotes a contemporary letter of 1630 to show that Cardinal
Federigo's real behaviour during the plague was not so reckless as Manzoni described.   He had himself carried through the lazaretto in a litter enclosed entirely
with glass.   In the plague of 1576 his uncle, St Charles Borromeo, had servants
around him with sticks hitting anyone who came too near.

Manzoni's own curious and typically inadequate description of his novel later was 'more or less of a charity ball.' Was there a touch of ironic self-persuasion in this remark, an attempt to prove to himself that he was writing mainly with a moral purpose in view? Monsignor Tosi, now Bishop of Pavia, was still hoping for a sequel to *Osservazioni sulla Morale Cattolica* and was horrified at the news that he was starting on a novel. To an inquiry by Monsignor Dègola in 1825, when the novel was more or less finished, Manzoni replied rather defensively: 'How very good of you to interest yourself in the trifles that come out of my pen. Do you know what kind of work it is at which I am drudging away as if it were something of importance? It is that kind of composition to whose authors our Nicole [of Port Royal] used unceremoniously to give the title of "public poisoners" [1] [*empoisonneurs publiques*].' But he went on to say that he had all his answers ready and intended to defend his book against the accusations of 'perniciousness and uselessness.' The time had not yet come when, due partly to his own moral objections to imaginative fiction, he was to write nothing but essays.

Temporarily he was swept away on a tide of creative delight rare to him. 'To get up in the morning,' he told his son-in-law Giorgini years later, 'with the image of the day before lively in the mind, to go down into the study, to take out of the drawer some of those characters I know so well, to dispose them in front of one like so many puppets, to observe their movements, to listen to their conversation, put it on paper, and then read about them again, was for me a delight as lively as that of a satisfied curiosity.' In August 1823, when he was just finishing the first draft, he wrote with muted exultation to Fauriel:

All I can tell you of it in conscience is that I have tried to know exactly and to paint sincerely the period and country in which I have placed my story. The materials are rich; everything that shows up the seamy side of man is there in abundance. Assurance in ignorance, pretension in folly, effrontery in corruption are, alas, among many others of the same kind, the most salient characteristics of that period. Happily

---

[1] From Nicole's attack on Racine in his *Visionnaires*: 'A maker of novels and a dramatic poet is a public poisoner, not of the bodies but of the souls of the faithful, and must regard himself as guilty of an infinity of spiritual murders.'

there are also men and traits which honour the human race; characters gifted with a strong virtue, remarkable by their attitude to obstacles and difficulties, and by their resistance, and sometimes subservience, to conventional ideas. I've tried to profit by all this; how I've succeeded only God knows. I've stuffed it with peasants, nobles, monks, nuns, priests, magistrates, scholars, war, famine . . . that's to have written a book!

II

From the beginning he found he was taking much longer over it than he had expected. In November 1821 he had to put it aside for a time to finish the last draft of *Adelchi*, and the studies and plans for *Spartaco* were not abandoned until late in 1822, partly as a result of criticisms of *Adelchi*. In March 1822 he was able to write with wry relief: 'Within two or three days the last pages of *Adelchi* will go to the copyist, thence to the censor's, thence to the press, thence to the public, thence to oblivion.' By September 1822 he was half-way through the second volume of *I Promessi Sposi*; according to his original calculations he should have been at the end of the third. It was not till mid September 1823 that he finished the first draft.

During the autumn of 1822 his nerves were troubling him again; he was only well enough to work for five or six days, 'the others, filled by an almost absolute incapacity, have seemed rather long to me.' Yet Fauriel, away in Paris, was apt to hear more about his nerves than his intimate friends who saw him every day, with whom his tone was sometimes almost jaunty. 'You won't get banquets, balls, and jousts here at Brusuglio,' he wrote, inviting Tomasso Grossi to stay that summer, 'but I hope you will find here that calm good humour so suitable to men of study which, between ourselves, is what we are, and of whom the humblest herewith sends anticipatory greetings'; and to one of his endless demands for books to Cattaneo he added: 'I promise you that once this fine work I'm on now is finished, I'll write nothing but lyric poetry, for which there is no need of positive information as all one has to do is wait with one's mouth open for inspiration.' Summer storms, the friends at La Maisonette were told, had caused great damage to the Brusuglio crops: 'They were completely beaten down by hail, the corn

had to be cut, the cocoons hung from above,' wrote Donna
Giulia to Mme de Condorcet, adding in a burst of introspection:
'Your friendship is strong and generous, mine is rather com-
plaining.' Alessandro took up the refrain in July. 'My good
Henriette, without being actually bedridden is nearly always
ailing; my mother has been tormented these last few days by a
swelling in a finger joint, which completely prevents her from
thinking of anything but the pain. Henri and Cristina have
scarlet fever. . . .' Then he broke suddenly into a note of deep
and genuine pain: 'This is just a part of the things which have
made this year one of the saddest that I have yet spent.' It was
a glancing allusion to the Carbonari trials which had taken place
that spring.

Just as these plaints reached Fauriel, disaster was overwhelm-
ing the *ménage* at La Maisonette. In August 1822 Mme de
Condorcet became seriously ill. For a time she rallied, then
while letters of congratulation on her recovery were on the way
from Italy, on 8th September she suddenly died. The shock
for Fauriel was appalling; his entire life, he felt, had collapsed
about his ears. On top of it, he hinted to Manzoni that 'there
are accessories and circumstances to my disaster which are very
bitter to me. . . .' It seems that Mme de Condorcet's daughter
and son-in-law, the O'Connors, who had been so friendly before,
now rapidly cooled, and he found himself isolated as well as
homeless in his sorrow. Even the devoted Mary Clarke forgot
herself in a cruel outburst of jealousy from Ilfracombe. For a
week after the death he had been supported at La Maisonette by
his great friends Thierry and Cousin, but it was over a month
before he regained 'a certain degree of calm and assurance,' and
was able to write to Brusuglio. To avoid falling into despair, he
wrote to Manzoni, his great need was to seek old friends and make
new plans. By now he had left La Maisonette and was in rooms
in Paris. 'I feel the imperious demand, moral as well as
physical, to revive the whole of my shaken being by plunging it
into a new atmosphere, with old friends and new scenes. And
d'you know where I'll find all that? I hope, dear friends, you
can guess: near you.' He went on to suggest his coming to
Brusuglio, where he could work with 'mon cher Alexandre' and
try 'to produce, by his side, something worthy of him'; and

he asked for a quick reply, to give him some hope to set his heart on.

The idea of his mentor coming to stay just when he was in the middle of his most important work filled Manzoni with excitement.   Only a year before, when studying sources for *Adelchi*, he had written to Fauriel: 'How often have I cursed more than usual the distance that separates us when after useless researches in these imbecile chronicles to discover some important information on the state of medieval society, after even more useless reading among our opinionated moderns, I should have liked to turn to you, and find all that there was to know, or be assured that there was nothing to know.'   Now he wrote off at once to say that there was no need for Fauriel even to ask if he could come: they had been expecting him for years.   He should come straight away, he went on, or join them in a projected expedition to Tuscany which they were thinking of making for Henriette's health, once *I Promessi Sposi* was at the printer's.   But the trip to Florence was held up by 'my boring hotchpotch' 'which has taken more time than I had thought of giving it; and to carry it away half done to finish elsewhere would be too much of a nuisance, as I have to consult every moment a quantity of books, manuscripts, even vellums, many of which are rare, even unique, and which I can only borrow on the spot.'

Fauriel's trip was delayed again and again, and it was another year before he appeared at Brusuglio.   Letters may have gone astray, as no news of him reached the Manzonis for three months.   In March 1823 Mme de Rance, a friend of Donna Giulia's visiting Paris, was asked to let them know if he was ill. In August Donna Giulia's maid Fanny went to Paris to see her mother, and took him a message.   But Fauriel seems to have buried himself in work that winter.   He was held up, among other things, he finally wrote, by trying to get *Adelchi* adequately reviewed in France.   He had also started a new work, an anthology of Greek songs, *Chants populaires de la Grèce moderne*.

Before Fauriel arrived Manzoni had finished the first draft of *I Promessi Sposi* (on 17th September 1823, as he noted on the margin).   When, in early November 1823, Fauriel did finally reach Brusuglio, he stayed there the whole winter, most of the next summer, and the spring and summer of 1825; during this period he spent a good deal of time working with Manzoni on the completed draft of *I Promessi Sposi*. In between he made trips to Venice and Trieste with the Greek poet Mustoxidi to search for Greek popular songs for his new anthology. There were not many to be found among the Greek exiles in Venice, he wrote, but more among the Greeks in Trieste who had wives, children, and servants '. . . and it's this ignorant part of the population which knows best the things I'm looking for.' One unexpected development during this stay at Brusuglio was that Manzoni and Fauriel found that one or both of them were suspect by the police, for when they went out walking they were followed by agents, who would sidle up and try to overhear their scholarly conversation.

Fauriel's suggestions for *I Promessi Sposi* were mainly aesthetic and structural. Although his own search for popular songs was paralleled by Manzoni's attempts to find a living language for the novel, he dissuaded his friend from going too far and rewriting the book in Milanese dialect.[1] That not only Fauriel but a number of other friends made many suggestions can be seen by their notes on the margins of the original manuscript. It is curious to find both Fauriel and Monsignor Tosi in agreement about cutting the episode of the Nun of Monza, though for very different reasons: Tosi from fear that it might be considered as an attack on monastic life in general, and Fauriel because he thought it overbalanced the book. Between them they managed to make Manzoni take out a superb description of the nun's love-affair with the bravo Egidio. In the finished book, after the bravo had first spoken to the nun, this was cut short with the pregnant phrase, 'the wretched woman replied.'

In details of language there were few changes between the first draft *Gli Sposi Promessi* and *I Promessi Sposi*, while the revision of language was the entire purpose of the third version published in 1840–2. But this first rewriting eliminated much of the preaching style carried over from *Morale Cattolica*. Also cut was a whole dissertation against writing about love, 'there being,' wrote Manzoni deprecatingly, 'at least six hundred times more love in this world than is needed for the conservation of our

---

[1] Raffaele Masi, a friend of Manzoni's, and Jean Gosselin, in his preface to the second French translation of the book, wrote that this was seriously considered.

revered species'; and more sombrely: 'After history passion is the cruellest and stupidest things there is.' Yet oddly enough the first version contained more clear hints of sex, even apart from the development of the story of the Nun of Monza, such as an insistence on the effect of Lucia's eyes on her captor, the 'Unnamed.'

The rewriting made the whole tone of the book subtler and lighter, and further removed also from any influence of the *Tales of Terror*, with their sublime loves and fatal heroines. Fra Cristoforo, at first a Savonarola-like figure, was brought down from the pulpit and made the human character of the final version. The touches of almost savage bitterness, which linked parts of *Gli Sposi Promessi* to the spirit of *Adelchi*, were modified as the Carbonari failure sank into memory in the silence of Brusuglio. Possibly, too, the friendship with the gently optimistic philosopher Rosmini, whom Manzoni met for the first time during the correction of the second draft, was already beginning to affect his views.

The endless corrections and rewritings, which preoccupied Manzoni for two years even after finishing the second draft, may well have been encouraged by the habits as well as the suggestions of Fauriel, whose tendency, like Manzoni's, was to be for ever correcting and improving his work. Manzoni would sometimes chide Fauriel for this: 'Do you want perfection in everything?' he had written a few years before, when Fauriel was contemplating entirely rewriting his French translation of *Carmagnola*, 'or must one always say to you, as to Alceste, that you must accustom your mind to endure what it produces?' And about another of Fauriel's dragging works, *The History of Southern Gaul*, he had written: 'I know that it is not from fear of other people's judgments, but from conscience that you are so exacting. But you have read so much that you know better than I do how many new, profound, and true works of the highest imagination would never have seen the light of day, had their authors not been resigned to mingling with them a good deal of "perhaps" and lots of "more or less."' The remark, like so many in his letters to Fauriel, seems to have been part of an argument with himself.

III

The exaltation he had felt during composition returned only rarely in correction. By the time the first volume had gone to the printer's he was writing: 'My work goes on very slowly, with long interruptions: I am completely disenchanted with it; the only thing that animates me a little is the hope of being rid of it once and for all: you know what verve that will give me.' He called it a 'rabâchage' (an endless repetition), and in Milanese dialect a 'thick mattress of writing.' But there were bright moments. 'Din don, fareum incoeu, faremm diman' (Ding dong . . . on . . . on to-morrow), he wrote in dialect to a friend after a good bout of correction, before getting into a carriage for a drive. But sometimes correcting a single chapter would take weeks. 'Alessandro is contented,' wrote Donna Giulia in the spring of 1825. 'He's happy with his rewriting at the moment.' By August 1825 the corrected manuscript was in the hands of the copyist. In October it was at the printer's. At this stage Fauriel left, regretted by all at Brusuglio. 'Do turn back your steps,' wrote Donna Giulia, 'and return to this solitude which is yours as much as it is ours.' He was now travelling in Tuscany with Mary Clarke and her mother.

The delivery to the printer's did not mean that Manzoni's preoccupations were over. Corrections still went pouring in to the wretched compositors, with long pauses in between. 'My uncertain and shrewish health is preventing me from finishing the "rigmarole,"' he wrote to a Turin bluestocking, the Contessa Saluzzo, in March 1827. It was coming on 'word by word, letter by letter.' One day Tommaseo called while he was correcting the proofs and putting them out to dry. 'You will see I've got something out in the sun, too,' he said, smiling, as if they were figs or tomatoes on some peasant's terrace.

To Grossi, who was composing his epic poem on the Lombards at the First Crusade at the same time, he wrote from Brusuglio: 'My novel is coming panting along slowly behind your poem, like an old servant escorting an ardent young cavalier.' When in Milan he and Grossi would meet in the passage that divided their studies and show each other how many pages they had written. 'Have you given her [i.e. the book] a good doing to-day?' Manzoni would ask in dialect.

The censor had stamped the manuscript on 3rd July 1824. On 5th June 1827 young Giulietta Manzoni wrote to her god-father Fauriel sending him some more proofs for the French translator. 'As you see, we can finally hope that this eternal novel will be published, and heaven knows it is time, as papa is bored with writing it and others with waiting for it.' The book finally appeared on 15th June 1827, though the title-pages of the first two volumes bore the date 1825 and the last 1826. While it was printing and various friends, such as Berchet and Visconti, had read the first volume, the subscription list went up from 600 to 1,600. 'C'est sans example,' Manzoni wrote to Fauriel, who was back in Paris, homeless, with a poste restante address. He was looking after the French edition, which was to be published by Baudry, as the printer Didot had made so many mistakes in the combined edition of *Carmagnola* and *Adelchi*.

Young Giulietta Manzoni gave Fauriel the first news of how the book was going in Italy. On 7th July she wrote and apologized for her father's not writing—surrounded by congratulating friends he was busy adding more corrections, though the book had been published three weeks before. 'I must tell you,' she went on, 'that we've been delighted at the success of papa's work, which has surpassed not only our expectations, but every hope. Six hundred copies have been sold within twenty days: "c'est une vraie fureur." Father is overwhelmed by visits and letters of every kind and from every rank of society. He has even had some reviews, all favourable, and others announced.' When, a week later, Manzoni set off with his family for Genoa, *en route* for Florence, he must have left with an agreeable combination of relief, surprise, and delight. The 'rigmarole' over which he had sweated for so long was to prove a landmark in the history of Italian publishing.

IV

Nothing could be simpler than the plot. The theme of a marriage prevented by evil circumstances has been a common one throughout literature from the earliest times. It was used by Plautus and Lucian, by Machiavelli in *Clezia*, by Voltaire in *Le Droit du Seigneur*, by Lessing in *Emilia Galotti*, and by Beaumarchais in *Le Barbier de Seville* and *Le Mariage de Figaro*.

The plot may be simple, the final effect limpid as a work of art, but the book contains an extraordinary complexity. The luminous surface, at first sight, only hints at currents in the depths, at storms that could blow up any moment. Perhaps it is the unfolding impression of hidden layers of meaning that contributes so much to the fascinating humanity of the book. Something of this Manzoni had acknowledged himself when he wrote about *Carmagnola* of the two interests which a reader or spectator could draw from drama:

The first comes from seeing men and things represented in a way which conforms to the type of perfection and desire which we all have within us; and this, in infinite grades of meaning, is the admiring interest aroused by many characters of Corneille, Metastasio, and innumerable novels. The other interest is produced by the representation, as true to life as possible, of that mixture of greatness and pettiness, of reason and madness, which is seen in the events, both great and small, of this world: and this interest comes from an important and everlasting part of the human mind, the urge to know what is really true and to see as much as possible into ourselves and our destiny on earth. Of these two kinds of interests the deepest and the most useful to arouse I consider to be the second. . . .

Before *I Promessi Sposi* was made into one of the Italian national monuments, contemporary comments showed an awareness of its fundamental contradictions, whose control and expression give it its vitality. The marriage of Renzo and Lucia is prevented by a racketeering nobleman, by the social and political conditions of the time, and then by the scourges of war, famine, and plague. Providence seems to stretch out a long arm to solve the two young people's difficulties. At the very end there is a wry discussion between Renzo and Lucia, now married and settled, on the lessons they have learnt from their experiences.

'I've learnt,' said Renzo, 'not to get into riots; I've learnt not to make speeches in the street; I've learnt not to raise my elbow too much; I've learnt not to hold door-knockers when there are excited people about; I've learnt not to fasten a bell to my feet before thinking of the consequences. And a hundred other things of the kind.'

Lucia, however, without finding these doctrines false in themselves, was not satisfied with them; it seemed to her, in a confused sort of way, that something was missing. By dint of hearing the same refrains repeated again and again, and thinking them over each time: 'And I,' she once found herself asking her moralist, 'what d'you think I've learnt? I never went looking for troubles, they came looking for me. Unless you mean to say,' she added, smiling sweetly, 'that my mistake was to love you, and to promise myself to you.'

Renzo at first found himself rather in a difficulty. After discussing the question and casting around together for a solution, they came to the conclusion that troubles often come to those who bring them on themselves, but that not even the most cautious and innocent behaviour can ward them off; and that when they come—whether by our own fault or not—confidence in God can lighten them and turn them to our own improvement. This conclusion, though it was reached by poor people, has seemed so just to us that we have thought of putting it down here, as the juice of the whole tale.

But was it, in fact, quite the 'juice' of the whole tale? One school of critics has called this ending 'tired.' Others have thought it was a call for resignation before the world's injustices, as this kind of trust in God and Providence, so far from being an active force for good in this world, almost, they considered, implied inertia. This interpretation may have had its conveniences, but it was an arbitrary selection of one facet of the book. Although Manzoni insisted on the value of kindliness and simplicity of heart, of humility and tolerance even amid war, foreign occupation, famine, and the plague, he also hinted clearly and with acid irony that these scourges come largely, not from Providence, but from the folly of men. Stripped to essentials the dualism in the book is between the religion which reposes all hopes of a just and happy life in the next world, and the rationalism which satirically, acidly, hints that the irresponsibility of a limited class not only aggravates injustice, war, famine, and plague, but in essence causes them.

This fundamental ambivalence in the book was reflected in the variety of contemporary criticism, and has caused controversies which continue in differing terms even to-day. Even praise was sometimes contradictory. 'Such a book,' wrote Giuseppe Verdani, 'could only be written by a profound philosopher, by one with a real knowledge of the human heart, and

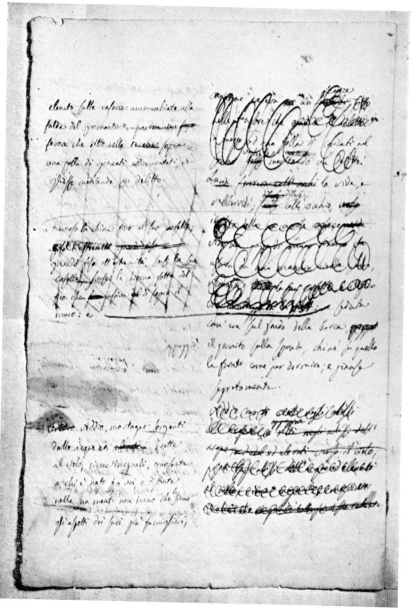

A page of the original manuscript of *I Promessi Sposi*, now in the Braidense Library, Milan. 'Addio, monti sorgenti dall' acque . . .' is now one of the most famous passages in Italian literature

by a pen guided by the liveliest feelings of religion and patriotism.
. . . It's a book which will never perish and will always do
great honour to the nineteenth century in Italy.' But he went
on to remark that the pictures of the horrors of the world almost
blotted out the hope that the author put in faith. Count Somis
had reservations, though pleased at 'la gloria di Don Alessandro.'
'I forgive the author for the various things that could have been
better done, and which he wanted to do in that way in spite of
his own good sense. . . .'

Goethe received a copy from Manzoni in July 1827, and praised
it at once. 'If I were younger,' he said one evening, 'I would
translate *I Promessi Sposi à la Cellini* [a strange juxtaposition!].
Manzoni has sentiment but not sentimentality, the situations are
clear and strong, his way of treating his subjects is as limpid and
lovely as his Italian sky.' But in conversation with Eckermann
he said that Manzoni had abandoned his poetic self too much
for the historian and that he found the descriptions of the war,
famine, and plague dry and unpalatable. The German translator, he suggested, should cut this part by a third; but 'as soon as
the characters in the novel reappear Manzoni returns in his
glory.' The author himself, incidentally, was uncertain
whether he had made the historical parts too long, and in a letter
to Fauriel before publication, after praising the 'aimable et
héroique résolution' of a M. Tronchon to translate the book,
added: 'I approve in advance any cuts he feels he ought to make
to my *plague*. I myself felt it was too long, generally speaking,
but here it is like family gossip, which can have its value.'

One after another the European figures of the day pronounced
their opinion of the book. Chateaubriand's recorded remark
was laudatory but vague: 'Walter Scott is great, but Alessandro
Manzoni is something more!'[1] Lamartine's impression was
'New, strong, and vital. . . . Never have I read pages on

---

[1] The admiration was never reciprocated. Manzoni disliked in Chateaubriand's
writing what he disliked in Tasso's: the atmosphere of illusion and dreams. Also
particularly unsympathetic to Manzoni was Chateaubriand's combination of *ennui*
and pride. Forty years later Mme Colet incautiously exclaimed to Manzoni that
he resembled Chateaubriand in appearance. 'If the feelings, as I think, imprint
themselves on the face and end by moulding it, I should not have any resemblance
to Chateaubriand,' came the reply. 'His genius is not one of those that touch and
fascinate me . . . his style is good, but only out for effect. His *Génie du Christianisme*
is a work of rhetoric and not of conviction.'

G

religion which moved me so much as yours, when you gave yourself up to the religious feeling which breathes in all your works,' and again: 'One of the three or four books which I have read with most enchantment in my whole life.' The anti-Catholic Sismondi called it 'une bonne action,' but Stendhal's only recorded comment was: 'Far too highly praised.' Grossi, considered Stendhal, was 'without contradiction the better writer or at least the one with the most genius.' In England the novel received less notice than had the plays. 'An example of what we must consider as an indifferent novel, written by a highly respectable dramatist,' wrote the *Quarterly Review*, which found the plot artificially managed. It noted, however, 'how differently the banditti scenes are managed in a real Italian novel, and in our own romances of the Radcliffe school,' as in the latter 'background and landscape excite the imagination, but figures have no characters.' In the plague the *Quarterly Review* noticed an attitude which had been introduced by both Thucydides and Boccaccio, that the 'selfishness, the indifference, and reckless jollity of man increase on such occasions, the nearer he seems to approach the end of his career.' Although 'Manzoni's power as a novelist is certainly not equal to his ability as a dramatist . . . even in this tale he displays no inconsiderable portion of talent, always excepting his attempts at humour, which we cannot help considering as very tragical mirth.' Other English reviewers found it 'feeble and imitative,' such as the *Westminster Review* in 1837, which accused Manzoni of 'inciting people to patient suffering rather than action'; and pronounced the book 'unequal to the necessities of the times and the demands of his country.'

In Italy its popular success was undoubted and immediate—nine editions were sold out in the first six months. This caused general exultation in Milan. 'Finally we have a Walter Scott! Finally Manzoni has filled the great void in our literature.' 'It has made people weep, so several people who have never wept for years have told me,' wrote Costanza Arconati from exile at Wiesbaden to Mary Clarke at Ilfracombe. And a canon of the church of San Babila wrote that he did not dare criticize the book in Milan for fear of being 'hounded out of the town.'

Professional literary men in Italy, however, were apt at first to hold aloof. There were many disturbing things for them in

the book.   Some raised shocked eyes at the treatment of the
governing classes.   'Are peasants . . . worthy heroes to be linked
to any historical epoch?'   'Why two peasants as hero and
heroine?   Surely passion enters less strongly when the heart is
still crude?'   The dialogue, they noted with horror, was written
in current slang.   The binder, it was said, had repeated whole
passages to the author in dialect.   Not for some time was it
realized that the book, whatever its merits and demerits, had
done something of capital importance for the diffusion of Italian
books: it had broken down for the first time the old barriers
between the literary world and the general public.

There was, too, a feeling among the cultivated classes at the
time that Manzoni had lowered himself and them all by writing
a novel.   For novel-writing was still considered so dubious
socially that even Walter Scott had had to publish anonymously,
so as not to endanger his position as Clerk of the Edinburgh Court
of Session.   A change of opinion on the standing of novelists was,
indeed, already on its way from Paris.   In 1826 *Le Globe* noted:
'For the last ten years a serious person has had to hide to read a
novel.   Now, unless he's a Jansenist, he doesn't make any
mystery about it.'   Manzoni's remark to Degola about novelists
as 'empoisonneurs publiques' showed he was well aware of this
attitude in Italy still.   Later he himself almost came to agree with
it, in spite of his earlier defence of the drama against the attacks
of Bossuet and Rousseau.   A year or two later, when he was
becoming more insistent on the moral role of art, he was to
write: 'If art aimed at amusing that class of person who do
practically nothing else but amuse themselves, it would be the
last, most frivolous, most servile of the professions.'

Though some priests considered the book as 'a model of
tolerant and useful religion,' others, including Don Bosco,
found it irreligious and immoral.   The first reaction from Rome
was more than dubious.   There the character of Don Abbondio
appeared to be an attack on the clergy in general, an attack
which seemed particularly unfortunate in the eyes of the Curia,
as the North Italian clergy at the time were notoriously sub-
servient to Austria.   The episode of the Nun of Monza, as
Monsignor Tosi had seen when he had implored Manzoni to cut
it out, could also be interpreted as criticizing all monastic

institutions.   At one moment there seems even to have been
some discussion at the Vatican about putting the book on the
Index.   Writing from Florence on 16th September 1827
Giuseppe Montani, one of the chief contributors to *L'Antologia*,
the Florentine equivalent of *Il Conciliatore*, told a friend that he
had just seen a letter from Rome dated a fortnight before, from
someone who had been assured by the Roman bookseller Agazzi
'that the sale of Manzoni's novel has been forbidden under new
orders.   The Master of the Sacred Palace (*Maestro del Sacro
Palazzo*) had passed it.   Others, more zealous, have remedied
his dangerous compliance!'   The sale of the book was suspended in Rome for about a fortnight, then the ban, if ban it was,
was lifted.   But for the first year or two criticisms persisted
there.   In November 1829 Enrico Mayor reported to Vieusseux,
the editor of *L'Antologia*: 'One is scarcely allowed to say a word
here in praise of Manzoni, and I can imagine no subject that
more annoys the Roman *literati*.   I remember last year Contessa
Lenzoni told me that many literary men in Rome kept away from
her *salon*, because Manzoni was praised there.'   In the spring
of 1829 Father Salvagnoli Marchetti, the same priest who had
attacked the *Inni Sacri*, launched into a furious tirade in the
Giornale Arcadico.   'Manzoni writes not as a man of letters, but
as a carter, a porter, a fish-vendor might write, clumsily, taste-
lessly, atrociously.   He is a writer without construction, flimsy,
cloudy, whom no one can understand . . . a master in guile, a
hidden Voltairean who laughs Olympically at everything and
everybody.'   In the book Father Marchetti discovered 'doctrines which overthrow every divine and human law, which
reduce society to a pack of wild beasts, draw the mind to error,
and the heart to disorderly passions. . . .'[1]

During the winter of 1829–30 something happened in Rome
to change the climate of opinion.   In March 1830 the philosopher Antonio Rosmini was writing to Manzoni from Rome:
'Here *I Promessi Sposi* is applauded by the flower of Rome; and
those who praise it most and recommend it to their students
are the Jesuits.'   This must have seemed particularly odd to

---

[1] This opinion has been echoed in recent years by a modern commentator,
Giovanni Papini, who wrote that Manzoni was 'rich with the most poisonous
juices of French illuminism, and saw in Catholicism only a social humanitarianism.'

Rosmini, who was not only to become Manzoni's greatest friend, but one of the chief opponents of the Jesuits within the Church. The new Jesuit attitude towards the book was confirmed by a remark in a letter from Count Monaldo Leopardi to his son Giacomo from Rome in June 1830, that the Jesuits in Rome were recommending it to their penitents. Yet, though *I Promessi Sposi* was set at the period of the Counter-Reformation when the Jesuits were at the height of their power, the only Jesuit mentioned (in an acid footnote) was an astrologer, 'that fatal Delrio, who would surely be one of the most renowned of authors, if their fame were in proportion to the good or evil produced by their works.' The Order that appears and provides one of the heroes of the book is that of the humble and self-effacing Capuchins. Perhaps, in spite of the persistent coldness of the Vatican towards the author (a coldness which is understandable in view of Manzoni's later attacks on the Temporal Power), the Jesuits realized the political importance of harnessing the novel to their policy. That their interpretation was accepted even by many of their opponents can be seen by an attack on the book in *Nuova Polemica* as 'preaching resignation to assassinated Italy, perhaps because of which the Jesuits recommended its reading to their penitents.' This was the precursor of an attitude still general in Italy to-day.

While the Church, in spite of some doubts, took the book more or less under its wing, it was the liberals and anti-clericals who were and continued to be most critical. Leopardi was one of the earliest to express this critical view. In spite of, or perhaps partly because of, remarks by a father with whom he dared not openly disagree, in 1827 he wrote in a letter to his friend Mamiani: 'The fact that Manzoni has chosen for the setting of his novel one of the most wretched and servile periods in Italian history must hide many reasons, and deep ones too. But they certainly don't appear, and what seems instead to come out of his account is the deplorable conclusion that one must not complain of the present, as Italians have been much worse off at other times, and the Austrians are pure gold compared to the Spaniards.' This unfair and inaccurate conclusion about Manzoni's attitude to Italian independence was even repeated just after his death. 'With Manzoni's way of expressing the conception of Italy we should still perhaps have the Austrians and the pontifical Zouaves here. The idea exists in Manzoni's writings, as there's linen in certain stuffs, but subtly interwoven with wool.' Luigi Settembrini went even further:

To write and publish in 1827, in the darkest and most ferocious time of reaction, when the priests were in command, the Austrians were terrorizing Venetia and Lombardy, and tyrants were up in arms everywhere, a book which praised priests and friars and advised patience, submission, and pardon, meant (Manzoni certainly didn't want this, but it is the necessary consequence of the book) to advise submission to slavery, the negation of patriotism and of every generous sentiment.

The crudest of all the anti-clerical attacks reached Manzoni in an anonymous letter: 'I've read *I Promessi Sposi* and it's annoyed me because you're working for the "shop" (clerical of course), and like all those who work for the "shop" you are carried along by it.' In *L'Indicatore Genovese* in 1828 Mazzini defended Manzoni. He defined the Italian romantics as 'men for whom truth is the *aim*, and nature and the heart the *means*. . . . They are not slaves of foreign ideas; they want to give Italy an original national literature, a literature which is not just a sound of fugitive music, but one which soothes the ear and yet interprets the emotions, ideas, and needs of the social movement.

There were also anti-clericals such as Montani who, more subtly, saw 'something intimate and secret which reveals itself little by little and warms rather than seduces.' But the most acute contemporary comments of this school came perhaps from Giovita Scalvini, a sensitive and intelligent Carbonaro exile writing from Paris. He began his notes to *I Promessi Sposi* by a plea to equate Liberalism and Christianity—an argument which would not have sounded unfamiliar to Manzoni himself. 'Christianity,' wrote Scalvini,

and that which is called Liberalism by those who understand it, work towards a single aim: which is to revive the love of one's neighbour, to abolish all the vicious reasons for inequality, and to establish the reign of justice. And if anyone asks why we see some hostility between Christianity and Liberalism, if both have the same aims, many things could be said in reply to dissipate the doubts of the timid, and to warn them against the fallacies of those who find it useful that such a truth should not be spread.

'Dogma,' he went on, 'has for a long time violated doctrine to obtain pre-eminence, and vice versa doctrine has been able to violate dogma for the same end, but a day will come when they will be seen to be reconciled.' Manzoni's religion, he said, 'has obviously drawn its wisdom and breadth from modern philosophy, from that philosophy which, while it seemed busy hiding the faith from human minds, was spreading in the world without realizing it, those teachings for whose love human minds accepted the faith.' Scalvini saw Manzoni as resolving Catholicism into Liberalism, not Liberalism into Catholicism. But although he commented on Don Abbondio's interview with Cardinal Federigo that 'his [Manzoni's] more thoughtless and wayward readers are like chicks in the talons of a hawk among his arguments, as Don Abbondio is himself with those of the cardinal,' he also, like Benedetto Croce, considered Manzoni's religion to be born in part from an historic pessimism. 'He has raised his disillusioned eyes from the earth and turned them to heaven, and just as he saw everything down here as darkness and pain, so he saw everything above as happiness and light.'

Scalvini noticed, though, that under the apparent pessimism of the book was a rationalist, almost revolutionary, undertow. The concept of oppression stifling innocence and truth can have an earthly as well as religious connotation. Renzo in his cups was the simple anarchist swept by the hope that the men in the street, 'the decent chaps,' would unite to abolish injustice and establish freedom. 'My poor Renzo,' said Fra Cristoforo on returning from his fruitless mission to Don Rodrigo, 'if men of power who wanted to commit acts of injustice always had to give their reasons, things wouldn't be as they are now.' Scalvini saw more than just bombast and self-righteousness in the decrees against the bravoes. The Governor-General of Milan, he considered, made little real effort to discourage the bravoes, because their disorderly conduct kept people's minds off the inefficiency and profiteering of his administration. This somewhat tortuous argument sounds familiar to-day.

V

From the first, most foreign reviewers were inclined to consider the novel to be just a dull imitation of Scott's. The *Gentleman's Magazine* for February 1828 called Manzoni 'the author of a fourth-rate novel, modelled on those of Walter Scott.' The *Encyclopaedia Britannica* in the edition of 1849 labelled him 'one of those literary traffickers who need to borrow most of the capital in which they deal.' The *Literatischer Zodiacus* said that Manzoni stuck to his model Scott 'like a sheet to a skin.' And Barbey d'Aurevilly repeated the same opinion a month or two after Manzoni's death. Even Edgar Allan Poe, hailing *I Promessi Sposi* in the *Southern Literary Messenger* for 1835 as 'a work which promises to be the commencement of a new style in novel-writing . . .' went on to say: 'It might be too much to say that the novel is in every sense original. The writer is obviously familiar with English literature, and seems to have taken at least one hint from Scott.' The first serious comparison between Manzoni and Scott was in the *Christian Remembrancer* of April 1845. 'In Scott the wilderness of human nature is left to its own direction. In Manzoni, that wilderness is brought under control of a power above it. The Church overshadows the ground like the cathedral arch, and the groined Gothic roof overhangs, from its solemn height, all the stirs and commotions of the crowd below. . . . Manzoni's Church is not a pictorial but a practical one. . . .'

It is Italian critics who have gone most deeply into the differences between these two. Some of them also point out that Scott himself was not entirely the originator of the historical novel, and may have drawn his ideas from his early translation of Goethe's *Goetz von Berlichingen*. Scott said himself he was inspired as a fiction writer by the *novelas* of Cervantes.

The Waverley novels had aroused a wave of enthusiasm throughout Italy after the Napoleonic Wars.[1] They were widely read by all classes; the bookstalls were full of cheap translations of them, nearly all made by Manzoni's friends,

[1] The name Ivanoe is still used as a Christian name there, e.g. Signor Ivanoe Bonomi, the late Prime Minister.

Fra Cristoforo bids farewell to Lucia, Renzo, and Agnese. A scene from the film directed by Mario Camerini in 1941. Operas, plays, ballets, films, marionettes, and costume parades at country festas have helped to make the characters in *I Promessi Sposi* household words in Italy

The sacking of the bakeries. From a woodcut by Francesco Gonin in the 1840–2 edition, lavishly illustrated by Gonin and financed and supervised by Manzoni

Don Abbondio meets the Bravoes. From a lithograph by Roberto Focosi, *c.* 1835. These lithographs were used as bases for the large coloured prints of scenes from *I Promessi Sposi* widely distributed in Italy later in the century and still to be seen in many homes to-day

including one by Tomasso Grossi. Young Giulietta Manzoni,
writing to Fauriel in 1826, mentioned that she was reading
Woodstock. 'What do you think of it? It's Walter Scott, so one
must keep quiet. . . . This Englishman is a bit of a torment to
me, as people are for ever trying to get me to talk about him.'
Popular plays and operas were based on the novels; scenes from
them were portrayed in pictures, particularly in the new art of
lithography. There was a sudden spate of historical novels by
Italians. Carlo Varese's *Sibilla Odaleta* and Gianbattista Baz-
zoni's *Castello di Trezzo* both appeared a few months before
I Promessi Sposi, and like Guerazzi's *Battaglia di Benevento* were
directly influenced by Scott. But *I Promessi Sposi* was actually
written before any of these, and, in spite of the delay in publication due to rewriting and correction, can claim to be the first
Italian historical novel chronologically.

Manzoni himself told Fabris: 'Had there not been a Walter
Scott the idea of writing a novel would never have occurred to
me.' He also called Scott 'the Homer of the historical novel';
though this was in a later essay when he was attacking the
historical novel as an art-form (and he went on to say he found
the *Odyssey* full of bragging and lies). 'Can you indicate to me,'
he asked in this essay, 'many works among ancient and modern
read with more pleasure and admiration than those of a certain
Walter Scott?' And he replied himself: 'That these novels
have pleased, and not without good reason, is an undeniable
fact.' Both Manzoni and Thierry had been particularly impressed by Scott's picture in *Ivanhoe* of social upheaval during
the Norman invasion, and they found the book contained more
real history than most historical works, in contrast to the contemporary historians' insistence on dynastic events. Thierry
devoted an article to praising *Ivanhoe* in the *Censeur européen* of
May 1820. The novel, he considered, reflected his theories
about the conflict between the conquerors and the conquered:
'. . . two peoples, two languages; customs that contrasted and
struggled against each other; tyranny and insolence on one side,
misery and hatred on the other . . . a real development of the
drama of conquest of which the Battle of Hastings was but the
prelude.' Manzoni was first put on to *Ivanhoe* by Fauriel, and it
was read to him during one of his illnesses in 1819 or 1820. He

* G

read it a second time after his return from Paris, during the
winter of 1820–1, and at the same period he also borrowed *The
Astrologer* and *Waverley* from Cattaneo at the Brera library.   But
he did not entirely share the enthusiasm of Fauriel; in spite of
Scott's description in *Ivanhoe* of the social results of invasion,
he still found it contained too much romantic falsification of
history.   He thought the picture of Richard Cœur-de-Lion
defective.   'When historical events and characters are mingled
with a story I think they must be represented in the most strictly
historical manner.'

Manzoni derived from Scott not only the idea of an historical
novel, but details and touches scattered over *I Promessi Sposi*,
which could be traced to memories, probably unconscious, of
various passages in the Waverley novels.   There are parallels
between Gertrude's parents and Lucy of Lammermoor's, the
scholar Don Ferrante and Luke Lindon in *The Abbot*, Don
Ferrante's library and Oldbuck's in *The Antiquary*, Lucia's hair
and Alice Lee's in *Woodstock*, Lucia's relations with the Nun of
Monza and Margaret Ramsey asking Lady Hermione for help in
The Fortunes of Nigel.   But although Renzo and Nigel both had
to face unknown cities because of bullies at home, the difference
between the two writers showed in the varying depths of conception of these characters.   Nigel, as he acknowledged himself,
was a sort of puppet created by others.   'I became a courtier
because Heriot so advised it—a gamester because Dalmazo so
contrived it—an Alsatian because Lowestoffe so willed it.
Whatever good or bad has befallen me has arisen from the agency
of others, not my own.'   But there is something warm and
instinctive about Renzo, who remains inwardly a free agent even
in the most adverse circumstances.   The difference between
Scott's and Manzoni's treatment also shows by comparing the
scenes of Nanty Ewart's drunkenness in *Redgauntlet* and Renzo's
in *I Promessi Sposi*.   Manzoni's description not only has the pictorial observation of a Dutch picture, but treats into a wider
dimension with Renzo's incoherent hopes for freedom and justice.

There is a strong possibility that the influence of Scott on
Manzoni may also be partly reciprocal.   A novel of Scott's,
The Fair Maid of Perth, published in 1828, could have been written
after reading *I Promessi Sposi*, to which it shows great similarities

of plot if not of treatment. It was written very rapidly and is not one of Scott's best. It is also the tale of a marriage postponed by bullies and by public events. Catherine is persecuted by Rothsay, who also attempts to kidnap her, against a background of Rothsay's conspiracy, struggles among the highlanders, and the end of the weak government of Robert III of Scotland.

The fundamental divergence between Scott and Manzoni was one of attitude. Scott, by his rediscoveries of picturesque legends of romantic Scotland, of heroic deeds and old poetic traditions, provided a flight from reality, and he avoided spoiling entertainment by disturbing any prejudices. 'I have tried to unsettle no man's faith, to corrupt no man's principle,' he said himself. It was this lack of depth that Balzac deplored in Scott. 'There is no passion in Walter Scott,' the young novelist Daniel d'Arthez is made to say to Lucien de Rubempré in *Les Illusions Perdues*. 'Either he is himself without it, or it is forbidden by the hypocritical laws of his country'; [1] and later he made d'Arthez advise Lucien to 'portray the passions, then you will have at your disposal immense resources that the great Scottish novelist had to forgo in order to provide family reading for the prudish English.' Taine later remarked that Scott 'sees and gazes at the outside of things and forms much longer than at the inside and the feelings.' Manzoni, although he submerged the passions, was out to shake complacency, to deride cant, to find the fundamental springs of history, perhaps to state a view of the powerlessness of the individual before the State. 'While Scott set down carelessly thought-out ideas to give pleasant entertainment,' observed Benedetto Croce, 'Manzoni set down all the tragedy and human comedy of a subtle moral conscience.' [2]

[1] Honoré de Balzac, *Lost Illusions* (*Les Illusions Perdues*). Translated by Kathleen Raine. John Lehmann, 1951.

[2] According to a story in many literary histories which probably originated with Cantù, Scott and Manzoni met and exchanged mutual compliments. Manzoni said that *I Promessi Sposi* owed everything to Scott, to which the latter gallantly replied: 'In that case it is my finest work.' According to Donna Teresa, Manzoni's second wife, this remark was made by Scott in London to Panizzi, the Carbonaro exile who became director of the British Museum, and who was a friend of Manzoni's. The meeting between Scott and Manzoni himself is most unlikely chronologically. It was only possible during Scott's journey to Italy in 1832, and he was then in the grip of his last illness and hurried back to London from Rome, without, so far as is known, stopping in Milan. During this visit, in a conversation at the castle of Bracciano, Scott expressed 'great admiration' for Manzoni. And on another occasion he told Sigismondo Trechi that all he wanted to see in Milan was Manzoni—and the cathedral.

VI

A deeper and much more permeative influence on Manzoni, and one which he freely acknowledged, was that of Shakespeare. Though Manzoni only once wrote of Dante, which has annoyed some Italians, he left pages of enthusiastic praise about Shakespeare, '*il mio* Shakespeare' as he called him when replying to an objection by the first English translator of *I Promessi Sposi*, the Rev. Charles Swan. 'I was struck,' Swan had written in the preface to this translation, published at Pisa in 1828,

as everyone who reads it must be, with the parenthetical remark in which the author styles the King of Bards 'a barbarian not entirely destitute of talent.' Indignant, as a loyal subject should be, at the aspersions of a rebel, I dared to fling the gauntlet at his feet; and in a letter to Mr Manzoni . . . I charged him zealously, if feebly, with his crime. In the reply, which I am permitted to annex at foot, he condescends to rebut the charge, and extend a friendly hand where I looked for a hostile glare.

Swan, though accepting the explanation of the passage as ironical, was apparently rather confused by the involved style of Manzoni's defence, for he added: 'While admiring the ingenious mode by which he deprecates our English prejudices, let him [the reader] recommend to this highly gifted individual henceforward to be less frugal of a note of admiration: and let him add, in the language of one among the consummate masters of irony that England has had to boast:

> To statesmen when we give a wipe
> We print it in Italic type.

Manzoni's defence was that he had used the contested phrase 'in the supposition that my readers (of whom, as you must have noticed, I foresaw much smaller numbers than fate gave me) would know my admiration for Shakespeare. . . .'

Do you remember that character in comedy who, bullied and beaten by his wife from jealous suspicions, congratulated himself on her anger and praised her blows, which were to him a proof of love? Now that is almost my feeling at seeing you angry with me in defence of my Shakespeare. Although I do not read a word of English and only know the great poet by means of translation, yet I am such a warm admirer that I am apt to get annoyed if others say they like him more than I do. And at a time when I took a warmer interest in poets and poetry than I do now I cannot tell you how angry I was at those ill-considered sentences of Voltaire and his disciples about Shakespeare. And perhaps more than the insults I disliked that strange way of praising him, of saying that in the midst of a series of extravagances he (Shakespeare) comes out now and again with a wonderful flash of genius: as if the voice of genius which raises a cry, as it were, in those places were not the same which speaks elsewhere; as if the same power which stands out so strikingly in one passage does not show itself, less obviously but with marvellous continuity, in the depicting of so many different passions, in the language—so human and so poetic, so unexpected and so natural—used for numberless characters and situations . . . as if the same power does not appear in the choice, in the conduct, in the progression of events and effects, in the order so apparently neglected yet so followed in effect, that one does not know whether to attribute it to an admirable instinct or to an admirable artifice . . . yet both are there to an extraordinary degree.

He repeated the praise, and the criticism of Voltaire, in his essay *Del Romanzo Storico*. 'Anyone who wants to write poetry must read Shakespeare: how he knows all the feelings!' he exclaimed later. In Shakespeare's plays he found, as he did not, he added, in those of Racine, 'a progressive series of circumstances and events gradually developing the passions.' Manzoni's admiration went so deep that he expressed it almost in religious terms: he felt that Shakespeare expressed a concept near his own heart, of Providence lightening the desperation of reality, a sense of mysterious forces shaping human lives. To Shakespeare, indeed, he was apt to ascribe 'a highly moral purpose' which few critics, except possibly the Marxists, would allow to-day. Shakespeare also disregarded the unities with a liberty to which the romantics aspired, and showed a fearless search for hidden truth, an anti-heroic realism that Manzoni found particularly sympathetic. *Adelchi* and *Carmagnola* are very unlike any play of Shakespeare in form (though there are parallels between some characters such as Hamlet and Adelchi), but Manzoni considered he had found in Shakespeare their combination of moral idealism and tragedy. His appreciation of Shakespeare had been increased by correspondence and conversation with Fauriel and by the writings of Schlegel and Mme de Staël.   And the mixture of the serious and the comic in *I Promessi Sposi* was perhaps influenced by Schlegel's enthusiasm for this mixture in Shakespeare.

In *I Promessi Sposi* Manzoni was influenced by Shakespeare more in the conception of his characters than in the scenes.   He had analysed Richard II and the complex moral essence of Othello as Goethe had done with Hamlet, and drawn from them the *riflessione sentita* (deeply felt reflection) which impregnates the novel.   Yet, as de Lollis has remarked: 'The differences between *I Promessi Sposi* and Shakespearian tragedy are like those between the Lake of Como on a summer day and the Channel in November.'   But the calm of the Lake of Como can be deceptive.

VII

Ignorant of any English, as he had told Swan, Manzoni almost certainly read his Shakespeare in the French translation of Le Tourneur, a set of which can still be seen in his library in Milan. But apart from Scott and Shakespeare there are hints in *I Promessi Sposi* of other English writers whose works were translated into French or Italian: of Goldsmith's *Vicar of Wakefield*, more perhaps of Sterne's *Sentimental Journey*, a magnificent translation of which by Ugo Foscolo we know Manzoni read enthusiastically, until it was removed by Monsignor Tosi.   Manzoni's ironic, rather complicated humour, his deprecating self-laughter, have considerable links with Sterne's.   Defoe's *Robinson Crusoe* was mentioned in *Gli Sposi Promessi*, though not in the final version. A French translation of Defoe's *Journal of the Plague Year*, which Manzoni may have read, has recently been discovered.   But apart from the fact that the Milan plague of 1628 was the same one which reached England fifty years later, similarities of incident in such descriptions are inevitable.   For instance, a number of observations made by both Defoe and Manzoni appeared recently in Albert Camus's *La Peste*.

All his life Manzoni read French with more ease and pleasure than he did Italian, and *I Promessi Sposi* is steeped in the influence of the French literature with which he had spent his youth.   The

great French religious writers of the seventeenth century—
Pascal, Bossuet, Massillon—mingled in his mind with the rationalist, logical thinkers of the Enlightenment, whose impact he
had felt at such close quarters during those formative years
among the Idéologues in Paris. The dimension of psychological
analysis in *I Promessi Sposi*, which was quite new to the novelists
of the time, except possibly to Richardson and Laclos, and
which sometimes appears to foreshadow Proust, may be due in
part to the observation of the contradictions of human behaviour
by the Fathers of the Church, developed by the seventeenth-
century French moralists. Some of the more leisured passages
in *I Promessi Sposi* recall, too, the grand style of the French
seventeenth-century theologians. 'La philosophic,' wrote Massillon, 'découvrait la honte des passions, mais elle n'apprenait
pas à les vaincre: et ses préceptes pompeux étaient plutôt
l'éloge de la vertu que le remède du vice.' Joseph de Maistre,
a contemporary Catholic with whose politics Manzoni particularly disagreed, once remarked in an aside (that might have
been made by Pascal, with his 'le moi est haïssable'): 'I don't
know what the conscience of a rogue is like, I only know my own,
which is the conscience of a decent person, and it is enough
to make one shiver.' Perhaps Manzoni saw every believing
Christian as something of a Don Quixote, going through life
with certain principles which he is unable to carry out—unless
he has the tenacity of a saint.

When, after his conversion, he soaked himself in the moral
analysis of La Bruyère, La Rochefoucauld, and Vauvenages, Voltaire's final judgment of man as either a hypocrite or a fool came
to seem shallow. In 1817 he had handed over his magnificently
bound eighteenth-century edition of Voltaire's complete works
to Monsignor Tosi, who solemnly burnt it volume by volume in
his presence. He only kept three volumes back, and there were
none in either of his libraries when he died. But the influences
of youth remain ingrained and cannot be so easily dismissed.
The irony, the rationalism, the narrator's attitude of combined
judge and satirist in *I Promessi Sposi* all seem influenced by
Voltaire. In the *Lettre à M. Chauvet* he attacked Voltaire as a
playwright and analysed *Zaïre* and *Othello*, but he was interested
in him as a historian, though he considered that the attempt in

the *Henriade* to combine poetry and history showed that they were impossible to reconcile.   There is a remark in Voltaire's *L'Ingénu*: 'I'm going to recount quite simply how this happened, without putting in anything of my own, which is no small effort for a historian' that is curiously reminiscent of Manzoni's comment about the behaviour of the Commissioner of Supply during the riots: 'What else he did we cannot tell, as he was alone, and history can only guess.   Luckily it is quite used to doing so.'

Whatever Voltaire thought of other historians, history, for him, was nothing but a field of follies where the few just and wise had to conduct a perpetual rearguard action against the assaults of rogues and fools; if the only weapons of the just and honest are good faith and sincerity, they run the risk, as in *Candide*, of meeting even more disillusionments and disasters than did Don Quixote.   There is a hint possibly of this attitude in *I Promessi Sposi*, where, as one modern Italian critic has put it, it becomes 'the *accedia* of the anchorite rather than the decision of the soldier girding himself for the fight.'   One part of Manzoni saw humanity as poisoned in will and thought from the beginning— a conception influenced too by Jansenism—and the work of regeneration as slow and wellnigh hopeless.   In this view most of the social edifice was built on violence; iniquity and oppression have been codified into laws which sanction and protect the privileges of the strong—so forming that insidious network which we call civilization: this order is in essential contrast to evangelical principles, and the strident contradiction is bound to torture any sensitive mind.   Manzoni's attitude in *I Promessi Sposi* was that legal justice is a myth, and laws mere instruments to keep the oppressed in their places.   The official representatives of law and society in the book are all made to cut a very poor figure, except for Cardinal Federigo.   Lawyers and magistrates, mayors and councillors, police and military, are all either servile or stupid.   The Governor-General of Milan, Don Gonsalo Fernandez de Cordova, tries to blame the riots in Milan on Renzo to the Venetian resident, and the merchant at Gorgonzola ascribes all the ferment to agitators, while in the plague imaginary sorcerers and mysterious anointers are made scapegoats for the follies and inefficiencies of the governing class.

Although of course deploring, after the conversion, Voltaire's sardonic attitude to religion, Manzoni continued to approve, as he noted on the margin of his copy of *Le Siècle de Louis XIV*, Voltaire's 'attacks on abuses and excesses.' 'La famine, la peste, et la guerre sont les trois ingrédients les plus fameux de ce bas monde,' Voltaire had written in his *Philosophical Dictionary*, and these ingredients make up almost half of *I Promessi Sposi*. Benedetto Croce has noted a number of details in the novel which are reminiscent of Voltaire. The Abbé de Kerabon, at the beginning of *L'Ingénu*, and Don Abbondio are introduced almost in the same words: both dates, 'the evening of 15th July 1689' and 'the evening of 7th November 1628,' being brought in to give an ironic touch of mock solemnity to the normal stroll of a country priest; and 'Tout-à-tout' in *L'Ingénu* has a strong resemblance to the lawyer Azzeccagarbugli of *I Promessi Sposi*. Voltaire's play *Le Droit du Seigneur* has almost the same plot. It starts with a bet between the local noble and his cousin that he will get the peasant girl; her kidnapping by bravoes to a lonely château is followed by the chevalier's conversion. The moral at the end of Voltaire's stories ranged from some acid or ironic comment to the resigned acceptance of human weakness in the *Histoire des voyages de Scarmentad*: 'Je fus cocu, et je vis que c'était l'état le plus doux de ma vie.' The deprecating shrug of the manner, though scarcely the matter, of this remark, might be Manzoni's.

VIII

For a man with Manzoni's background the influence not only of Voltaire but of the other Encyclopaedists was permeative. His incisive and objective attack on the abuse of monastic institutions in the story of the Nun of Monza was different in tone to the eloquent and passionate onslaught of Diderot, whose short story, *La Religieuse*, published in 1780, had partly inspired it,[1] as it later inspired Verga's *Storia di una Capinera*. Diderot's nun Susanna was pushed into a convent because she was illegitimate;

---

[1] Other French writers whom Manzoni must have read also treated the subject of forced entries into convents. Massillon had preached a sermon on this theme, while Marivaux's *La Vie de Marianne* contains whole passages of striking resemblance to Manzoni's.

to prevent her, with her beauty and natural gifts, getting off with a prospective husband intended for her half-sister. Yet the ways by which the abbess of the convent persuades her to take the veil are very similar to those of the cold and calculating Abbess of Monza, obsessed by the advantages of having Gertrude's father as a patron.

'What are you being asked to do? To take the veil!' urges the French abbess when Susanna hesitates to take the first vows. ' "Why not take it? What does that bind you to? To nothing! To live with us for another two years. One doesn't know who will live and who will die: it's a long time, is two years! Lots of things can happen in two years . . ." and she added to these remarks so many caresses, so many protestations of friendship, so much falsity in fact! . . . So I let myself be persuaded.' Susanna is a clearer representative of the rationalist Enlightenment than the more turgid Gertrude, for, unlike Gertrude, she hates the convent not from pride, or lack of faith, or a yearning for outside pleasures, but because she sees no logical reason why she should die in slavery. Diderot, crude, realistic, obscene, and warm-hearted (he was found in floods of tears when writing the story), described the progress of Susanna's love-affair in detail, and did not allow himself to be deflected by advice as Manzoni was. Yet Manzoni's account has a restrained force and a subtlety of observation which make this episode one of the most moving in I Promessi Sposi.

IX

In the margin opposite a passage in Marmontel's Éléments de Littérature which runs, 'The feeling of difficulties overcome enters more than one thinks into the pleasure given us by the arts,' Manzoni wrote: 'The pleasure that one gets from art does not consist in observing the means which the artist uses, but in feeling their effect.' And it is in the effect of all-pervading humanity that I Promessi Sposi lives; for no influences can explain a book so fused into an artistic whole. Realism and social satire, poetic lyricism and Christian belief, mingle with a humour stemming from a compassionate view of human weakness which is, perhaps, an essential part of Manzoni's Christianity. It is 'the poem of humility and pride,' as one modern Italian critic has called it, of 'the psychology of sanctity and the psychology of the half-hearted' according to a modern English one, 'a picture of life with all its cruelty and jokes,' according to another.

Benedetto Croce, although he found much to criticize in the book, considered it to be 'among the most balanced and perfect in all literature,' adding that he saw two sides to it, 'the vast, historical panorama' and 'the satire on human folly' which 'from top to bottom is a tale of moral exhortation measured and guided with a firm eye towards that end.' This statement opened a controversy as to whether the book was fundamentally a work of lyrical artistry or of moral exhortation, which split the Italian literary and academic world for generations, until Croce refuted his own earlier opinion on rereading *I Promessi Sposi* a few months before he died.

Although Manzoni's indictment of evil is devastating, there are times, amid the analysis of motive, when we are left wondering whether the conditioning effects of society do not raise a great question-mark above conventional ideas of right and wrong. Who is wrong, for instance, Don Abbondio who puts off the young couple's marriage through fear of the local tyrant, or Renzo and Lucia who then force their way into the priest's room and disturb his peaceful classical reading to try and bring off the marriage by a trick? This is left to the reader to decide, as he must decide between action and resignation, between logic and Providence. Seeing the world through the experience of the Revolution and the Napoleonic Wars, Manzoni expressed the sense of a search for values amid fundamental upheavals which brings *I Promessi Sposi* closer to our shaken generation than, possibly, to any since it was written. And with the disillusionment and the muted irony at human folly there runs a thread of hope in human nature, in kindliness and humanity, which is quite unsentimental, and which he applies to this life quite as much as to the next.

CHAPTER TEN

I

WHEN *I Promessi Sposi* was published Manzoni was forty-two.   He
was to live for almost another half-century before his pall passed
through the black-draped streets of Milan amid the mourning of
a nation.   Yet his creative work as an artist was done.   Into the
novel on which his fame rests he put most of the experience,
personal and emotional, religious and philosophical, that had
shaped his life.   What he wrote before was a preparation for
it, what he wrote afterwards a consequence.   *Il libro per tutti*
(everyman's book), in which so vast and varied a public have
found something that reflects themselves, marks the culmination
of his work as an artist.   Whether it was a work which expressed
'divine persuasion' or the equilibrium of contradiction, the
book was the focal point of his past and future.   It was symp-
tomatic that he was never to cease correcting it throughout the
rest of his life.

Henceforward he was to show a growing distaste for poetry,
and indeed for any work of the imagination.   He had exhausted,
he said, his lyrical instinct.   'I realized,' he told Mme Colet in
1860, 'that the muse was no longer pursuing me, but that I had
to pursue her.'   Except for a few moving lines at the death of
Henriette in 1833, there are no poems of any interest by him
after this period.   Drama he had already more or less discarded
in spite of his earlier defence.   The Philodramatic Society of
Florence must have been surprised to receive Manzoni's acceptance of their honorary membership in February 1829, with the
rider: 'I must confess that since their publication [i.e. of *Carmagnola* and *Adelchi*] my ideas have gone much further along the
good or bad road on which I had entered; so that my actual
opinions in this particular tend altogether towards the anarchy,
not to say the destruction, of the art itself.'   In February 1827
he wrote to a versifier who had sent him his poems and asked to

meet him: 'I must warn you in all conscience that the man you propose to honour (with your acquaintance) is one from whom the only thing to be gained is the exercise of patience, a man hindered in brain and tongue, and with whom it would be providential to avoid talking literature, as the little he thinks and the less he can express are scarcely other than heresies.'

Apparently the novel-form was consciously abandoned as early as January 1828, when he wrote to a lawyer at Nice who had suggested translating his next novel: 'The material for your very amiable project is lacking, as I have no new novel either ready to appear or in preparation . . .' adding with his exaggerated and rather double-edged modesty: 'I am very flattered that my first and probably my only work in this *genre* should have been worthy of your observations. . . .' In September 1829 Sismondi wrote to a friend to say how sorry he was that Manzoni, instead of writing a new historical novel, was preparing a book against such works, the essay *Del Romanzo Storico*. The moral effect of *I Promessi Sposi* particularly interested Sismondi: 'There was genius in *I Promessi Sposi*; there is at the same time something in that kind of book which can, in spite of the censorship, make a most general and useful impression on the Italian public.' In July 1830 Sismondi wrote to Pietro Verri's daughter, a family friend of the Manzonis, asking her to pass on to Manzoni his admiration, and regret that 'he did not continue along the career he had so gloriously entered. . . .' For, he repeated, 'there is much more in *I Promessi Sposi* than a fine work of literature, much more than a new kind of writing for Italy, there is a good action [*il y a une bonne action*].' Thinking, perhaps, of his own experience as a historian, he urged Manzoni to go on: 'By serious books one diffuses serious thoughts only among those who already have them; but he [Manzoni] has introduced them into a new category of people who have never reflected, who have never mingled the best emotions of the heart with its amusements.' Ten years later Sismondi, still wondering why Manzoni never wrote another novel, gave a possible reason which was later to become current: 'He is perhaps wiser not to repeat. When one is a man of great talent it is a danger to have to be compared to oneself; people would not fail to say he was not up to *I Promessi Sposi*—for the public would have demanded of him to be both always the same and always different. It would want to feel again the emotions it had already felt, yet in a new way.'

In 1829 Manzoni wrote a pendant to his chapter on the plague in *I Promessi Sposi*, which was published under the title *Storia della Colonna Infame* (the 'Column of Infamy' put up on the spot where the anointers were executed), and attached to the 1840–2 edition of the novel. The rumour had gone round that this was a new novel, and it was eagerly awaited. The Austrian censors and police were alarmed at what they heard of the new book and particularly at the publisher's announcement that it was 'written in as democratic a sense as could be admitted.' This turned out, instead, to be an essay on the attitude of the judges towards the so-called 'anointers' during the plague. This subject had been treated by Pietro Verri in *Osservazioni sulla Tortura* as a straightforward argument against torture. Manzoni, in cold, legalistic prose which hid an underlying sense of horror, tried to show that the judges did not condemn the wretched accused because they believed either in the anointing or even in the efficacy of torture, but because they were carried away by the terror and passion of the moment—'How blind is fury!' Behind the measured prose, as Galletti has noted, is a perplexed, almost tormented state of mind, due to the contrast between Manzoni's Christian belief in the hidden but constant work of Providence, and his acute observation of the incoherence (which could be considered absurd if it did not involve such misery) of many historical events.

Manzoni's doubts about the whole practice of imaginative literature were expressed when in 1832 Marco Coen, a young Venetian with literary ambitions, whose father was trying to force him into the family business, wrote to him for advice. Manzoni replied in a long letter. 'As for the so-called literature of the imagination . . . I am every day partly forgetting, partly discrediting the little I seemed to know of it,' he began, and he ended by firmly advising the family business. He favoured, he said, the effect on the brain of a profession which forced one to see the real relations between things and ideas. It was dangerous just to work away in isolation in one's study. The practical life, he implied, is the best school for a writer, and not books which are apt to contain ideas with no more truth than 'the fables of the centaurs and hippogriffs, but which unfortunately, unlike the latter, are not at first glance discernible as fables.' If it was true that young Coen had had no peace since he had agreed to his father's insistence and sat on his office stool, then

Why? For love of letters? But what letters are those which do not let a man feel happy in carrying out his duties in an occupation which has a useful aim, and which gives continual exercise to reflection and sagacity . . .? I fear that these letters with which you are so taken are just the ones that live by and for themselves, and you don't realize that they can only be effective where it is not just a question of playing with the imagination. I fear, in fact I believe, that this violent aversion to commerce is caused mainly by the impression made on you by those maxims, those doctrines which exalt and consecrate certain exercises of the intelligence and of human activity, and denigrate others born of the common feeling of men and the essential conditions of society. But detach yourself from these doctrines and look outside; and ask yourself what would embarrass the world most, to find itself without accountants or without poets; and which of these professions is most useful, I don't say to the comfort, but to the culture of mankind.

Later he was to define poetry as 'the quintessence of common sense,' an attitude already foreshadowed in *I Promessi Sposi*, where he had commented on Renzo's drunken remarks about poets: 'Among the common people in Milan and even more in the country the word "poet" does not mean what it means among all respectable folk—a sacred genius, an inhabitant of Pindarus, a votary of the Muses: it means a peculiar person who's a bit crazy and behaves with more wit and oddity than sense. What an impertinent habit this is of the common people's of manhandling words and making them say things so very far from their legitimate meaning!'

Fundamentally his concept of the artist was religious—to live apart in an ivory tower of the imagination is immoral, as men are all members of society and each has a duty to perform. Like Cardinal Federigo Borromeo he was 'convinced that life was not destined to be a burden for the few, but a responsibility for which each one has to render an account.' And he came to condemn the artist's desire for fame with startling severity: 'As with all feelings which spring from the urge for enjoyment and not for perfection, contempt of obscurity is anything but

noble; as with all feelings which are based on confidence in
ourselves and in our own powers, and as with all feelings which
aim at man's own satisfaction and not at the performance of a
duty, he has nothing to console him when he fails.'

He came to theorize more and more against the form of art
to which he owed his fame.   His preoccupation with reality
and truth even led him to wonder in the end whether they could
not be reached better directly, without any help from the arts at
all.   These ideas he expressed in *Del Romanzo Storico*, published in
1845, but written many years earlier, an essay in which he under-
mined the whole basis even of *I Promessi Sposi* as an historical
novel of poetic invention.   Possibly at the back of his mind he
foresaw the rise of the realist novels based on contemporary
customs or psychological analysis.   If so, he never found in practice a way of reconciling his love of art with his love for truth.

Henceforward his chief preoccupations, against the background
of the retired life of a country gentleman, were with history,
religious philosophy, and the problems of the national language.
But the ideas, particularly on the last of these subjects, of this
withdrawn contemplative had considerable influence on the
Risorgimento.   The acute analytical mind remained.   The
heritage of the Enlightenment in which he had been brought up
still showed in his opposition, ardent Catholic though he remained, to the Temporal Power of the Church.   And it was
fundamental to his attitude to language as the vehicle of knowledge for all.

II

As early as the autumn of 1827, when he visited Florence,
there was an aura about him of a national figure.   Yet he knew
very little of his own country, either then or later.   For years
his life moved regularly between Milan, Brusuglio just outside,
and one or two villas of relations or friends on the lakes within
easy reach of the city. . Turin and Genoa he had visited on
journeys to France in his youth, and later he was to be a regular
guest in Piedmont of old friends, the Arconatis, exiles from
Austrian territory.   Tuscany and Siena he came to visit again
later in life, thanks to his children's marriages, but Sicily, Naples,
and most surprising of all, Rome, he was never to see at all.

Manzoni in 1848. From a drawing done 'in two rainy hours', by his stepson Stefano Stampa, and now in the Casa del Manzoni, Milan

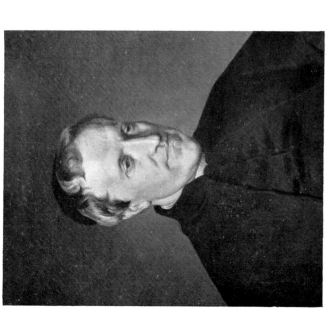

Abate Antonio Rosmini. From a portrait by Hayez

When a journey to Florence was first planned as early as December 1822, he had mentioned as an inducement for Fauriel to join them there an interest in the Tuscan language. The trip, when it finally took place, was largely undertaken in the hope of curing an eye trouble of Henriette's. Yet its effects, summed up in Manzoni's famous phrase about 'rinsing my linen in the Arno,' were to be historic for the renovation of the Italian language.

Henriette had been having continual trouble with her eyes since the autumn of 1822, and had been advised by the doctors to seek a 'more active air.' She had been taken to Como for a change in the summer of 1827, but this had apparently not been effective, for early in July she was so weak that she nearly fainted every morning. Sea-baths had been recommended as an infallible cure for the eye trouble, and on 15th July the whole family set off with her for Genoa. The party numbered fourteen, including Donna Giulia, six children, and five servants and nurses. After an excellent luncheon at Pavia with the bishop, old Monsignor Tosi, they set off boldly in a thunderstorm. Near Genoa the carriage overturned without, apparently, anyone being hurt. 'Heaven will always help such a virtuous family,' wrote the printer of *I Promessi Sposi* from Milan when he heard the news. At the Genoese frontier there was an agreeable episode when an old soldier put his head into the carriage window and recited whole paragraphs of *I Promessi Sposi*. 'Whoever would have said,' murmured Manzoni in Milanese dialect as his old valet undressed him that evening, 'when I was racking my brains over that book that it would make such a stir.' On 18th July they were settled at the Albergo delle Quattro Nazioni in the middle of Genoa.

Stimulated by the change of air and habits, the feeling of relief and achievement, Manzoni led quite a lively social life in Genoa while Henriette was occupied with her baths. The Intendant-General of the Sardinian Navy, Alexis de St Real, showed him round. *I Promessi Sposi* was being read everywhere, and he was a welcome guest at the literary *salons*, which from the names he mentioned in his letters seem to have been filled with civilized liberals who had either been active in the Carbonari or were to take part later in the struggles of the Risorgimento. He often went to the delightful home high above the

town, 'La Villetta' (now a public garden), of Marchese di
Negro, the widower possibly of his early love 'Luigina,' who
had died prematurely in 1810. Manzoni commented slightly
maliciously on this Maecenas, who had frustrated literary
ambitions: 'Di Negro is a man whom one should like, at whose
table one should eat, and whose verses one should not read.'
In the garden above the view were numerous grottoes scattered
with busts of the great, where Manzoni attended recitations and
improvisations. 'When one's in the dance, one dances as best
one can,' he wrote back to Milan with a deprecating shrug at this
unusual activity. His letters from Genoa breathe a spirit of
liberated enjoyment rare in that absorbed and self-contained
correspondence.

The family stayed on longer than they intended, particularly
as they heard alarming reports from Livorno. 'Some acquaintances whom we found here and some new ones we have made,'
he wrote to Grossi at the end of July, 'have begun to set us
against Livorno and the heat which they say is appalling, and
certain mosquitoes which change the whole shape of one's skin
and give one fever; and these things were said in such a polite,
cordial, and altogether sincere way, that between the fear of
these dangers and the attraction of this place, we looked at each
other and said let's take the baths in Genoa, and already my wife
has taken five, a third of her quota.' Little Pietro was becoming
an excellent swimmer, taking to the water wonderfully, he said,
diving from the boat and swimming underneath it.

Finally on 10th August they set off for Livorno, stopping at
Spezia and Pietrasanta on the way. Ambling slowly along the
Ligurian coast the almost continual views of 'sea and lovely hills,
oranges, laurels, olives, figs, and pretty villages are a real delight.'
'There were spots, however, which though I wouldn't call them
dangerous alarmed my mother who, as you know, is frightened
of being precipitated into places where anyone who wanted to
commit suicide would find difficulty in meeting their needs; but
she enjoyed the journey as for love of us she kept her fears silent,
and fear gets bored and leaves when it can't speak out.' The size
of their party sometimes made accommodation difficult. At
Livorno they had to put up with very uncomfortable quarters,
after changing hotels with the sleepy, hungry children; but the

local banker, M. Guithard, called next day and found them better
lodgings.   'We ended up in new beds: I mean new ones for us.'
Though roomier, the position on the main thoroughfare, and
a magic lantern performance in the courtyard below, made
Manzoni compare the new lodgings to 'the bastion of Porta
Orientale (the Hyde Park of Milan) in carnival time,' while
young Pietro Manzoni, with rather a heavy attempt to fit into
the family sense of humour (he never fitted into any family
activity very well), suggested that the continual clatter around
the hotel was caused by endless games of hopscotch from chairs
yards apart.

Perhaps it was the noise that cooled Manzoni's first elation at
travelling, for acquaintances now mentioned that he 'suffers
from nerves, makes no visits as he doesn't want to.'   In spite of
this, the family spent a fortnight at Livorno, from 12th to 26th
August; from there he wrote to Grossi about the effects of
travelling and of continuous packing and unpacking: 'I've
noticed that irritation and ill humour are extreme in the first
moment and gradually diminish when one is in a place for some
time, and finds that one is passably comfortable.   I believe, in
fact I am ready to bet, that if one examined travel books, one
would find that the worst-tempered passages were those describing a town where the writer only spent one day.'

On the 26th, stopping at Lucca and Pisa for meals, the party
reached Florence, and put up at the Locanda delle Quattro
Stagioni, now the Palazzo Gianfigliazzo, on the Lungarno.

III

Tuscany, as Manzoni had written to Fauriel when inciting
him to join them there in 1822, not only had the advantage of
good air, but 'that of being one of the few countries in Europe
where there are less passions in movement and suffering, less
irritation and pain: advantages particularly precious for myself
who feel an inexpressible desire not only to feel but to see
tranquillity.'

For the first twenty years after the Napoleonic Wars, Tuscany
was the most liberal state in the Italian peninsula.   Since the
days of Leopold I, when it had been one of the centres of

enlightened innovation, it had retained more autonomy than any other of the Hapsburg dependencies. In 1822 young George Bancroft, the future historian of America, sent home an endearing little picture of the modern Grand Duke, Leopold II: '. . . a good fellow to be sure, quite a radical, an honest man who wears a blue coat and a white hat and is drawn about by six horses.' The Tuscan character has always been more ironical, more suavely sceptical than any in Italy; surrounded by repressive regimes, the Government was now lazily paternal, and the Prime Minister and Minister of the Interior, Don Neri Corsini, an amiable cynic who believed in *laissez-faire*.

Although Stendhal found the atmosphere *assoupissant*, Florence had attracted the best of the persecuted writers, historians, and sociologists from all over Italy. In *L'Antologia*, a review started by Pietro Vieusseux in 1821, they found a successor to *Il Conciliatore* in keeping alive the spirit of unprejudiced thought and open-minded research. As Leopardi, who was then living in Florence, wrote: 'When I think that a paper like this is made and published in Italy in this period, I feel I'm dreaming.' The main supporters of *L'Antologia* were prosperous burgesses, or nobles such as the great historian of Florence, Gino Capponi, but it contained widely differing views and carried articles by some of the more original minds in the peninsula, such as Mazzini, Pepe, Coletta, Niccolini, Carlo Cattaneo, and Lambruschini. Vieusseux, a Swiss who had settled in Florence, was a fervent and active believer in the diffusion of culture. As well as *L'Antologia* he founded the Gabinetto Scientifico-letterario, which was to be a centre of Italian intellectual life for half the century, with its members ranging from the Countess of Albany, Stendhal, Lamartine, Montalembert, and Sismondi to Louis Napoleon and Ruskin. Florence, for those twenty years, until the Government panicked during the revolutionary movements of 1833, suppressed *L'Antologia* under Austrian pressure as a 'revolutionary paper,' and instituted measures as repressive as any other contemporary regime in Italy, was a literary and cultural centre of international importance. Its visitors were not then so entirely devoted to gossip and studying the monuments of the past as they are apt to be to-day.

Manzoni had been eagerly awaited since early in August, and

the first to greet him was Vieusseux. Due to customs difficulties, the first copies of *I Promessi Sposi* had arrived in Florence only a few weeks before the author, who found a pirated edition already announced there. (Since he refused to allow reprints of the first edition while he was preparing the corrected version, for years he had trouble with pirated editions.) But his fame had gone before him and he was received with sympathy and deference. 'You will see a man who by the very absence of singularity appears to everyone as singular and admirable,' Tommaseo had written to Vieusseux a year before. 'He is of average height and has a long, dark, pock-marked face, inspired by that goodness which genius, if it does not spoil it, makes more genuine and deep. His voice is modest, almost timid, and is helped by his very stutter, so that the words seem to come out more mature. His clothes are quiet. A gentle wisdom reflects on all around him.' In spite of his reserve, he was soon an undoubted success among some of the most observant and critical people in Italy. 'Manzoni is here adored by everyone,' wrote an acquaintance. 'We agree about Manzoni,' wrote Giordani, 'an excellent painter though rather Flemish. He is here now. A very amiable and modest person, revered and loved by all and much honoured by the court.' And again: 'His face obviously shows both kindness and high wit. In Milan I never sought him out, so as not to disturb the solitary life he liked leading in the midst of his family. . . .' 'To enjoy this interesting man,' reported Vieusseux to Capponi,

one must go to his home, for his life is entirely a family one, and he fulfils his duty as a son, husband, and father with religious care. His illness and timidity make it almost essential for him not to go out; he stutters much in talking, and his nerves sometimes make conversation impossible for him. This is a great pity, for in spite of his stutter it is of the liveliest interest; he only gets animated when talking of romanticism or religion, but there he is on his own ground and one likes to lead him there. Conversation with him is rarely cold or languishing. He is sweet, affable, and modest, but he also realizes his own worth; he prizes more highly the success of his novel than, I think, that of any of his other works.

In spite of these remarks about his shyness and stutter, he was soon appearing in public unusually often, particularly at

the evening gatherings of Gaetano Cioni and of Vieusseux
himself. Vieusseux even persuaded him to attend a meeting
of the Gabinetto Scientifico-letterario. At these gatherings he
could be paradoxical. An acquaintance commended his open
expression and gentleness of manner, but was horrified at the
attacks he made on some of the accepted Italian literary idols,
such as Tasso. One evening too he forgot his stutter, and held
the room in a religious discussion with Pietro Giordani, an
atheist who had just left a Benedictine monastery. Sometimes,
although the company pleased him, he would find the lionizing
was rather irksome. 'I have seen him very disturbed by the
endless praises showered upon him,' wrote Leopardi's friend
Mamiani. 'He would reply with a few confused words and
blush just like a girl.'

Often Leopardi himself was present at these apotheoses. His
Operette Morale had also just come out, but were then being read
only by a few friends. 'And I,' wrote Mamiani, 'seeking him
huddled up alone, while the flower of the literary men and
scholars flocked round Manzoni, asked him to tell me what he
thought. "It's excellent," he began. "I'm delighted that
the Florentines haven't forgotten their former hospitality and
wonderful warmth towards the arts."' But after this general
remark he went on to object to the *divinizzazione* and adulation of
Manzoni: 'Excesses are never praiseworthy. . . .' There was an
undercurrent of acidity in most of Leopardi's references to
Manzoni, though he was careful not to show it when writing to
his father, who he knew was an unqualified admirer. His first
reference to *I Promessi Sposi*, writing to a friend in early August
1827, had only repeated a judgment of others: 'So far I have only
heard a few pages read out loud. I'll tell you in confidence that
here it is found inferior to expectations by people of taste.
Others generally praise it.' He was sharper in another letter
written on the day of Manzoni's arrival. 'Have you seen his
novel, which makes so much noise and is worth so little?' But
to his father he wrote: 'I'm pleased you've read the Christian
romance of Manzoni. It is a really beautiful work and Manzoni
has a very fine mind and is a very nice person.' In reply he
received a copy of *Inni Sacri*, printed at Recanati, with a foreword
by his father himself.

The encounter between the two major figures of modern Italian literature does not seem to have meant much to either of them. Manzoni's religious convictions prevented him admiring the poetry of Leopardi, whom he pitied, he said, for letting himself be drawn along by the incredulity of his friend Giordani. But a year or two later he remarked about Leopardi's essays to the German philologist de Sinner: 'Not enough attention has been paid to this little volume. Nothing better in Italian prose has been written in our day.' For on language they held similar views, although Manzoni was surprised, he said to Tommaseo, that Leopardi, having lived so long in Florence, had not absorbed more of the Tuscan idiom into his writing.

In spite of these inadequate exchanges, they had something more in common than an attitude towards the language. Both, though their conversions were in opposite directions, shared a heritage in the Enlightenment. Both drew from it the lucidity of thought which, in the words of Professor Momigliano, 'kept Leopardi's despair this side of inconsistency and Manzoni's faith this side of vagueness and mystical transports.' Sometimes, too, the anguished Stoic and the tortured Christian, whatever their views of a hereafter, appear perhaps not to have been so far apart in their view of life on earth. Their sensitive and tormented temperaments seem to meet in Leopardi's remarks on despair: 'Hope is a most turbulent passion, for it necessarily carries with it a great fear of failure; and if we abandon ourselves with all our strength to hoping and consequently to fearing, we shall find that despair and sorrow are the more bearable.'

This glimpse of the Stendhalian *sombre Italie* was repeated in Lamartine's view of Manzoni as 'a suffering genius, an accent of pain enclosed in a sensitive man.' Lamartine had been at the French legation in Florence since 1825. It was a year since the Carbonaro exile Gabriele Pepe had challenged him to a clamorous duel for describing Italy as the 'land of the dead,' when in his *Pélérinage d'Harold* he had called for 'men and not human dust.' Lamartine had not much liked *Carmagnola* or *Adelchi*, but had been so excited by *Il Cinque Maggio* that it had moved him to write his own ode on Napoleon. His enthusiasm about *I Promessi Sposi*, which he read a month or so after meeting Manzoni in Florence, made him, he wrote, 'long to give up diplomacy and live in the country and write.' He then advised Manzoni to abandon history and try a modern theme. 'You can do it, your third volume is that already.' Manzoni, in an elaborate letter of thanks for the praise and advice, added that he wished the other had marked some passages he had thought superfluous.

The acquaintanceship endured. In 1848, when Lamartine was head of the Provisional Government of France, Manzoni wrote to support the Italian request for French help, adding: 'You have here, among the many people thinking of you, an old friend, a Christian who, incapable by nature of taking an active part in the affairs of this world, implores the assistance of God on those who are entrusted with them.' But he cooled when he observed Lamartine's handling of foreign affairs; and Mary Clarke, by now Mme Mohl, remarked sharply at the same time that Lamartine 'has been mad with vanity for years,' adding: 'But that is rather an advantage in public life.' Cantù, at the very end of Lamartine's life, met him, now poor and discredited, hobbling along on a nephew's arm in the Place Vendôme, and the old man said: 'If M. Manzoni remembers Florence and me, say I remember too, which is always homage when it goes to a man like him.'

Although Manzoni considered Lamartine's poetry too ethereal to express definite ideas, he may have pondered in later life the other's sombre remarks: 'The proof that liberty is the divine ideal of man is that it is the first dream of youth, and that it does not disappear from our minds until the heart softens and the spirit grows bitter and discouraged. There is no mind of twenty which is not republican, and no old heart which is not servile.'

IV

So amiable was the languid air of the Grand Duchy that Manzoni found himself being received with voluble informality by the Grand Duke Leopold himself, twice within a week. Leopold had a very high opinion of *I Promessi Sposi*. A year later he had seven dramatized scenes from it performed for his birthday, and later the great hall at Poggioreale was decorated with life-size frescoes from the novel, by Nicola Cianfanelli. 'I think it is certain,' he wrote to the author, 'that the book has done, is doing, and will do much good. For it sows the seeds of good

Donna Giulia in old age. From a drawing now lost, reproduced by Dott.
Marino Parenti in *Immagini Manzoniane*. Hoepli, 1941

and diminishes the seeds of evil, as it circulates in even the remotest parts.' Leopold also did his best to prevent the failure of *Adelchi* when it was staged at Florence a year later. 'Without the presence of the court,' wrote an observer, 'things would have gone worse than they did: for three Acts there was nothing but laughter and yawns; but the chorus and the fifth Act pleased the public.'

By the Grand Duke's request Manzoni was dressed for the interview 'without etiquette, in a frock-coat, a round hat, and trousers.' As an avowed republican Manzoni felt he had to excuse these visits when describing them to his old confidant Grossi in Milan. Grossi, he wrote, would think him mad with vanity, 'but I must tell you that it was not an impulse of vanity in me, but excess of goodness on his part.' By the end of the audience he had almost got over his nerves and enjoyed talking to 'a very cultivated, very amiable man of excellent intelligence and heart.' And he threw in artfully that the Grand Duke had talked most flatteringly of Grossi's poem *Ildegonde e le Crociate*. But Manzoni could not resist a typical aside: 'I know well that anyone who manages to talk to princes always exalts their qualities of intelligence and heart, particularly their goodness, as this implies that one has been well received.' With his son Pietro he also went out to Poggioreale where the Grand Duchesses Maria Anna and Maria Ferdinanda received them and talked literature. So high did he stand in the Grand-ducal favour that Leopold, on a visit to Milan the next year, asked to see Manzoni (signing himself 'Yours affectionately, Leopold'), and graciously advised him to get on with another novel: it was an echo, in its direct royal way, of what people were saying all over Italy. Manzoni, wrapping himself in the elaborate style his grandfather had caricatured in *Il Caffè*, and signing 'l'umilissimo obbedientissimo servitore,' replied firmly that he was planning no other novel at all.

'Princes are the greatest romantics on earth,' the Grand Duke's chamberlain once wrote to him feelingly, 'for they never take time or space into account. One has to be there as soon as they ring, anyone they ask for has to come like lightning, with no thought of the time needed to cover the space. And so we courtiers must be in good training too, and have strong legs.'

H

The relations with Leopold were the nearest Manzoni was ever to come to being a courtier.

But neither these favours, nor the fascinating talks on language and on corrections to *I Promessi Sposi* with Cioni and Niccolini, could keep the home-lover from his own hearth. 'Milan, a cosy corner, a sofa, a fire-place with or without a fire, old, dear friends, that's enough for me,' he wrote to Grossi on 17th September. His health was disturbing him, and Henriette's too seems to have worsened. 'Though well provided with material fortune,' wrote an observer of the visit, 'neither he nor his wife enjoys good health.' We catch a glimpse of Henriette in Florence from Capponi, 'most beautiful and rather silent, but by this and her bearing one felt that she was the real inspiration of Manzoni.'

Besides, old Donna Giulia was not happy. Her urge to travel, her yearning for Paris and the dear Maisonette, her antipathy to Milan with all its dreary memories of the past—all these were beginning to leave her as old age settled in. She had lost her appetite, she felt vaguely ill, she was longing for her own domains. Her unhappiness in Florence she put down to the climate. This seems a possible explanation, for the dusty and sirocco-haunted Florentine September is scarcely refreshing, and one wonders how Henriette's eyes could possibly have been expected to improve in that glare, years before the invention of sun-glasses.

Manzoni left with regret. 'I am the only one who can say I have profited by this visit, and am almost ashamed of it,' he wrote to Cattaneo on 18th September. 'The sea-bathing, the movement, the idleness of mind, being in Tuscany have really given me new life.' They set off on 1st October. 'Our journey had no inconvenience other than that we drew at every pace further away from Florence,' he wrote back sadly from the first halt. 'What could I say that would be equivalent to those delightful conversations of Via Campuccio and the Lungarno? Nothing, except that the wish, the regret, and the memory of them will last as long as my life.' But later he told Tommaseo that he might have returned to Florence earlier if he had found there less literary ceremony and more heart.

The posting arrangements for the journey were made by the Grand Duke's chamberlain, and they took the quickest route back to Milan, straight over the Apennines and down into the Emilian plain. The only echo we hear from this journey is of family laughter at finding the famed pass over the Apennines so small after the Alps. 'All these shadows of danger which were tormenting my mother so much vanished the moment they took shape: the devil of the Apennines was not so bad as he was painted, but almost by contrast appeared beautiful; and at that terrifying Passo della Futa, the earth, the air, everything was so flat and calm that we all burst out laughing together.'

If Manzoni returned from Florence with happy, light-hearted memories, he also brought back with him a preoccupation that was to oust almost every other interest except religion throughout his lifetime: the reform of the Italian language.

v

Benedetto Croce once asked if Manzoni's deepening interest in the problems of language was not 'a simple obsession, born in the tired mind of an ageing artist and produced by a spirit that was always subtle and somewhat sophistical, then followed by the many who are always ready to take part in a "question of the day."' This interest seems, rather, to have been linked to the deepest roots of his being, to both his religion and the radical and humanistic traditions of his youth. For he considered, in the words of Professor Momigliano, that 'Art, like truth, should be accessible to all; that, as everyone's soul is the same at bottom, so every clear beauty, every certain truth, is the domain of everyone, of Cardinal Federigo as of Perpetua.' Manzoni praised Condillac, even when he came to disagree with his philosophy, for first observing that words were indispensable to make men put the rational into action; for him the love of clarity, of rational belief, all led to the love of words. It took some time for the implications of this to be realized. The gap between language and literature in Italy originally worried the romantics because it narrowed the reading public to a small and inevitably privileged class of the community. But as the movement for national independence gathered force, the creation of a living Italian language became a matter of immediate political importance, an essential part of the unification of the peninsula.

Even at the age of seventeen, during his short period in Venice, Manzoni had been struck, as a working poet, by the divergence between contemporary written Italian, with its pompositics and circumlocutions, and the living ripple of Venetian dialect, based on common experience and renewed from everyday life. He had been delighted particularly by the dialect theatre of Goldoni and its warm contact with the audience; and both he and Stendhal had a lifelong admiration for the Venetian dialect poet Pietro Buratti. In those youthful days, however, he had considered linguistics as pedantry: 'One must care about things, not words.' When he came to realize the importance of finding universally accepted words to bridge the gap between culture and literature in Italy, he had even considered at one moment the possibilities of basing a national language on the Venetian dialect. This idea was not so fantastic then as it seems now, for if no living and universally accepted Italian language existed, why not begin from scratch and base it on the supplest dialect to be found? From these beginnings he was to become more and more absorbed in the vaster problems of language and the mysterious links which unite feelings and ideas to words.

At the beginning of the nineteenth century the use of Italian as a current, spoken language was almost regional to Tuscany; when used for verbal communication between inhabitants of the various parts of the peninsula it was apt to sound as cumbrous and stilted as ecclesiastical Latin. Most of the population of Italy spoke only one of the twenty or thirty dialects: most of these were very different from one another, and were based on varying and immemorial roots. In Manzoni's home, as in other well-to-do households in Lombardy, Milanese dialect was always spoken. Foreign languages were spoken officially and at court; French at the Bourbon courts of Naples and Parma (though Ferdinand's frequent use of Neapolitan dialect was largely responsible for his popularity with the *lazzaroni*); Spanish in Milan until late in the eighteenth century; and then, after the Napoleonic interlude, German.

The problem of finding a language of general communication, which had preoccupied Manzoni even when writing *Adelchi* and *Carmagnola*, confronted him with all its difficulties when he began *I Promessi Sposi*. 'Imagine,' he wrote to Fauriel, 'a language never written as it is spoken and used by very few inhabitants of Italy; a language never used to discuss great questions verbally . . . a language corrupted and disfigured. There is a complete lack of feeling of communion with the reader, of the certainty of handling an instrument which is known equally to us both. . . .' And in another letter to Fauriel: 'I agree with you that to write a novel well in Italian is one of the most difficult things.' Years before, during his first visit to Paris, he and Fauriel had discussed the question of language in general when he had noticed how French poets and dramatists of both present and past had absorbed and used the everyday speech spoken in the streets of Paris. He returned to this as he began *I Promessi Sposi*:

When a Frenchman tries to render his ideas, you see what abundance and variety of means he finds in this language which he has always spoken, in this language which has grown up so long and continuously in so many books, in so many conversations, in so many discussions of every sort. With him there is a rule for the choice of expressions, and this rule he will find in his memories, in his daily habits, which give him an almost sure sense of the conformity of his style to the general spirit of the language: he hasn't to consult a dictionary to know if a word grates or if it will pass: he asks himself if it is French or not, and he is more or less sure of the reply.

He also found in English a 'familiarity,' 'in which writing is a kind of more meditated speech.' What could be done about Italian? In 1827 he wrote to another enthusiastic philologist, Padre Cesare: 'As Voltaire said of French that it was a poor proud woman on whom charity had to be forced, so it seems to me that our language might be called a careless and absent-minded lady whose property should be forcibly restored to her; it's a property which she has not consciously abandoned but lost through maladministration, and an attention which she refuses, not because she doesn't need help, but because she doesn't want to show that she does.' [1]

When he started *I Promessi Sposi* the problem became urgent. The divergence between his characters and the language he

[1] Dr Barbara Reynolds has pointed out that this somewhat autocratic concept of imposing a language was later modified by Manzoni, who in the end came to consider the task of the student of linguistics as being simply to record and in no way to direct usage.

found himself putting into their mouths preoccupied him more and more.   The 'stile togato' (toga-ed style) of the *Dizionario della Crusca* seemed totally unsuitable for either simple peasants or men of the world who were used to expressing themselves pithily and directly.   Milanese dialect was the only one he knew thoroughly, and on his return from Paris in 1820 he had become increasingly fascinated by the poems in Milanese dialect by Carlo Porta, although deploring their obscenities.   But dialect, both Milanese and Venetian, had to be abandoned, as its *colore municipale* would narrow his audience too much.   From this idea of Milanese dialect he went on to toying with a compromise between Milanese and Tuscan.   Tuscan was fascinating him more and more; he was beginning to consider it to be the 'richest speech capable of expressing the highest thoughts most adequately.'   This increasing interest in Tuscan was due to the quality of the language and not to any pre-eminence it had acquired since Dante.[1]   As late as 1836 Giovita Scalvini wrote to Tommaseo that he knew of no Italian spoken language: to which Tommaseo, who had compiled a Tuscan *Dictionary of Synonyms* and was then well under Manzoni's influence, replied that he had not spent enough time in Florence.   But when Manzoni visited Florence in 1827 he had not yet made up his mind about how far to use Tuscan in the recorrection of his novel.

Hearing Tuscan for the first time on the spot filled Manzoni with delight.   When on the third day out from Genoa they lodged at Pietrasanta, he wrote from Livorno: 'There began the pleasure of hearing with my own ears that language which seemed as delicious to me then as it does here in Livorno, and as it will be in Florence.'

Once there he began going over his manuscript with Cioni and Niccolini.   In this intensive rewriting, which was to continue with varying tempo for the rest of his life, he began to include Tuscanisms which he hoped would thereby become accepted as current Italian usage throughout the peninsula. Examples of differences between Milanese and Tuscan usage

---

[1] Dante himself, although 'the father of the Italian language,' had made a plea in *De Vulgari Eloquentia* for a poetic style based on all the Italian dialects.   The main upholders of Tuscan as the standard language for Italy had been Tasso and Machiavelli.

poured in to him from all sides. In the years 1828–9 he concentrated so much on linguistics that his health suffered. But the book which he appears to have started during the first rewriting of *I Promessi Sposi*, and which was, apparently, more or less finished by 1830, never saw the light. He is thought to have burnt most of it as his ideas kept on changing.

'You privileged Tuscans,' he wrote back on his return from Florence, 'cannot have the first idea of one whose job is scribbling and who is ignorant of most of the language in which he has to scribble . . . or knows it without realizing it, as words are said to be slang which are part of the living language.' He found that dictionaries, not being based on the living language, very often lacked words; sometimes he even used a French-Italian dictionary to trace an Italian word or phrase through the French. There was, he considered, little hope of a rapid change in this situation. 'As for seeing this [the Tuscan language] known, diffused, and used more or less generally by Italians, who have no other; as for seeing it treated like other living languages such as French, for example, that is a thing I do not aspire to see in my day: perhaps my grandchildren may.'

In 1828 the Grand Duke Leopold wrote to Manzoni, holding out as an inducement to him to return to Florence that: 'Here in dealings with many people, even the commonest, I've often noticed the simple but energetic words in which they express both the tenderest and the most violent passions'; and he went on to tell Manzoni how a mountaineer had described a first visit to Florence in terms very like those of Renzo's arrival in Milan. Step by step Manzoni's enthusiasm for Tuscan was mounting. In his letter to the Società Filodramatica of Florence in 1828 he hailed Florence as 'the cradle of Italian culture, which still possesses the essential means of promoting it.' In 1831 Henriette, loyally following her husband's interests, wrote to Costanza Arconati:

The changes in language which he proposes to make God knows when to *I Promessi Sposi* limit themselves to inserting words and expression which come from the living Tuscan language, and are now only to be found in a few books and dictionaries; for he is convinced that apart from that, one can definitely not find anywhere in Italy what constitutes all languages, namely usage. He even has a plan for a work on this subject, in which he hopes to include all these wretched questions, to compare them, resolve them, or dismiss them so as to satisfy and convince every party and stir the indifferent.

On the basis of Tuscan he was now inclined to accept any usage, even foreign: 'It doesn't matter where or when words enter into use in a language; the important thing is their being there'—a remark which showed the basic realism of his approach. 'A living language, which is by its nature a mixture of the actual and the potential,' he wrote later, 'is, in consequence, the sum, never however determinable, of what is universally accepted and what can be most easily accepted.'

The problem of using Tuscan called up vast numbers of doubts and difficulties. Some linguistic experts were inclined to hark back too much to what Manzoni himself hailed as 'that golden fifteenth century, that century in which everything was pure, classical, beautiful, and simple, when good language was breathed, as it were, through the air, and attached itself to all writing so that, incredible but true, even the kitchen recipes and public edicts were written in good style.' But it was hopeless to try, like the Abate Cesare, to base modern Italian on this. Manzoni was somewhat disturbed, however, as he told Tommaseo, that Florentines with such a wonderful spoken language wrote little in it: to which Tommaseo made the unhelpful comment: 'Perhaps as a gentleman should not say what he thinks, so he should not write what he says.' Then even in Florence he had had to struggle with the academic mind. When reading *I Promessi Sposi* out loud to Cioni he had stopped from time to time to ask if such and such a word was used in Florence. 'Yes, Lippi [1] has it,' Cioni would reply. To which Manzoni's rather sharp rejoinder was: 'I'm not asking if Lippi has written it, but if it is said in Florence now.'

By the middle of the 1830s the Manzoni house in Milan was becoming a sort of 'linguistic laboratory,' where the notes on Tuscan usage, streaming in from friends in Florence, were sifted by Manzoni and his collaborators. Chief among these was Signorina Emilia Luti, an old Florentine governess who had been lent to Manzoni by his son-in-law Massimo d'Azeglio. She

[1] Lorenzo Lippi, a seventeenth-century Florentine painter and poet, who wrote burlesque poems using extensively the Florentine idiom of the day.

read *I Promessi Sposi* out loud to Manzoni, substituting Tuscan words as she read, and her innumerable corrections had a decisive influence on the wording of the rewritten edition of *I Promessi Sposi* which began publication in 1840. The technical difficulties appeared endless. As he had written to the Contessa Saluzzo, who had been visiting Tuscany in 1831: 'Without realizing it I am plunging into an argument out of which I shall never find a way.' The 'linguistic laboratory' was even sifting claims about pronunciation from sections within Tuscany, such as Siena. 'This predominance given to Siena over Tuscany and even over the rest of Italy,' Manzoni wrote to his son-in-law Giorgini in 1851, when he had finally decided on complete Tuscan supremacy,

is one of the many things which show me how far we are from any common sense about language. Can there be any stranger conception than this, that a language is to be found in one place and its pronunciation in another? If only they were at least thought to be in the same place! But no, a bit here, a bit there, a bit in the present, a bit in the past, a bit in the possible. Fantastic things, but things that happen in Italy [Cose dell' altro mondo e dell' Italia].

His various essays on the problem of language were rewritten over and over again, so that the phases of his changing ideas are sometimes difficult to trace. The final result of the labour of nearly fifty years was the long and theoretical *Della Lingua Italiana*. This was unfinished, and published in part after his death, one section under a suggestive title *Sentir Messa* (i.e. *sentir messa* or *udir messa*, which points out the confusion in the verb *sentire*—'to feel' or 'to hear'). He concentrated his main arguments in a report *Dell' unità della lingua e dei mezzi di diffonderla*, to the Minister of Public Instruction of the new Italian Kingdom in 1868, when he was asked to preside over a commission to decide on standardization. But in appendices and other essays he continued to amplify his ideas almost till his death. On his theories, too, was based almost entirely the introduction to the new State-sponsored Italian dictionary, written by his son-in-law Giorgini. 'Manzoni's ideas,' wrote Giorgini, 'circulated among scholars and lexicographers,' but he added a candid aside which is said to have displeased its subject: 'After having given us his doctrine and its most illustrious

* H

monument . . . he drew to one side and enclosed himself in a silence which is perhaps a mystery even to himself. . . .'

'Twenty years ago,' wrote Manzoni in an appendix to his 1868 report on the language, 'amid the various opinions about the political organization which would be most suitable for Italy, there was one which many called a "Utopia," and sometimes even a "fine Utopia." Let us hope that the writing of the Italian language may be a "Utopia" like the unity of the Italian nation.' As time went on his interest in language became almost an obsession. Its aims and origins seemed forgotten and it developed a life of its own, became almost a separate entity. Having begun by considering language as a vehicle for thought, he ended by concentrating entirely on detached words and phrases as a near-abstract study. Language became to him an overriding factor even in judging the general situation of other countries. Portugal, he said, would never unite with Spain because it had Camoens, and Greece, he thought, would never be a nation as it had no modern literature. His judgment became distorted. When in 1862 the rival claims of Turin, Rome, and Florence as capitals of the new Italy were being hotly discussed from behind the cloistered walls of Manzoni's study came a pronouncement in favour of Florence. 'The capital of the nation should be the capital of the language.' Later he said that if Rome became the capital of Italy and a great city, there was no reason why its dialect should not, in time, become the language of the whole country. In October 1869, three years before he died, his interest in language was still so intense that he could write to Stefano Stampa: 'I have spent a number of evenings very enjoyably, listening to most of the letter A of the dictionary being read out loud.'

Such concentration is seldom without its reward. His stamp on the language has endured. As a result of his interest the whole question became livelier and more actual than it had been for centuries. Although, as Croce has observed, it was impossible from the very nature of the problem for him to reach a solution, he gave it a practical turn which was badly needed. To him can be largely traced the anti-rhetorical language and style which has persisted among a few in Italy ever since, although again and again it has seemed to be swept away by the floods of romantic rhetoric, typical early examples of which were the novels of Guerrazzi. After the Risorgimento there was a reaction to simple ordinary words, to a more precise and technical vocabulary for domestic life; this coincided with the new realist trend in literature, the 'lirica di tono basso' (low-toned lyric) as Croce called it, whose chief exponent at the end of the century was Verga. The reaction into neo-baroque in the prose of d'Annunzio, which started at the same time and from 1900 onwards influenced the style of newspapers, letters, and even telegrams throughout the whole of Italy, culminated in Fascist bombast. The contrast between the inflated language of 'the seven million bayonets' and that of simple direct common sense could be clearly seen during the Italian civil war of 1943–5, when the style of the communiqués on each side seemed to show a different attitude towards reality.

VI

The preoccupation with language forged one of the first links with a new friend, who was to become increasingly significant in his life, Antonio Rosmini. When, early in their acquaintance-ship, Rosmini reported in a letter that Manzoni had returned from Florence 'very pleased with the information about the language that he has gathered there,' he was himself working out a place for linguistics in the philosophical system he was just forming. This was a Christian system based on the concept of the Idea of Being,[1] which stemmed from Plato through Aquinas, Leibnitz, and Kant. It was some time before Manzoni was to come to see the Rosminian concept of the origins of ideas as indissolubly linked with the origins of language. For years Rosmini tried to persuade Manzoni that in his obsession about

---

[1] Rosmini considered that the Idea of Being (or Existence) enters into all our acquired knowledge, that it is essentially objective and distinct from the mind that sees it, and that 'being' and 'truth' are convertible terms in the vision of which the mind cannot err, as error presupposes a judgment, and there is no judgment here, but a pure intuition affirming nothing and denying nothing. He proceeded by a series of propositions to show that 'being,' naturally shining in the mind, is what we call the 'light of reason.' He developed this to include all knowable ideas of morality and reality, the two forms under which 'being' manifests itself. He particularly insisted, and here he found common ground from the beginning with Manzoni, on distinguishing morality from utility, as the first is the cause and the latter the effect.

language he was putting the cart before the horse. 'Manzoni
has written me a fine letter,' he wrote to his confidant Tommaseo
in 1831, 'in which he admits much, in fact all, of the things I
say about the Idea of Being; but then he wants this idea to enter
into us by a virtue *sui generis* of language, almost as if language
could create an idea entirely, instead of simply indicating it for
the attention to contemplate.' Eventually, in *Dialogo dell'*
Invenzione, Manzoni came to defend Rosmini's theories on the
origins of ideas, which, he set out to prove, only God can
create. This led him, in *Esame della dottrina del Locke e del*
Condillac sull' origine del linguaggio, to show that only God could
create language. For in the end he came to accept the whole
vast Rosminian system.

The relations between Manzoni and the leading Catholic
liberal thinker in Italy were from the first those of pupil and
master. These were soon infused with an affection and warmth
which made Rosmini take the place, if a friend of youth can ever
be replaced, of Claude Fauriel. As mutual interests between
Manzoni and Fauriel faded and meetings became only a memory,
communication between them got rarer and rarer, until about
1830 it seems to have faded away altogether, so that Manzoni
only heard through the newspapers of Fauriel's appointment to
the new Chair of Foreign Languages at the Sorbonne in 1832.
Yet occasionally a spasm of yearning would return for those happy
hours of flowing, interlocking ideas. Once, years later, according to his daughter, Manzoni suddenly jumped up from his chair
in the middle of a discussion and exclaimed: 'Oh, if only Fauriel
were here—what a talk we'd have!'

When Manzoni met Rosmini he had been feeling for some time
a need to integrate the philosophical basis of his faith with his
other beliefs. This need was emphasized a year or two later by
the conflicting interpretations of his novel and the accusations
of being a doubtful Catholic. 'The evidences of the Catholic
religion,' he wrote in January 1828 to the Contessa Saluzzo of
Turin, now a close pen-friend,

fill and dominate my intellect. I see it at the beginning and end of all
moral questions: wherever it is invoked, wherever it is excluded. The
truths which can be found without its escort do not seem to me complete, well based, conclusive, except when they lead back to it and

appear as what they are, the consequences of its doctrine. This conviction must transpire naturally from all my writings, if for no other reason than that when one writes one wants to be strong, and such a strength can only be found in one's own convictions. But the sincere expression of this may induce an idea (which is, alas, in my case false) of a faith always lovingly conserved, and whose prize is continuous recognition: I, on the other hand, have often repudiated this faith and contradicted it with my thoughts, with my speech, with my conduct; even since an access of mercy restored this to me, it still fails to stimulate my feelings enough and govern my life.

In the autumn of 1828 the Abate Cesare, emboldened by being an acknowledged expert on linguistics, asked him frankly if he adhered to Jansenist opinions, as was rumoured among so many. His reply was carefully phrased: 'With the Church . . . I am and wish to be one in this as in every other point of faith; with the Church I want to feel, explicitly where I know its opinions, implicitly where I don't know them; I am and wish to be with the Church, as far as I know, as far as I can see and further,' and in the same letter he stated: 'The protestation of my unlimited adherence to the teaching of the Catholic Apostolic Roman Church, says everything.'

Antonio Rosmini first met Manzoni in 1826, when as a young priest he came to Milan to study at the Ambrosiana for his first philosophical work, *Nuovo saggio sull'origine delle idee*. Early in their acquaintanceship Manzoni read part of his manuscript of *I Promessi Sposi* out loud, with Rosmini walking up and down the room, smiling with admiration and murmuring: 'What knowledge of the human heart! What truth! What goodness, which spills over everywhere from a heart full of it!' Rosmini had been one of the few who even considered that the book would open 'a new epoch in Italian literature.' He had also advised changes between the first version and the second, and particularly helped to tone down the note of heavy pessimism reminiscent of the gloom of *Adelchi*. On first meeting him Manzoni gave a small luncheon-party at the Via Morone, the guests at which were almost symbolic of their host's spiritual travels. Apart from Rosmini there was old Bishop Tosi and the gay agnostic philosopher and friend of Fauriel, Ermes Visconti. Visconti, though himself later to plunge into a piety which even Manzoni was to find excessive, still held at that time many ideas in common with Manzoni, which both drew from their rationalist influences. In 1826, wrote Tommaseo, Manzoni was 'Catholic in faith, but in philosophy he followed the French doctrines of the last century, only refuting the consequences which Destutt de Tracy deduced from them, and opposing at the same time the dubious and elegant metaphysics of Cousin, his valued guest and friend.' He still agreed, for instance, with Visconti's philosophical works on aesthetics, which were based on the system of the Sensists and its development by Tracy.

For a long time, in spite of a growing personal veneration for Rosmini, Manzoni was to struggle in letter after lengthy letter against the full acceptance of the new ideas, possibly influenced by the contempt which so many of his friends had for Rosmini as a philosopher. 'Oh, if the Idea of Being could only enter Don Alessandro's head,' Rosmini would exclaim. For years, until he succumbed completely to these theories, Manzoni's admiration went to other qualities in Rosmini, particularly his blend, so unattainable to Manzoni, of thinker and organizer. A similar admiration, in quite other terms, he had once given to Foscolo.

The priest who finally, after a struggle lasting nearly ten years, succeeded in drawing the residue of Manzoni's rationalist heritage into the coherent and intransigent system of Catholicism, was himself scarcely representative of many of the official attitudes of the Church. The sole heir of an important and wealthy family with an old tradition of Austrian Imperial service, he had taken orders as a youth against opposition from his parents. When he first met Manzoni he was just back from his first visit to Rome, where at the age of twenty-six he had conferred with the powerful Abate Cappellari, afterwards Pope Gregory XVI, about a scheme for founding a new congregation of the Fathers of Charity; he had even, it appears, obtained the consent of the reigning Pope Pius VII to an attempt at reforming religious philosophy. To study for this he came to Milan in his own carriage, to his own apartments, and supported by two familiars. One, Niccolò Tommaseo, was to become a confidant of Manzoni in politics, religion, and linguistics; and finally, rather surprisingly, the chief lieutenant of Daniele Manin during the glorious defence of Venice against the Austrians in 1848.

Rosmini spent the next three years in the study of philosophy, mainly of St Thomas Aquinas, and working out the principles (which he called of 'passivity' and 'indifference') on which he based the rules of the Institute of Charity, founded in 1828 with the encouragement of the Marchesa di Canossa. The Institute was approved by the Letters Apostolic 'In Sublime' of 1839. His ideas on religious organization had some parallels with those of the founder of the French Constitutional Church, Grégoire. Although Rosmini's Fathers of Charity flourished, both he and Grégoire failed in their broader aims, when they came up against the internal interests allied to the apparatus of the Church. To this, in Rosmini's case, was added strong Austrian opposition. As early as 1823, when he had read at Rovereto his 'Panegyric of Pius VII,' he had made clear his opinions about the independence from foreign interests of both Italy and the Church. In *Delle cinque piaghe della santa chiesa* he attacked the formalistic and dictatorial trends in the Church since the Council of Trent: 'Seminaries were invented that the clergy might be maintained in ignorance, as the catechisms were invented to ensure the ignorance of the masses.' He also advocated more personal responsibility for the bishops. In his *De costitutione civile* he pleaded for the Church to return to its democratic origins and for Latin to be abolished in religious services; he even made the bold suggestion that bishops should be elected by their own priests and flocks. *Delle cinque piaghe* is fundamentally a plea for a poorer, less materialist Church that would appeal to the people's hearts.

In 1829 Rosmini made another journey to Rome in search of support for his ideas. But, although he obtained the *Nihil Obstat* of the Holy Office for his philosophical work the *Nuovo saggio*, he found the atmosphere of Rome particularly thick with intrigue and overshadowed by terror of the Austrians, and returned saddened to Rovereto.[1] From there he published in

---

[1] The atmosphere of Rome and the intrigues both with the Carbonari and the Consistorio at this period were described with obvious inside knowledge in a remarkable novel, *Rome souterraine*, by Charles Didier, published in 1833. Chateaubriand, who had arrived as French ambassador the year before Rosmini's visit, gave scathing accounts in his official reports of the confusion and intrigue in the Eternal City. On

1839 his *Trattato della coscienza morale*, which led to a controversy with the Jesuits that was to go on for fifteen years, except for a three-year truce when Gregory XVI enjoined perpetual silence on all the disputants: it was to flare up later and continue years after his death. His next visit to Rome was even more disillusioning. In 1848 the Piedmontese Prime Minister Gioberti, filled by the election of Pope Pius IX with hopes for the realization of his theories about papal independence, expressed in his famous book *Il Primato*, sent Rosmini down on a mission to the new pope. Pius, swaying between opposing forces, yet attracted by the idea of the papacy as a regenerating force that might unify Italy, made Rosmini one of his chief ministers for a few hours. But by the same afternoon he was soothing the Austrian ambassador and declaring that the new minister did not enjoy his confidence. Rosmini loyally submitted and even followed his master on his flight to Gaeta.

Manzoni had not himself supported Gioberti's scheme for a pacific league of Italian states headed by the pope; but he was amazed to hear that Rosmini had been forced to leave Gaeta by the Bourbon police, and to find two of his books, *Delle cinque piaghe della santa chiesa* and *De costitutione civile*, condemned by the Congregation of the Index sitting at Naples, while all his other works were put under examination as suspected of pantheism and other heresies. The subsequent vicissitudes of these books reflected the internal struggles of the Church. By a papal *Dimittantur* of 1854 they were declared free of censorship 'as having nothing in them against faith or morals.' But in 1876 Catholic papers in the north of Italy began to insist that the *Dimittantur* decree could be interpreted as leaving the works still open to criticism, and *L'Osservatore Cattolico* of Milan was silenced by the Prefect of the Congregation of the Index. The attacks started again after the death of Pius IX and the accession of Leo XIII. Forty propositions from Rosmini's books, ranging from his opinions on ontology to those on the eucharist, were condemned, while the Rosminian centre at Rovereto was put

---

reading the diary of the Jesuit General Pavani he wrote: 'I had thought Pascal a calumniator who had bequeathed an eternal lie, but he did not exaggerate,' and he noted how the scattered movements for the unity of Italy 'were mistaken for the machinations of a handful of Jacobins.'

under papal sequestration. For a time he was generally considered to have been almost a heretic. The controversy about
the propositions was still continuing between Cardinal Mazella
and an erudite layman, Professor Morando, as late as 1905, when
some of Rosmini's ideas were being developed by Modernists
such as Fogazzaro and Father Tyrell. Rosmini missed a cardinal's
hat during his lifetime for his opinions on the Temporal Power,
and after his death a movement to canonize him has been held
up indefinitely by theological difficulties.

After 1849 he withdrew from active participation in public
affairs and spent the rest of his life in the north of Italy, increasingly immersed in the development of his philosophical
system and in the organization of his new congregation of the
Fathers of Charity. The Rosminian Fathers, devoted to preaching, education, and charity, have now branched all over the
world, and are particularly numerous in England.

Rosmini, like Manzoni himself, is a difficult figure to place in
the apparatus of the Church. Although they bowed to its
discipline, both had a trust in the free play of reason, a trust
which was also partly responsible later for the troubles of
Fogazzaro. 'Liberty,' declared Rosmini, 'is the very air that
keeps the Church alive.' It was perhaps this tendency which
caused the attack that appeared in a Jesuit paper after Manzoni's
death.

A terrible responsibility which we put on Manzoni and which we
could put on Rosmini, and which weighs on most of their followers, is
this corruption seething in our society, which has invaded schools and
barracks, triumphs in the theatre, permeates journalism and novels.
If one should lay the blame on the masters for the work of inept pupils,
it would not be possible to absolve Manzoni and Rosmini from having
laid the foundations of the inclined plane down which so many intellects
have slithered to ruin.

It was on Rosmini's return from his unfortunate last mission to
Rome, when he had settled at Stresa on Lake Maggiore and
Manzoni was at Lesa avoiding the Austrians, that the two really
became intimate. They were only an afternoon's stroll apart,
and saw each other constantly until Rosmini's premature death
in 1855. Manzoni was now attracted more and more by the
all-embracing character of the other's thought, and immersed

himself in philosophical studies in order to understand it.   He
came to consider Rosmini, he told Tommaseo, to be 'one of the
six or seven philosophers who have most honoured humanity
. . . such a man is only created once in centuries.'

Manzoni, acute and subtle as his mind was, never aspired to
be an original philosopher.   He had been a Sensist, then an
Idéologue, and passed on to his own form of eclecticism.   Now
in the coherent and all-embracing system of Rosminian idealism
he felt he had found, at last, the vindication and logical demon-
stration of truth, 'the natural heritage of man.'   This system
appeared, as he wrote in *Dialogo dell' Invenzione*, to fulfil his
hopes of dissolving all contradictions between dogma and
mysteries on the one hand and exigencies of reason on the other
—the dream of any agnostic who turns to religion.   'Should a
philosophy in order to remain free,' he asked,

have to admit *a priori* that there is a contrast between reason and
Revelation?   That would indeed be anti-rational, anti-philosophic, to
say the least.   Why should it be surprising that as reason and faith
come from the same principle, one should receive light and vigour
from the other to proceed independently?   Just as scientific errors can
be obstacles to faith in the mind of man, so revealed truths can be
helped by science, for by showing their relation with the supernatural
order they naturally make this better known; so too science can proceed from a vaster background to its own researches and discoveries.

Following Rosmini, he then set out to show that the artist,
too, does not invent but discover, and he discovers by fixing
himself on the truth, with a mind free of illusion.   Art, in
Rosmini's philosophy, was the means of demonstrating the ways
by which the divine order shows itself in reality.   This theory,
it may be noted, Manzoni never followed in practice.   Did he
have certain doubts about the nature of man which Rosmini
hadn't?   A pervading sense that even if Redemption had
given the spirit power of winning over matter, the struggle
between them was still raging?   Not for Manzoni was Rosmini's serene optimism, which, as Galletti remarked, would have
made Browning his favourite poet.   For Manzoni the struggle
between good and evil was too fierce and actual.   For him the
duty of the poet—although he himself no longer produced
imaginative work—was to develop in others the moral strength

to dominate and to judge the passions.   And he ended this essay by considering that the task of the historian was moral analysis, an aim more valid than any artistic pleasure.

Some of Rosmini's remarks in the letters that flowed from Stresa to his flock all over the world have a wry humanity which suggests a reciprocal influence between Manzoni and himself.   'If we know ourselves we shall have an unbounded kindness and indulgence for others.'   Another almost echoes Cardinal Federigo, with whose character Rosmini's has some remarkable parallels: 'Of praise, usually, I take little account, for I know too well that it is not always sincere.   But advice and admonition and even reproofs from friends, these are never deceptive: they are gifts from the heart.'

Here and there in Rosmini's writings there are, however, passages touched with that mysticism which Manzoni always managed to avoid; this trend is particularly noticeable in parts of the opening chapters of Rosmini's *Book of Love*:

We should reflect that though the souls in Purgatory suffer, yet they do so willingly.   Even were it in their power, they would not return again to this world.   They are truly happy in hope, honoured by the angels and raised to the dignity of spouses of God.   Their glorious destination is secure for ever.   There only remains a brief delay of that happy moment when they will see their Divine Spouse and, all beautiful and resplendent with glory, will be led by Him into His Nuptial Chamber.

We have no indication of what Manzoni thought of such passages.   Expressions of this kind were quite alien to him, whose attitude both to mystical raptures and to miracles was decidedly withdrawn.   There must have been doubts too in Manzoni's mind about some of Rosmini's ideas on general politics, although they were agreed in deploring the Temporal Power.   Manzoni, wrote Tommaseo, was apt to feel certain 'bold and fruitful desires for novelty.'   'He could not praise in his much-admired Rosmini the concept of property, I mean the ownership of material possessions, as a condition for the exercise of public rights, which he considered meant the representation by matter of a man's spirit.'   According to Rosmini property rights were founded on nature and reason, and he added, with a swerve in the argument, that parliamentary votes should be reserved for men of property, 'as poor deputies representing poor people would be bound to swamp the others by their numbers and sow confusion.' Commenting on St Paul's Epistle to Timothy, he wrote that the insatiable greed for property was 'an error of the heart' not 'an error of understanding.' 'The root of all evil is cupidity.' And Rosmini's conclusions were as comforting to property-holders as the 'Third Way' of Moral Rearmament: 'The property of man is not to be reformed, but the man of property is. . . . Faith and charity amongst all: justice and piety amongst the rich; patience and meekness among the poor.' These sound like caricatures of the trends in *I Promessi Sposi* for which Manzoni was attacked by the radicals of the day.

In spite of these differences, the agreement between Manzoni and Rosmini on religious and eventually on philosophical fundamentals, joined to a warm personal sympathy, made the friendship stimulating and inspiring for them both. On the path above Stresa where they used to meet, there is now a plaque with a quotation from Fogazzaro, 'Duplice vertica sublime di unica fiamma' (Sublime double point of a single flame). Manzoni would say he was raised by their conversations 'to heights which one feels one cannot attain alone.' And when Rosmini sat down to write of 'the divine in nature,' he would imagine himself to be talking to Manzoni and 'seeking for inspiration in his stimulating presence.' The unexpected sound of Rosmini's carriage in the courtyard at Lesa would bring 'il veneratissimo e carissimo Don Alessandro' almost clattering down the stairs, almost as the arrival of letters from Fauriel had done at Brusuglio thirty years before.

At Rosmini's premature death-bed they had a last conversation which showed how impregnated with religious feeling their friendship had been. 'No, no one is necessary to God,' Rosmini answered a remark of Manzoni's. 'As for myself, I'm not only useless but fear to be harmful, and these fears not only make me resigned to death but desire it.' To which Manzoni exclaimed: 'Ah! For the love of heaven, don't say that, what shall we do?' And Rosmini replied: 'Adore, be silent, and rejoice.' Then he kissed Manzoni's hand and Manzoni, outdoing him in humility, tried to kiss his feet.

CHAPTER ELEVEN

THE LAST FORTY YEARS

I

IT IS doubtful if any period in Manzoni's life could really be called golden, except perhaps for the few years between his conversion and the return of the Austrians to Lombardy. If the gold of the period when he was writing *I Promessi Sposi* might seem, under its even glow, to hide alternating patches of burnish and tarnish, it was the last really bright one of his life. The death of Henriette on Christmas Day 1833 began a long series of family disasters which continued regularly until the death of his eldest son Pietro forty years later, only a month before his own; while his greatest friends, Guisti, Torti, Grossi, died within a few years of Rosmini. These losses confirmed the secluded habits of his life and intensified the melancholy conclusions he drew from the workings of Divine Providence. The periods of unforeseen content, the return of absorption in his work, the patches of occasional gaiety, and the rarer bursts of enthusiasm when his unruly spirit broke through the bonds he had imposed on it, go to show that the spirit of a human being is too diverse to fit into any biographer's pattern. Dull as the last half of his life might be considered seen as a whole, it affords an example of retirement which appears rare only because it is associated with the name of the chief figure in modern Italian literature.

Up till 1830 Henriette had still been producing children with monotonous, and as it proved, exhausting regularity. With Matilde, born in July 1830, she had had eleven pregnancies, including one miscarriage, in twenty years. These she had accepted with a resignation that was sometimes restive. Indeed she had a good deal to put up with. In 1821, after confiding to her cousin: 'Add the worry and bother caused by my husband's health to the cares of looking after five children and a large household, and you can well see, my dear Charlotte, that I cannot have much time to myself. And now new pains make me fear that I am pregnant again: this will be my ninth

confinement; I assure you that this task is very difficult to fulfil
. . . but one must resign oneself to the will of God.' Later,
when Manzoni one day was warmly expounding the doctrines
of Malthus, she interrupted sweetly: 'Aren't you ashamed of
supporting such ideas before these seven children?' Her eye
troubles were a symptom of long-standing weakness. In the
summer of 1832 she became seriously ill and was ordered by her
doctors to return to the seaside. She went, though Donna
Giulia, now strong as ever and happily in command again, had
written to her little grand-daughter Vittoria the year before:
'You know when we are at Brusuglio we always have so many
things to do that it is very difficult for us to tear ourselves away.'

This last trip in 1832 was one of the rare occasions when
Henriette and Alessandro travelled alone together, for Donna
Giulia decided this time to remain behind. One morning of
early July in the Lombard plain they rose before dawn, and
using their own and then their agent's horses reached Pavia by
eleven, lunched with old Bishop Tosi, and in the cool of the
evening took post until, suffocated by the heat and dust, they
reached Genoa by midday next day. There they stayed until
the middle of August. The sea-baths seemed to do Henriette
good. So much better did she feel that, before turning home,
they went on to visit their eldest daughter Giulietta, Fauriel's
god-daughter, who the year before had married that remarkable
figure, the Marchese Massimo d'Azeglio, and was now living at
the old castle of Azeglio above a lake in Piedmont.

Giulietta had hesitated for a while whether to accept her
brilliant and rather erratic suitor. But by July 1831 she was
settled happily at Azeglio and enjoying her short period of
married life. Massimo, she reported, was at work on an historical
novel, *Ettore Fieramosca*,[1] 'devoting several hours a day to it
among those he gives to painting and music.'

The charming, versatile, and rather facile Massimo d'Azeglio
was a total contrast to the family he married into. ('Massimo
was born seductive,' was Manzoni's slightly malicious comment
on him.) He had already been a cavalry officer and embassy

---

[1] *Ettore Fieramosca*, like *I Promessi Sposi*, set out to expose the evils of foreign
domination, and to awaken national feeling. It also achieved great popularity.
There is little other similarity, although Manzoni is said to have rewritten the end.

attaché, and was a student of painting when he first appeared in Milan with an introduction from his brother Robert, who had met the Manzoni family during their stay in Florence three years before. Among the old-world Piedmontese circles in which he had been brought up, painting was considered such an ungentlemanly occupation that it was apt to be confused with house decorating. But in his youth Massimo d'Azeglio was an innovator and a breaker of conventions. He was one of the first from his enclosed country who 'depiedmontized' (*spiemontizzò*) himself, and became Italian through an experience far more varied than Alfieri's. Bolton King obviously disliked him, perhaps because of his later political evolution: 'He had painted pictures, written novels, done nothing very well. His democratic veneer came more of ostentation than of conviction; his slender purse, his frank manners, his obtrusive if shallow profusion of democratic sympathies, won him the liking of the democrats, and his novels made his name a household word throughout Italy.' Yet this apparent adventurer not only wrote one of the most sincere and rousing books about the condition of the Papal States in 1845, *Gli ultimi casi di Romagna* (for which he was expelled from Tuscany), but he was to become Prime Minister of Piedmont. He supported the Gioberti plan for a league of Italian states under the pope, and when this failed inaugurated the policy which with Cavour was to end triumphantly in unification. On resigning he went on missions to London to enlist sympathy for this policy. His last official post in his old age was director of the Turin Art Gallery. By then his growing conservatism and atavistic attachment to the House of Savoy had drawn him away from his famous father-in-law, whose feelings he had already hurt by remarrying only a few months after Giulietta's death. This second wife also came from the Manzoni circle, for she was Luisa Blondel, the widow of Henriette's brother. The marriage was not successful, as d'Azeglio was notoriously unfaithful. Husband and wife played Box and Cox, avoiding each other; and the story goes that when she hurried to his death-bed he looked up and smiled: 'Ah, Luisa, you always arrive just as I'm leaving.'

D'Azeglio could be a penetrating observer as well as a colourful character, and some of his remarks in his memoirs, *I Miei ricordi*, the best book he ever wrote, must have pleased Manzoni. After noting, for instance, that in Milan in 1833 the singers of the Scala were much more highly favoured than writers and painters, he commented: 'This shows the need for revising opinions about the sagacity and subtlety of the Austrian Government, which can be said to have governed Lombardy for so many years by means of the Scala Opera House. And one must admit that up to a certain point it succeeded well.'

II

There must have been some hereditary weakness in the Manzoni family. His daughters Giulietta, Cristina, Sofia, Matilde, all died young, and Clara never came out of babyhood. Those who lived spent their lives nursing their health. With the sons, on the other hand, all of whom were failures of varying degrees, the weakness seems to have taken the form of an instability which was either hereditary or possibly partly conditioned. Unlike the daughters they never went to school, but tutors were apt to be unsatisfactory. Ballantyne, a Scot, recommended by Fauriel, came to as bad an end as most of his pupils. Possibly one reason for the sons' reactions was that as time went on Manzoni's treatment of his children became stricter. His grown-up daughters were very rarely allowed out even to the theatre, and never to dances outside the family.

Could Henriette's combination of sweetness, firmness, and common sense have saved the whole family had she lived? She died, really of exhaustion, on Christmas Day 1833. At the end, reported Costanza Arconati, she had become so detached from life that even if she could have returned to it she would not have wanted to. Life at Brusuglio must have had its hidden strains, which, like so much else in Manzoni's life, we can only guess at. There seems no doubt that Manzoni felt her death profoundly, though Costanza Arconati noted that Alessandro choked down his grief, while Donna Giulia showed more signs of sorrow. In a copy of *I Promessi Sposi* given to his granddaughter Enrichetta, Manzoni wrote: 'To my dear grandchild Enrichetta! A sweet, sacred, blessed name for one who knew her in whose memory it was given: a name which signified faith, purity, good sense, love of family, kindness for all, sacrifice, humility, everything which is holy, everything which is amiable.'

Thirty years later, when Mme Louise Colet, in one of the surprisingly intimate conversations into which she managed to coax Manzoni, told him that her daughter's name was also Henriette, he exclaimed: 'It was that of my well-beloved wife, of the inseparable companion of my life, of the mother of my children: the only grief she ever caused me was that of dying before me. She had so identified herself with my mind that she thought, so to say, with my ideas and believed with my faith. . . . She was an angelic mixture of sweetness and firmness, which no suffering ever altered.' The character of Lucia in *I Promessi Sposi* is said to have been partly based on that of Henriette; like so many nineteenth-century descriptions of women, this has a certain insipid sweetness which may well be superficial and hide a real strength of feeling. A rarely expressed intensity appears in the lines of Adelchi to Ermengarda, written when Henriette was seriously ill.

> . . . nè tutta mai
> Questo labro pudico osato avrà
> Dirti l'ebbrezza del mio cor segreta.

(Nor has this modest lip ever dared tell you all the secret rapture of my heart.)

Whatever his feelings were for Henriette, he remarried within three years of her death. The arrangements were made once more by Donna Giulia, who although overwhelmed by Henriette's death was soon, with her eighteenth-century realism, facing the fact that her son needed someone to live with him, and to look after the younger children.

Donna Teresa Stampa Borri was first pointed out to Manzoni, on one of his rare visits to the theatre, by two mutual friends, Grossi and Rossari, the latter of whom was both Manzoni's walking companion and tutor to Donna Teresa's young son, Stefano Stampa. She was a widow, then aged thirty-seven, whose husband Count Decimo Stampa had died fifteen years before. The Borris were old Milanese nobles of the Verri school, with a tradition of public service and latterly of hatred of Austria. The Stampas were more cosmopolitan, and her husband had been educated in France at about the time Manzoni was there with his 'Idéologue' friends. Donna Teresa read Shakespeare in her limp-bound English edition, and even collected foreign travel books on Italy. Small, fluttery, with large, mobile eyes, she seems to have captured Manzoni at once, for next day he got Grossi to take him to call. With them went Donna Giulia to look Donna Teresa over. 'Fascinated, and almost in love myself,' was Donna Giulia's exaggerated way of expressing her approval, in a fit of enthusiasm which she was soon to regret. Alessandro proposed in August. The marriage took place four months later, in December 1836.

The public reaction to the marriage was a sign of Manzoni's growing elevation into a national figure, almost a myth. Henriette, who had become fused in the public mind with the images of Ermengarda and Lucia, seems to have become almost a symbol of conjugal love; and included among the domestic virtues which the Manzoni household was considered to enshrine was the ideal of fidelity towards a dead wife. But 'the once so proud Alessandro' had broken convention once again. The whispering in Milan was a curious throw-back to those distant scandals which had eddied round the Manzoni family years ago, and still echo among the equivalent group in Milan to-day. Costanza Arconati, whose criticisms, like those of so many intimate friends, might have come from the worst of enemies, began a letter by generalizing on the 'imprudent marriage' which 'takes away some of that sublime aura which surrounds Manzoni,' and added: 'It's natural the public should judge Manzoni more severely than another.' She found it an act of weakness, though she added that she understood it, and ended with the unexpected question: 'What does Fauriel say?' Fauriel had not even written to Manzoni on Henriette's death, but his humane comment on this second marriage to a friend in Paris was: 'People should do what they want; and he needs happiness.'

Tommaseo, whose early contact with Rosmini had left little imprint of Christian charity, was soon reporting other rumours. 'Here,' he wrote from Paris, 'they say she [Donna Teresa] is an unbeliever and has been a flirt [*galante già*]. Do please tell me what the truth is.' Rossari, who had introduced her to Manzoni, was rumoured to be her lover. The family friends soon had something definite to criticize in the rapidly worsening relations between the new wife and old Donna Giulia.

Donna Teresa appears to have adored Alessandro from afar ever since she had read *I Promessi Sposi* in the very first month of its publication. She has been accused of being something of a literary snob: 'the priestess of the Grand Lama,' a contemporary called her. Certainly she always took a great interest in her husband's work, and in that first happy year took notes of his conversation which are considerably fresher than the various other compilations of his talk. She loved to learn from Alessandro's conversation, she told her brother, after they had been discussing what would happen to industry when coal-seams were exhausted; and in spite of her love of opera, she gave up going to the Scala so as not to leave him alone in the evening. But she was a nervous and delicate woman, and her constant ills made her appear as something of a valetudinarian. In spite of his friends' opinions of her, Alessandro remained deeply devoted. Their correspondence when he was away shows him eager as a youth to get back to her. In 1852, when he was sixty-seven, his letters were dotted with phrases such as: 'Good-bye, my dear Teresa, how much I love and desire you.' And another time: 'I remain in the hope of embracing you (till I hurt you) next week.' Once he enclosed a cyclamen.

Yet there was an undertone of nervous strain in the household at Brusuglio, for which visitors found different reasons. In June 1838 Tommaseo wrote that 'Donna Giulia is rather left in a corner: not badly treated, I hope . . .'; and when he dined at Brusuglio in September 1840 he noted mordantly: 'Manzoni makes me sorry for him: he is good; the wife sly; the mother distressed; the son Filippo without affection.' Although Donna Teresa had left the control of the household entirely to her domineering mother-in-law, Donna Giulia was soon spreading her discontent among relations and friends. She showed it in the house in various ways, criticizing Donna Teresa's adored only son, Stefano Stampa, even making petty little scenes about his washing and about the Stampas' favourite wine from their vineyard at Lesa. Stefano never got over his hatred for Donna Giulia for the way she had treated his mother. Giuseppe Borri, Donna Teressa's brother, visiting Brusuglio for the first time in

July 1837, found that already by then Donna Teresa and Donna Giulia were scarcely on speaking terms. The latter, whose exquisite manners had enlivened those gatherings in Milan and Paris at the turn of the century, spent the evening reading or pretending to read, turning over the pages with rustles of disapproval. 'If in Manzoni one seems to see the philosopher whom Rousseau would have liked to find in his democracy to dictate a code of laws, in his mother one seems to see Madame Aristocracy in person,' wrote Borri. 'Her speech is pompously courteous; her words, even when they flatter, keep you at a great distance: she is not the daughter of Professor Beccaria, she is the daughter of the *Marchese*. She speaks rarely, and in a considered and sententious way, nor does the slightest smile ever come to smooth her brow. In fact,' poor Borri ended an account of what must have been a singularly unpleasant evening, 'her face, her words, bring a mortal chill to the mind.'

Tommaseo, commenting that 'poor Alessandro had lost many years of health and study because of his mother,' added: 'It is true that even before, if the music-master was different, the music was the same.' For to console Donna Teresa, Alessandro seems to have hinted that Donna Giulia had sometimes behaved in the same way even with the self-effacing Henriette. Apart from this he gave up the attempt to make peace between the two women. 'He was always so resigned,' commented Tommaseo, 'that he even appeared not to care.'

This discord set Donna Teresa longing for her own villa on the lakeside at Lesa, far away from Donna Giulia and the close air of the plain. From 1839 onwards she and Alessandro would escape there for increasingly long periods. To be back on the lake again enchanted him, and he spent more and more time there. He would take his afternoon walks along the old road between Lesa and Stresa, often visit Rosmini, and return on foot. There is a story that these excursions stimulated him so much that he even began planning during them, partly possibly as a conversational amusement, a fantastic romance about someone who came into the world with aspirations which experience of life made him change completely. He was also touched at Lesa by the craze for magnetism and hypnotism, then sweeping Europe, and did experiments on a maidservant in the house.

These pastimes alternated with periods of hard work, so hard that his daughter Vittoria once wrote to Donna Teresa asking her to prevent him doing too much. These studies were now purely either philosophical or philological. 'I'm working slowly and painfully,' he wrote once, 'at that wretched appendix on the Utilitarian system; which obliges me to read and think a great deal, to say very little.' Some summers and autumns the villas along the lakeside were full of friends, such as that of 1850 when the Arconatis were at Pallenza, where Berchet was now almost a member of the family. Mary Clarke, now Mme Mohl, turned up again, and came to Brusuglio later to search for Fauriel's letters, 'with great waste of Alessandro's time and to his great annoyance and discomfort,' Donna Teresa wrote; but when sending the few she could find to Mary Mohl, she said they had been searched out by her husband and sent on as a 'sacrifice to friendship.' Lesa was a haven, too, from other family troubles. And Stefano Stampa, Donna Teresa's adored only son, became with his painting, music, and devotion to Rosmini a substitute for all the failures of his own sons.

While his daughters died off, one after the other, Giulietta in 1834, Cristina in 1841, Matilde in 1856, the careers of his sons can be called nothing less than disastrous. Pietro, a drunkard, appears to have been the least unsatisfactory, for he was finally installed in Brusuglio with his family and, until his own death, a month before his father's, did his best to keep him company. The other two, Filippo and Enrico, were partly ruined by finding that Donna Giulia had disinherited them on her death in 1841. There were continual scenes between Donna Teresa and all the sons. Filippo, without consulting his horrified father, who had ruled the theatre out of his life, married a dancer from the Scala. He was a hopeless spendthrift and spent some time in a debtor's prison, when his father, appealed to, refused to pay up. Enrico, who also made a marriage of which his father disapproved, was so incapable that he ruined himself in business ventures and ended his life distributing the books at the Brera library, and living in one room. As late as 1890 the families of Filippo and Enrico were constantly applying for help to Stefano Stampa, who had not only remained prosperous and reputable, but undertaken the task of defending his famous stepfather's memory. Stampa

was even to leave money at his death for a review to defend
Rosmini's philosophy.

The criticism of Manzoni's second marriage persisted among
his old friends. 'She weighs on my stomach like a round of
beef,' remarked Sigismondo Trechi crudely of Donna Teresa.
Vittoria Manzoni called her stepmother a neurotic valetudinarian,
'a shrew' who finally drove her out of the house and into the
care of her Aunt Luisa Blondel d'Azeglio, the second wife of
Massimo d'Azeglio. Vittoria, who in her youth had always had
'une tête un peu romanesque' (when she had even to be prevented from reading Byron), later regretted this outburst, and
after her own marriage she and Donna Teresa became devoted
correspondents. A more serious criticism came from Federigo
Confalonieri, who was now out of prison, having petitioned the
Austrian emperor for his freedom in 1836, on a promise of not
taking part in any political activities (his prison experience and
reconversion to Catholicism had made him into an ardent
quietist). 'Few things could surprise me more than the news
of Manzoni's marriage, and of his choice,' he wrote from exile;
'but such is the opinion I hold of him that I say to myself, if he
has done this he has done it for good reasons—and on that I fall
silent and wish it all success.' When in 1840 he returned to
Milan and dined with Alessandro and Teresa, his comment
afterwards was: 'I am saddened at seeing a couple who do not
seem well suited.'

Teresa, in fact, must have provided Alessandro with a refreshing change. Where Henriette had fused her life with his, and
subordinated everything to him even to the detriment of her
health, he now found himself looking after Teresa and attending
her in her numerous illnesses with understanding sympathy.
In his letters of this period there is less mention of his own nerves
than ever before. Her illnesses became almost continuous after
twins were born to her, dead, in February 1845. Sometimes
her face and even her ears would swell up. Sometimes she
would spend hours filling the cracks of doors with paper, or
dream of thieves and storms, and he would soothe her. Brusuglio
she disliked even when Donna Giulia, making her peace with all
(pending the reading of her will), died of pneumonia in 1841:
we catch a glimpse of the old lady on her death-bed reciting her

son's *Inni Sacri*. As the years went on Alessandro would leave Teresa in her villa at Lesa, surrounded by 'clusters of women' who were half companions and half servants, and set off to visit friends or relations in other parts of Northern Italy. She would then worry about his health in her turn, and her letters about it when he was away at Siena visiting his daughter in 1852 almost aroused him to protest. Their affectionate intimacy is shown by an ironic little description he sent her of the relations between his grand-daughter, d'Azeglio's child, and young Marchese Ricci at their wedding in 1852. 'There's a perfect uniformity of tastes between them. Just to mention one which hints at a number of others, they are both mad about balls, theatres, and noisy parties, just like you and me.'

III

The long self-imposed exile at Lesa to avoid the Austrian reaction after the events of 1848 cost him a heavy fine, which he found difficult to pay. The death of Donna Giulia had cut off a great deal of his income, and his fortune had been further depleted by the failure of the elaborate illustrated and rewritten new edition of *I Promessi Sposi* of 1840–2, which he had financed himself. The Austrian fine now reduced him even to giving up his carriage. It was the first time he had been directly affected by political events since that refusal of the passports for Paris over thirty years before. This new-found poverty preyed on his mind: he would alternate between a recurring obsession that he was ruined, and the attitude expressed in a letter to his daughter Vittoria: 'As for me I assure you that if it were not for the dear and piercing preoccupation about my children, poverty could not frighten me at all, old as I am and used in these months to living economically: if it were not such as to make me depend on others, I would even take a certain pleasure in it.'

The friends who had been more directly affected by political events were now beginning to reappear. Some, like Confalonieri and Pellico, were to spend the last years of their lives in religious devotion. The Arconatis, until they were allowed to return to Italy, had made their luxurious home of exile at the castle of Gaesbeck outside Brussels, which they had made a centre for

years for the more respectable Italian liberals.   Those among
the group who were able to circulate would stay now for
long periods with the Arconatis at Cassolo in Piedmont, just
across the Lombard border.   One day when Manzoni was staying
at Cassolo in the 1860s he looked around at the company, all
of whom had either been in prison or in exile, and exclaimed
with a touch of regret: 'And I wasn't there.'

Not that events since 1821 had left him unmoved.   He held
aloof from the festivities for the Austrian emperor's visit to
Milan in 1838.   He rejected the offer of an Austrian decoration
made by Metternich, and in 1858, when he was seriously ill,
refused to receive a visit from the young Austrian viceroy, the
Archduke Maximilian, who had called to find out how he was.

Never participating actively, he followed the developments
of the movement that was to result in the unification of Italy
with an apparent detachment that hid the depths of his interest.
The collapse of the Carbonari revolution in 1821 had driven the
movement underground after 1822, when the leaders who had
escaped prison or execution moved off to France.   In Paris they
mixed with radical exiles from every country in Europe, and as
a result the Italian Carbonari in exile became merged for a time
into the main stream of European Liberalism.   The influence
was reciprocal, and the French Carbonari under Lafayette took
over many of the Italian forms of organization.   In spite of
energetic leaders such as General Pepe, the former head of the
Neapolitan Carbonari Government, for a number of years after
1822 the Italian Carbonari exiles inevitably lost contact with the
main body of their sympathizers and adherents within Italy.
They ceased to have a local understanding of events, and in turn
efforts within Italy became sporadic and unco-ordinated, such
as the abortive uprisings in Romagna in 1830 and 1832.   These
risings broke out largely from exasperation with the repressive
governments of the Papal States, and the concept of a general
war of liberation was still to come.   The cry of the Bonaparte
brothers during the Romagna rising, 'Italy, Rome, Liberty,' was
more of an imaginative aspiration than a definite aim.

The events in France and Romagna in 1830 were followed
with close attention by the Manzoni household.   The overthrow
of Charles X was a delight to them, as it was to Fauriel, who

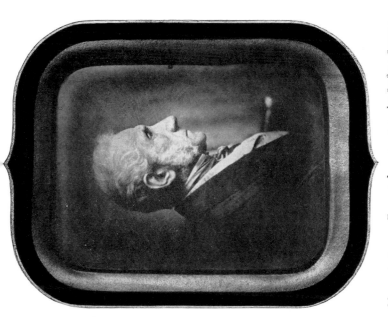
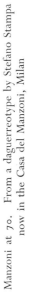

Manzoni at 70. From a daguerreotype by Stefano Stampa now in the Casa del Manzoni, Milan

Donna Teresa in her room. From a daguerreotype by her son Stefano Stampa now in the Casa del Manzoni, Milan

wrote to Mary Clarke of his 'delight' at this 'great and equitable event.' Just after the July Revolution had taken place Fauriel found Giovita Scalvini wandering about in the Tuileries gardens 'in a state of joy and admiration for which he could find no words.' 'Many English,' Fauriel also told Mary Clarke, 'have been superb.' At this time the Manzonis, Costanza Arconati reported, had 'seemed full of hope for the future: how can France see without sympathy so many joys which she has encouraged?' and she went on: 'Henriette let it be clearly understood that they were expecting a deliverance very soon. They had an air of being so sure of this and so happy about it'—Costanza Arconati was writing when the news of the collapse of the Romagna revolt had already reached her—'that it hurts me to think of them now. Must we endure all over again what we went through ten years ago?' The failure had been partly due to lack of arms, which had been promised by Louis Philippe, who had then taken fright. The defection disillusioned Manzoni and other liberals about Louis Philippe, who had shown himself conservative and materialistic after all their high hopes. 'I have suffered,' wrote Sismondi to Vieusseux with gentle despair, 'under the empire of Napoleon, under the allied reaction, under the Restoration, but at least I could offset the reality with my hopes and desires: now I suffer much more, as I do not know what to desire.'

Yet 1830 was to prove a spiritual turning-point for the Italian movement. The imprisonment of Mazzini for Carbonari activities led to the maturing of his political ideas in the calm of prison. When on his release in 1831 he was given the choice between supervision and exile, he moved to Marseilles, where he started the movement called 'Young Italy,' which was to have a vast influence on the Risorgimento. At the same time the advent to the throne of Piedmont of Carlo Alberto, who stood, as he himself said, 'between the daggers of the Carbonari and the poisoned chocolate of the Jesuits,' was to lead to important moves towards unification.

According to a contemporary, de Gubernatis, Manzoni and Mazzini met in 1860 when Italian unity was achieved, and congratulated each other on having both been among its few long-standing supporters. But Stefano Stampa, who was with

I

Manzoni almost continuously for the last twenty years of his life, said that though they never met, Manzoni had declared: 'Mazzini and I have always had faith in the independence of Italy, carried out and ensured by liberty.' After the disasters of Custoza and Novara in 1849–50, Manzoni at Lesa had begun a dialogue to show that 'if the unity of Italy was a Utopia, it was at least a beautiful Utopia'; and at the news of the disaster of Villa-franca he swayed to his feet, gripping his chair in agony. But to that detached observer Mazzini seemed irresponsible and his theories too idealistic and cloudy. 'The individual and the collective, the "I" and "We,"' wrote Mazzini, 'are both eternal elements of life, which is the manifestation of God on the earth; they are the two poles of the problem which troubles humanity since its birth. The real aim of democracy is to create a harmony between these two elements.' Yet as Manzoni grew older his criticisms of Mazzini were apt to be somewhat contradictory. In 1845 Manzoni attacked 'the twisted ideas of that man and of his colleagues, who want to achieve the regeneration of Italy by means of communism.' Some years later he was telling his brother-in-law Borri: 'They [the Mazzinians] were the worst of aristocrats, under the cloak of liberty.' Once he compared Mazzini's predictions about the unity of Italy to a friend's remark, 'It's going to snow at the first cool winds of September,' which was repeated when the cold increased in October and November, until when January came and it really did snow he exclaimed: 'I told you it was going to snow.' Though Manzoni himself never adhered to any party, most of the friends whom he saw at his evening conversations belonged to the party of moderate reform, which was alarmed by Mazzini's singleness of purpose and methods.

Mazzini had been brought up in strict Jansenist principles since the Abate Dègola had converted his mother. In the early days he was inclined to blame Manzoni, who he thought could be 'the Luther of Italian literature,' for 'being silent and throwing himself into Catholic interests.' And, anyway, art should be laid aside for political action. 'Italian art will flourish, if we succeed, on our tombs.' Later he was to write in his *Manzoni e Alfieri* (in warmer, if vaguer terms): 'We feel affection for Manzoni, and his name means sanctity and grandeur to young Italians.'

Alfieri, an aristocrat weakened by twenty years of gentlemanly laziness, was able to write a treatise on tyranny, but could not be revolutionary in politics or literature. Manzoni's aim, his belief, his perennial tendency, was the redemption of the people. The banner of Christian equality is more or less visible in all the productions of the followers of Manzoni. The choice of subject, the manner of treating it, everything shows that the high intention of the writers is to destroy the power usurped by the aristocratic principle.

Until after 1848 Manzoni had remained a republican. Finally he supported the Savoy monarchy because he became convinced that only the leadership of Piedmont could achieve the unification of Italy. When a friend wrote to say that the war of 1859 was the work of the Mazzinians, he replied flatly, with a total subordination of his argument to the facts: 'That party has ceased to exist, and a good thing too. . . . I mean all people of good faith who belonged to that party have changed their minds' —as all those able to bear arms, he went on to say, had enrolled under the banners of Victor Emmanuel, 'that king admirable for his bravery and loyalty.' He ignored the fact that Mazzini and his followers continued to think that Cavour saw unity not in terms of a popular movement, but as an expansion of the Piedmontese dynasty and power. Yet although in 1848 Manzoni at some personal risk during the street fighting signed an appeal for the intervention of Charles Albert, whom he had never trusted, to help the Milanese, he was against a plebiscite on the unification of Lombardy and Piedmont. If Manzoni thought he would succeed in making Charles Albert into a republican, d'Azeglio wrote to him, he had no hope of doing so with Pius IX. To d'Azeglio, Manzoni was always to seem 'a bit red.' This belief was perhaps justified by the terms in which he announced to his son-in-law his adherence to the Savoy monarchy: 'If something came up that promised better (and it doesn't look like it now), I'd turn my coat at once; and then,' he added with his usual ironic self-deprecation, 'I should do you as much harm as I now do you good—which is immense.'

He was frank about his incapacity for public life. 'I'm absolutely useless,' he declared flatly in September 1848 to the editor of *Concordia*, 'in any political discussion, and for a number of reasons.' When he refused at the same time an offer to become deputy for Arona, he explained to his nominators that he lacked, among the other qualities necessary for a politician,

just to mention one, but an absolutely essential one, that capacity for discerning one point from the other, and where the desirable meets the practicable, and when to hold on to the latter and sacrifice the former not only with resignation but with firmness. . . . Bold, as long as it is a question of chatting among friends, in putting forward, and no less tenacious in defending, propositions which are or seem paradoxical, everything becomes doubtful, obscure, complicated when words may lead to decisions. . . . In many cases, and particularly in the most important, my trend of thought would be to . . . deny everything and propose nothing. . . . To be a Utopian and irresolute are useless things, at least at gatherings where talk should lead to conclusions, and I should be both at the same time. . . . It is a sad and mortifying thing to find oneself useless in a cause which has been the dream of one's life, but *ipsos facit nos et non ipsi nos.*

'What I'm really good at,' he said ruefully, when he finally accepted a seat in the Senate of United Italy, 'is mixing the sugar in the water of the orator sitting next to me.'

The events of 1848 caused not only this frank avowal, but his only article for a newspaper and his only recorded public speech. During the five days' street fighting in Milan in March he watched, from the windows of his house in the Via Morone, the young men going to the barricades, some still in evening clothes and dancing-pumps, and wistfully noted their liveliness and gaiety. He encouraged his sons to go out and fight, and Pietro was captured by the Austrians at the Town Hall. One night he found two or three hundred demonstrators under his windows. 'Viva l'Italia! Viva Manzoni!' came up from the square below. Finally, reluctantly, Manzoni allowed himself to be urged on to the balcony, with a couple of lanterns held behind him. 'No, no!' he managed to shout. 'Viva l'Italia and those who fight for her! I've done nothing. It's just been my aspiration!' 'No, no!' came the shouts back. 'You've done a lot! You've given an initiative to the whole of Italy! Viva Manzoni, the champion of Italy!' But when the crowd began calling for him to write a hymn on the liberation of Italy, he prudently withdrew, muttering that he would do it if he could. But he had already written poems that were being sung all over

Italy. The ode *Marzo 1821* that he had written during the Carbonaro revolution thirty years before, and which would have sent him to the Spielberg had the Austrians found it—*O, giornate del nostro riscatto*—was being greeted as a revelation, and the choruses from *Adelchi* intoned as marching-songs.

The decisive phases of the Italian war of liberation he watched from the Borris' house at Torricella outside Milan. The city was not considered safe for him, in case he was taken off as a hostage as his son Pietro had been. He left Milan with Donna Teresa, who forced herself out of bed to accompany him, a week before the battle of Montebello, and returned just after the triumphant entry into the city of Victor Emmanuel II and Napoleon III.

His year of triumph was 1860. 'These great events which made Italy strong and free after so many centuries of decay, warm and reanimate my old age. I thank God for having let me live to see this unhoped-for hour.' For years he had refused royal decorations, from the Emperor of Austria, the King of Prussia, the Grand Duke of Tuscany, King Louis Philippe (who offered his through Victor Cousin), and put off approaches by the Emperor of Russia and the Grand Duke of Weimar. 'You know,' he wrote when refusing a decoration, 'how often demonstrations of honour bring dislike on the head of the person who is the object of them; and make those who would otherwise not have thought of it either denigrate, or in this case put in his place, the person whom others wanted to put too far forward. I prefer to remain in my corner rather than be thrust back into it.' But he had accepted the honorary membership and sometimes presidency (as long as he did not have to appear) of a large number of literary societies. One of his last recorded verses was written on receiving the diploma of the oddly named *Accademia dei Sepolti* of Volterra.

> Manzon qui giace ne' suoi versi involto
> Veramente accademico sepolto.

He was also an honorary member, apart from this relic of the Arcadians, of the Society of the Friends of Popular Education of Prato, of the Society of Mutual Help among the workers of S. Sofia Montano (of which Garibaldi was president), and of the

Society for Popular Reading at Impruneta. Now in 1860 he also accepted Cavour's offer of a seat in the Senate of United Italy; with it Victor Emmanuel offered a Civil List pension, which relieved his financial difficulties. 'It was you who in times of general discouragement,' Cavour wrote to him when passing on the king's offers, 'preserved pure and undefiled the glory of Italian letters.' To which Manzoni countered: 'You have all the qualities that make the statesman: you usually have prudence, but also imprudence at need.' In his last years he produced, rather incongruously, an essay on language to celebrate the marriage of Queen Margherita. He also copied out with his own hand *Il Cinque Maggio* for the commonplace book of the Empress Eugénie, as he had long admired Napoleon III for his liberal views and Carbonaro activity, and judged him 'greater than his uncle because juster.'

At times he was still capable of his old intransigence, and even of flashes of his old enthusiasm. 'Porci di siori' (filthy gentry), he once, in his extreme old age, hissed through the window of a carriage which had spattered an old woman in the street. In 1860 he followed excitedly the news of Garibaldi's expedition in Romagna, and when the hero visited him in 1862 he flung his arms wide and said: 'If I feel a nobody in front of any one of the Thousand, what should I feel for their general!' In 1864, against great opposition, particularly from many friends, he made his only visit to the Senate in Turin to vote for the transfer of the capital to Florence, *en route* for Rome. For even the Piedmontese liberals, in spite of their attitude to the Temporal Power, were loath to see Turin lose its capital status. Panizzi heard in London that the Arconatis and others had tried to bring pressure on him to stop him voting. D'Azeglio even got his confessor at the church of San Fedele, round the corner from the Via Morone, to write and try to dissuade him. The story goes that Manzoni received the letter after his arrival in Turin, read it, and without a word quietly put it back in his pocket. So strong was feeling in Turin that no one came to visit him. The day after the vote he went to see d'Azeglio, who kept the conversation during the whole visit entirely on his latest craze, spiritualism and table-turning. Then in a wild speech in the Senate he attacked Manzoni without naming him: 'In the tendency to move the capital towards Rome,' he shouted, 'there enters a great deal of hatred for the papacy.'

In 1872, while the whole of the Italian clergy was protesting against the occupation of Rome—which to them seemed almost the end of the world—Manzoni accepted the Freedom of the City from the Roman town council because it showed, he wrote, 'an acknowledgment of the constant aspiration of my long life for the independence and unity of Italy.' His disillusion with Vatican politics had lasted ever since Pius IX's defection from Liberalism. Already in *I Promessi Sposi* he had called the papacy 'that office which is so tempting to ambition and so disastrous to piety.' In 1862 he said to Mme Colet: 'In the early centuries the Church did not possess lands, and those were the days of its supreme grandeur. Then it walked resplendent in the world without the chains which bind it now. The doctrines of the Church must remain unchanged, for they come from God Himself. But that which belongs to human institutions must be transformed—it is both just and necessary.' 'I bow my head humbly before the Holy Father, and the Church has no more respectful child than I . . . but why confuse the interests of the Church with those of Heaven? The Roman people are within their rights in demanding their emancipation. There are times when nations and governments should not concentrate on what is to their advantage but on what is just.' Once, when discussing the Temporal Power with him, Leon Favre opposed 'Catholic interests' to the unity of Italy, and Manzoni interrupted sharply: 'Monsieur, you are reducing the Church to the rank of a Utilitarian school.' To the Contessa Maffei, who had used a similar phrase, he made the rejoinder: 'Interests of the Church? Just party phrases.' In one of his evening conversations he summed up: 'The Church will never be at ease on this earth.' It was no wonder that he was never wholly approved of by the hierarchy, was never asked to take part in any religious congresses, and never received any letters or blessings from the pope.

IV

'Oh! I am old,' he said to Cantù in the 1860s. 'I am of the past generation, which is taking a last look of affectionate interest at the efforts of the generation which is its heir. I look, I approve, I regret, I congratulate, I accompany it a step or two with my desires.' Right up to extreme old age his brain, sharpened by the habit of philosophical studies, remained acute. He would bring out ideas for analysis before his friends, hold them suspended as he observed their many facets, then make a sudden and unexpected synthesis which 'sometimes came from his bottomless erudition, sometimes from transporting the rules of one order of ideas into another with which they had a hidden link, discovered by him,' in the description by Fabris.

Alongside his language obsession there grew up in his last years another on the French Revolution. 'My two loves are the language—and Marie Antoinette,'[1] he said unexpectedly, showing how his views had changed since those far-off chats with Grégoire. The French Revolution had been an interest dogging him for years, and probably no other Italian knew so much about it: he had read all the books on it and even knew all the names of the members of the Convention. Yet his views came to be coloured more and more by his theology. In an analysis of Robespierre, written in 1841, after remarking on 'his belief, independent of any personal interest, of a new, extraordinary, and rapid perfection in the moral and material conditions of mankind,' he had gone on to discuss the conflict between the doctrine of original sin and the belief that all evil originates in social conditions—a belief which presupposes the innate goodness of man. In 1860 he started an historical essay comparing the Italian unification and the French Revolution, *La rivoluzione francese del 1789 e la rivoluzione italiana del 1859*, which was unfinished at his death. This long essay, influenced partly by Burke, and similar in its conclusions to Louis Madelin's, was a legalistic attack on the Revolution and an apologia for Louis XVI, seen as a reformist monarch swept off his feet by violence. Here was the same horror of violence as in *Colonna Infame*, the same insistence that it cannot be explained or excused on any grounds of necessity. What he called the Italian Revolution he saw as a legal one. The French, because theirs was not, had suffered as

[1] Still preserved at his house in Milan is the piece of embroidery on which Marie Antoinette was working in prison just before her execution. It was given to Donna Giulia by Mme de Condorcet.

a consequence great difficulites in setting up a government in place of the one they had destroyed. There was ironic disillusionment in his remarks on the fate of individual liberty, guaranteed by five successive French constitutions.

It did not begin to be something more than a vain name except in the constitution of 1814, and by the two most anti-revolutionary means that it is possible to imagine: the invasion of armies nearly all of which belonged to absolute monarchies, and the return of the dynasty proscribed by the Revolution. And can anyone say that to attain that liberty, which had already been offered by Louis XVI in 1789, it was absolutely indispensable to be dragged for a quarter of a century along a path that led in the opposite direction?

Though the essay is full of subtleties, particularly legal ones, there is no sense of the Revolution's importance or even its grandeur. For de Maistre the French Revolution had been satanism under a hypocritical mantle of rationalism, for Ballanche it was a holocaust caused by Divine Wrath and needing immolation and purification, for Victor Hugo the dawn of liberty and progress, for Carducci a prodigious expiatory rite. Revolutions for Manzoni in old age were legitimate only when they had a moral purpose or a logic, and in his analysis of the latter he was apt to get entangled in his own hair-splitting. In the end he came to regard the swing of politics almost with resigned and fatalistic detachment. Constitutional liberty, he once observed, led gradually to a republic; too much republican liberty led to anarchy; and anarchy inevitably ended in despotism, which in its turn revived the desire for constitutional liberty.

His routine, as the years went by, had become more and more stereotyped. He rose between five and six in the morning, lit his own study fire, and made his own chocolate on a spirit lamp. After his morning devotions he worked or read. At midday he prayed again. Prayers in the evenings for the family included readings from Bossuet translated by himself. All these devotions were short, and no rosary was said. 'The rosary is the psalter of the ignorant,' he declared; and the remark was used at his death by the Jesuits as a sign of his being 'against the Madonna.'

From eleven o'clock till one he received visitors and acquaintances in the study off the courtyard in the Via Morone. From three to six he went for a long walk, accompanied by a school-master and later by a local priest.   In the evening he received his few intimate friends in the drawing-room on the first floor, overlooking his own little garden and the larger formal gardens of the Palazzo Clerici.   This room is now the main library and catalogue room of the Istituto Manzoniano which occupies the old house.   On the walls were the portraits of his family: Henriette and himself surrounded by the heads of their children, Donna Giulia with him as a little boy, old Don Cesare Beccaria with his white wig.   The furniture was of the very simplest Empire style.   Manzoni's old arm-chair was always reserved for him by the fire.   He would stand with his back against the white marble mantelpiece, on which stood an eighteenth-century clock with a sculpture of Anacreon, dear to him as he had seen his eldest child Giulietta smile for the first time at the sound of it striking:

> Spira dei' nostri bamboli
> Nell' ineffabil riso. . . .

Snuff-box in his right hand, he would remain standing much of the evening, facing the small group of friends sitting in a half-circle round the fire.   This he would insist on looking after himself, as tending a fire, he would say, was one of the few practical things he could do really well.   But in spring the fire was a 'principe spodestato' (dethroned prince), as Manzoni called it, and conversation took place round the circular table near the door, on which were laid out papers and the numerous books received from writers inviting criticism and praise.   His practice with new books at the end of his life, we are told, was to glance at them to see if they contained anything irreligious. If not, and the writer showed signs of talent, he would send the author a visiting-card of thanks and lay the book out on the table for friends to see.   Irreligious books received no acknowledg-ment.   Criticisms either of his own work or his friends' he refused to read at all.

The group of intimates included one or two university pro-fessors, a librarian, a priest, and one or two noble literary amateurs, usually lifelong friends: these included Ermes Visconti in the earlier period, and later Giuseppe Arconati, Gabriele

Casati (Mayor of Milan during the five days' street fighting), and Giovanni Litta.   Although the professors, the librarian, and the chaplain had been intimates for years, it was only the nobles that Manzoni called by the familiar 'tu.'

Professor Cristoforo Fabris, a member of the group, gave a lecture in Venice in 1898 on his memories of those evening conversations.   But Manzoni lacked a Boswell or an Eckermann, and it is difficult to find a spark of life in these and other devoted recordings.   What does appear from them is that Manzoni, silent and stuttering among strangers, was surprisingly chatty, even garrulous, among those he knew well.   His conversation would switch from the verses of Buonarroti the younger to the Academy of the Crusca, from Monti and Parini to youthful memories, from Beccaria to Bourdaloue, Massillon, and the Temporal Power; and the most solemn theme might suddenly be invested with a light ironic anecdote or an unexpected paradox.   His staple subjects were religion, language, and the French Revolution, but he could range over the modern world too.   The renaissance of Catholicism in Italy, he said one day, would come from the example of England; at the objection that England was mainly Protestant he replied that the English people would become Catholics 'as more than any other people they have the strength of character necessary to carry out a similar transformation in themselves.'   Was parliamentary opposition necessary?   'One might as well say that to plough a field better one should add, behind the bulls drawing the plough, a horse or donkey pulling the opposite way.'   Diplomacy?

I find it quite useless.   Ambassadors are nothing but spies put to listen at the antechamber of powers that are called friendly.   This might have been all right at one time; but now that the press diffuses what it knows and doesn't know of courts and chambers, tell me, what use is an ambassador?   To receive a slap like Hübner, or like Cardinal Barrili, to assure that all goes well in Spain the day before the queen goes hunting?   Don't let Massimo hear me. . . .

Women?   'They have a pair of scales in their heads with stubbornness on one side and curiosity on the other, and can come down on either side. . . .'   'Thoughts are like women [when dogged by an idea which he said he must take down before he forgot it], and women do as Galatea did when she threw an apple: others hid, but of course she wanted to be seen before she hid.' Love? 'I have the idea, perhaps suggested by experience, that women boast about it, while men on the other hand are just butterflies of indifference.'

Very rarely did he talk about himself, apart from recounting anecdotes of his youth. Then, as Cantù wrote: 'It was in one of those pauses which follow an animated conversation, when his mind, not having any subject before it to occupy it, seemed to relax and follow for a while the unconscious thread of his thoughts.' But these moments of self-revelation were rare. Few men with such a reputation have cared to present so little of their inner selves to the outside world. He even hated having portraits done of himself. Once a painter commissioned to do his portrait had to follow him in the early morning to church and try, unsuccessfully, to sketch him from behind a pillar. One of the few portraits of him that gives a sincere impression of his personality is the one by Francesco Hayez, though it is doubtful if it fulfils the painter's bold assertion when he started: 'I'll try and put the plague of Milan in those eyes.' Manzoni's dislike of portraits of himself caused him to make one of the few remarks on painting recorded of him. 'In making a portrait that is a likeness it seems to me that painters must often feel like scholars who have to copy out an original manuscript full of mistakes without being able to make the necessary corrections.' He preferred to make the corrections in the privacy of his own mind.

v

Un tempio ed un uomo,
Manzoni ed il Duomo,

were, as Ippolito Nievo sang, the chief sights in Milan in the last thirty years of Manzoni's life. It became almost a duty for celebrities of every nationality visiting Milan to see both him and Milan Cathedral. Since young George Bancroft had included Manzoni in his European tour in 1821, after Goethe and before Byron, there had been other liberal American visitors. Bancroft had seen 'the family of Manzoni as too pure and happy not to be considered rare this side of the Alps.' George Ticknor was surprised in 1838 by Manzoni's knowledge of internal conditions in the United States, and found in him a combination of the characters of Fra Cristoforo and Don Abbondio.   To the novelist Catherine Sedgwick, visiting him in 1839 with intro-ductions from Pellico and Confalonieri, he regretted that *I Promessi Sposi* had not become more popular in America.   When Gladstone passed through Milan in 1832' Manzoni's fame had not yet apparently permeated the city to the extent it has to-day, for on asking the way to Manzoni's house outside his hotel he found that none of the passers-by had heard of him.   Gladstone noted that in some circles in Milan Manzoni was considered a 'bacchet-tone' (bigot), and he was surprised by Manzoni's combination of rigid piety and advanced political views.   Bulwer Lytton dedicated *Rienzi* to him 'as to the genius of the place.'   The Emperor Pedro II of Brazil, whose liberal policy towards the Brazilian slaves had aroused Manzoni's admiration, came two or three times; when he insisted on sitting by his host at the fireside instead of enthroned in a separate arm-chair Manzoni murmured whimsically: 'One is forced to obey tyrants.'   The emperor followed his translation of *Il Cinque Maggio* into Portuguese by quoting the poem on his visit to Egypt, under the Sphinx, 'with twenty centuries looking down.'   Newman passed through Milan on his way to ordination in Rome, and Manzoni wrote of his 'profound and tender admiration for him.'   Longfellow called, though he had fallen asleep over *I Promessi Sposi* ('The book does not exercise on me the fascination it has for others.')

In 1837 Balzac came.   His visit to Milan had aroused such expectations that at the Scala an Austrian guards officer was mistaken for him and received an ovation.   Balzac finally entered the theatre while there was a 'ballo di mezzo carattere,' *I Promessi Sposi*, going on.   His favour in Milan did not last long, for he was foolish enough to make a disparaging remark about *I Promessi Sposi* at a dinner in Venice when Milanese were present. This was reported back, and on his return to Milan Balzac found himself being attacked in the local papers as a sponger just out of a debtor's prison.   To set himself right with the Milanese literary world he hastened to visit Manzoni.   They began by talking about pantheism and cranioscopy, but when they discussed novels, Balzac shocked his host by his materialistic approach to the failure of his one religious novel, *Le Médecin de Campagne*. To treat *le genre religieux* successfully, said Manzoni when his visitor had left, it must be done with deep conviction and not as a kind of literary speculation. Balzac had ended what sounds like rather a sticky visit by suddenly gushing that he seemed to see Chateaubriand in Manzoni. No wonder that when he left Manzoni said he had had the impression, so out of key did Balzac's conversation seem, that he had not read *I Promessi Sposi* at all.

Verdi, though he only met Manzoni in 1868, had been an enthusiastic admirer for years. 'You don't know,' Verdi told the Contessa Maffei before visiting him for the first time, 'how much I admire that man, who I consider has not only written the greatest book of our period, but one of the greatest books ever to come from a human brain. It is not only a book, it is a consolation for humanity.' After their meeting Verdi wrote: 'I could have gone down on my knees before him, if one could adore men.' On Verdi's next birthday he received a typical card: 'To Giuseppe Verdi, from a decrepit Lombard writer.' Apart from the famous Requiem, Verdi also composed unpublished music for the choruses in the tragedies and for *Il Cinque Maggio*.

Sometimes with his visitors Manzoni showed a slightly dramatized view of the past. To Mme Colet in 1860 he talked of all the French liberals he had seen in that room in earlier days.

What passion! What fugue! What exaggeration, I might almost say, in their words! In philosophy as in liberty they overstepped the doctrines whose triumph they were trying to bring about in France and in Italy. Then they carried with a swagger the flag which has since dropped in their hands, and which they finally deserted when they treated us as revolutionaries. I can never see the convictions of the spirit darken and vacillate with age without a deep sadness. . . .

Did something of this sadness apply to himself, in spite of his firm religious anchorage? One current picture of him which has been handed down by those who did not glimpse his fluid and complex personality is of a smug old man, smiling with dubious modesty, sure of being right, and Olympically indulgent of errors in others. A truer view would be of a man discontented with himself and others, tormented with doubts and objections, dominating himself with an iron discipline under an elusive smile. 'La doute me tue,' he said, repeating Goethe's remark to Cousin. 'It is a misfortune to doubt,' Pascal had written, 'but it is an indispensable duty to search when in doubt. He who doubts and does not search is at the same time both unfortunate and unjust.' Very occasionally in his last years he would show the strain under which he lived by some remark such as: 'I've acquired the habit in the moments when I can do nothing but afflict myself uselessly, of taking my thoughts by the hair and holding them there. . . .'

His religion seems to have given him a certainty of feeling but not of thought. 'How can you, in your goodness, ever have succeeded in forgetting that I am the most useless person in the world at making suggestions?' he wrote in 1829 to Bishop Tosi, who had asked for advice about religious books to publish in Pavia. 'To throw doubts on things decided, to chatter about general principles when it is a question of deciding about a detail, to want something better without being able to decide what it is, that is what I'm really good at.'

Melancholy yet apparently serene, deprecating and slightly ironic, he would appear occasionally in public, surrounded by an atmosphere of veneration. Before he died 'ce déplorable Manzoni' as the Parisian Jesuits had called him, the 'irresolute Utopian' as he had called himself, was being exalted as the symbol of solidity and safety, of the patriot who was also a family man with all the Christian virtues: a national myth, particularly after the Unification, to be accepted with a slight yawn. In his last years he was elevated almost into the position of a local saint. 'Nostro grande santo uomo,' said the Contessa Maffei, as she cut the ivy off her balcony walls to send to friends in commemoration of a visit from him. We catch a glimpse of him on one of his afternoon walks just before he died, being recognized by crowds in the public gardens, who called out 'Manzoni! Manzoni!' and brought him their children to bless.

VI

Physically he remained active almost until the end. After the death of Donna Teresa in 1861 he travelled more about the northern part of the peninsula; he visited Florence again with Stefano Stampa and went on to his daughter Vittoria at Siena, and another time to Forte de' Marmi. Every autumn still he would spend some weeks with the Arconatis in Piedmont.

In the last months his faculties failed, but a touch of the old deprecating Manzoni remained. Sending his daughter Vittoria a photograph of himself in January 1873, he wrote:

> Occhi, orecchi, gambe e ahimè . . . pensiero
> Non ne ho più uno che mi dica il vero.

As the end drew near those few short years of irreverent agnosticism in his youth began to lie more and more heavily on his conscience, until they became almost an obsession. A few days before his last illness he told Fabris how frightened he was of making an impious death. 'I fear that in punishment for my former unbelieving, some thought against the Revelation may come to me, and the last voluntary thought. . . .'

On 7th May 1873, at the age of eighty-nine, he slipped one morning on the steps of the church of San Fedele when going alone to early mass. No member of his family was now living with him. He was carried home and fell into a state of alternating mania and delirium. His memory went; he threw all the papers in the room on to the fire; his past sins loomed sinister and tormented him with regret. 'The bill's a long and heavy one. What will happen to me?' he kept on repeating. His tendency to doubt, which Lombroso was to call 'la malattia del dubbio,' gripped him so that when a newspaper was read out to him he stuttered: 'I don't understand. I don't think either the original or the reading or the fact is true.' He confessed and communicated. But in his delirium he abused and denied the very faith that had upheld him for sixty years: 'With words of which he was not conscious, he confessed thoughts that he should not, to those he should not.' When a visitor asked him in his last hours why it was he got things all mixed up he answered, with a flash of his old wit: 'If I knew why it was, I wouldn't get them mixed up.' The last thing he read was a few pages, on his death-bed, of Propertius.

He died at the house in the Via Morone on 22nd May 1873.

The last photograph. Manzoni at the age of 85. From a photograph in the Casa del Manzoni, Milan

No. 1 Via Morone, Milan, now the Casa del Manzoni and centre of Manzoni studies, as it was at the time of his death

(By permission of Dott. Marino Parenti)

VII

For newly united Italy his death was a national bereavement. All over the peninsula schools, universities, and theatres shut. 'There is not a corner of Italy where it is not bitterly felt,' wrote Garibaldi to Enrico, Manzoni's only surviving son. Five hundred telegrams of condolence were received at his home. The Mayor of Florence offered a tomb in that sanctuary of the Italian great, the church of Santa Croce. The funeral and the lying in state at the Town Hall of Milan were at Government expense. The funeral procession on 28th May was interminable. Between closed shops, with odes and invocations placarding the walls, the funeral car moved slowly, drawn by six horses, between packed crowds. It was preceded by a squadron of cavalry and representatives of scholastic and workers' organizations; the flanking cords were carried by two princes of the blood, the presidents of the Senate and the Chamber, and the Ministers for Education and Foreign Affairs. At least a hundred poems on his death have been counted. Streets and squares were named after him all over Italy, so that one finds his name up on the corners of alleys in the remotest villages in Calabria. And the great Requiem of Verdi was performed and dedicated to him on the first anniversary of his death.

But amid the acclamations there were one or two discordant notes. A month after his death the Catholic *Giornale degli Studiosi* published an attack on him as a bad Catholic for having insulted the pope by accepting the citizenship of Rome with such pleasure. *L'Osservatore Cattolico* found a 'fine poison' in his writings. 'Manzoni was never straight in his thoughts: through the fault also, we may say, of those who adulated him and of those surrounding him who put him on the road to conversion. Poor Manzoni! How often we reread his writings and how often we have wept over the misfortunes of such an intelligent mind.' The head of the Milanese Jesuits came out flatly with: 'He was born a revolutionary.' The Vatican remained silent.

Obituaries from abroad showed a confusion and ignorance about him which has lasted since. 'The Italians for lack of great men labour to exalt the mediocre ones,' wrote the Parisian

K

La Liberté. 'The whole of Italy is upside-down because of the death of a certain Manzoni, a former Mazzinian conspirator, recently made a senator of the kingdom.' An obituary in the London *Quarterly Review* found in him 'much more of the Protestant than of the Catholic.' Even the Hachette *Almanac* for 1923, in a short note, attributed to him 'many novels. . . .'

He had himself written to Marco Coen forty years before: 'Glory is a sweet fallacy, a superb dolour, which never contains what it promises and would cheat one even if it did; however perfect and unclouded a man may imagine it to be, it yet carries with it an emptiness, a bitterness, a disquiet which both accuse and punish vanity.' For 'every fiction which shows man in moral repose is dissimilar to the truth.' Moral repose was just what remained unattainable for one who had written in 1828 to Victor Cousin:

I think I was born eclectic, for while receiving docilely, in the unity of a book, of a phrase, of a word, mixtures of ideas, principles, and hypotheses which are anything but a single thing, I have always had a disposition to make a choice among them, to reject something in what I had approved, to find something in what I had discarded among these artificially opposed unities. When I recognized this disposition in myself I tried to perfect it, to direct it, and apply it to everything in which I could exercise my reason.

The complexity of even the most apparently simple facts, the prismatic qualities of reality, drew him in spite of himself. Yet 'there is nothing so narrow as truth' he had written in 1829 to the rector of Geneva University. 'You, sir, have no way of seeing broadly either in mathematics or in morality. . . . You talk to me of liberty, but that is not what I ask, nor that which I should ask: what I ask is to believe, as it is for that I have an intelligence and for that there is a religion. To believe is my duty and my need . . . and the liberty you leave me is nothing but uncertainty. . . .'

'What a tangle is the human heart!' Just as tangled are the roots of creative inspiration.

BIBLIOGRAPHY

MANZONI'S WORKS

THE most recent and complete edition, in three volumes, and edited by Professors M. Barbi and F. Ghisalberti, was published by the Centro Nazionale di Studi Manzoniani (Casa del Manzoni), Milan:

Vol. I. *I Promessi Sposi* and *Storia della Colonna Infame*, Milan, 1942.

Vol. II. *Opere Varie*, Milan, 1943:
Inni Sacri.
Osservazioni sulla Morale Cattolica.
Il Conte di Carmagnola.
Lettre à M. C—— [Chauvet] sur l'unité de temps et de lieu dans la tragédie.
Adelchi.
Discorso sopra alcuni punti della storia longobardica in Italia.
Sul Romanticismo . . . Lettera al Marchese Cesare d'Azeglio.
Del Romanzo Storico e in genere de' componimenti misti di storia e d'invenzione.
Dell' Invenzione . . . Dialogo, and various writings on language.

Vol. III. *Scritti non compiuti.* Youthful poems and others, short or unfinished, written later. *La rivoluzione francese del 1789 e la rivoluzione italiana del 1859.* Scattered thoughts, comments, and extracts from letters. Milan, 1950.

Letters. Pending a new complete edition of Manzoni's correspondence projected by the Casa del Manzoni, collected letters of various periods will be found listed under Gallavresi, Rosmini, and Scherillo in the following bibliography. All letters, including those scattered in newspapers and reviews, have been indexed by Marino Parenti in *Bibliografia delle edizione a stampa delle lettere di Alessandro Manzoni*, Florence, 1944.

ENGLISH TRANSLATIONS OF MANZONI'S WORKS

Inni Sacri and *Il Cinque Maggio*
Translations of Poems Ancient and Modern, by Edward Earl of Derby, London, 1862.
Modern Italian Poets, Essays and Versions, translated by William J. Howells, New York, 1887.
Italian Gems. The Sacred Hymns and Napoleonic Ode of Manzoni, translated into English rhyme by Rev. Jo. Foote Bingham, London, 1904.

Osservazioni sulla Morale Cattolica

   A vindication of Catholic morality or a refutation of the charges brought against it by Sismondi in his history.   London, 1836.

I Promessi Sposi

   The Betrothed Lovers, translated by Rev. Ch. Swan, Pisa, 1828.

   I Promessi Sposi or *The Betrothed Lovers*, translated by G. W. Featherstonehaugh, Washington, 1834.

   Lucia, The Betrothed, translated by Andrews Norton, New York, 1834.

   The Betrothed, translator anonymous, London, 1834.

   The Betrothed, translator anonymous, London, 1844.

   The Betrothed Lovers, with *The Column of Infamy*, translator anonymous, London, 1845.

   The Betrothed, translated by Rev. Daniel J. Cooper, New York, 1924.

   The Betrothed, translated by Archibald Colquhoun, London and New York, 1951.

Storia della Colonna Infame

   The Column of Infamy.   (See 1845 translation of *I Promessi Sposi* above.)

Dialogo dell' Invenzione

   A Dialogue of the Artist's Idea, by Manzoni, the author of *I Promessi Sposi*, paraphrased from the Italian by Rev. J. A. Drewe, London, 1899.

A Short Bibliography of Books about Manzoni

This list only includes the more important studies. In J. F. de Simone's *Alessandro Manzoni, Aesthetics and Literary Criticism*, which deals exhaustively with all Manzoni's literary influences, will be found a list of articles comparing him with other European and Italian writers. Other general bibliographies will be found in A. Momigliano's *Rassegna manzoniana* and in the notes to Chapter V of G. Mazzoni's *L'Ottocento*. Modern studies are listed in G. Prezzolini's *Repertorio bibliografico della storia e della critica italiana dal 1902–32*, and in a later volume covering the years 1932–42.

Angelini, Cesare: *Manzoni*, Turin, 1942.

Angeloro, A.: *Il Caffè ed Alessandro Manzoni*, Gaeta, 1911.

Barbi, Michele: 'I Promessi Sposi e la critica,' Milan, 1942. (In *Annali Manzoniani*, Vol. III.)

Barbiera, Raffaele: *Il Salotto della Contessa Maffei*, Milan, 1920. (About Milan and Manzoni in his last years.)

Beaumont, J. P.: 'Manzoni and Goethe,' Cambridge, 1939. (In *Italian Studies*, Feb., No. 7, Vol. II.)

Bellezza, Paolo: *Curiosità manzoniane*, Milan, 1923. (Particularly 'Genio e follia di Alessandro Manzoni.')

Bindoni, G.: *La topografia del romanzo 'I Promessi Sposi,'* Milan, 1923. (For pilgrims to the Manzoni country.)

Bognetti, G. P.: 'La genese dell' Adelchi e del Discorso e il pensiero storico del Manzoni fino al 1821,' Milan, 1951–2. (In *Giornale Storico della Società Storica Lombarda.* The latest researches on Manzoni at this period.)

Bondioli, Pio: *Manzoni e 'Gli Amici della Verità,'* Milan, 1936.

Bonghi, Ruggiero: *Colloqui col Manzoni*, Milan, 1944. (See under Giardini, C.)

Borri, Giuseppe: *Colloqui col Manzoni*, Milan, 1944. (See under Giardini, C.)

Bowen, C. M.: 'Manzoni and Scott,' Dublin, 1925. (In *Dublin Review*, Vol. CLXXVI.)

Busetto, N.: *La genese e la formazione dei Promessi Sposi*, Bologna, 1921.

Calosso, Umberto: *Colloqui col Manzoni*, Rome, 1948. (Not conversations, but a charming modern introduction to the subject.)

Cantù, Cesare: *Alessandro Manzoni; reminiscenze*, Milan, 1885. (Lively and often inaccurate reminiscences.)

Carducci, Giosuè: *A proposito di alcuni giudizi su Alessandro Manzoni. Discorso di Lecco;* and other writings on Manzoni. Bologna, 1937. (In Vol. XX of the Carducci collected edition.)

Christesco, Mlle: *La Fortune d'Alexandre Manzoni en France*, Paris, 1943.

Colet, Louise: *L'Italie des Italiens*, Paris, 1862–3. (Confidential conversations with Manzoni in 1860.)

Croce, Benedetto: *Alessandro Manzoni. Saggi e discussione*, Bari, 1930; *La Poesia. Introduzione alla critica e storia della poesia e della letteratura*, Bari, 1937.

Custodi, Pietro: *Mémoires*, Bordeaux, 1906. (Fragments published in *Annales de la Faculté de lettres de Bordeaux et des universités du Midi. Bulletin italien*, No. 4, Vol. V.)

De Gubernatis, A.: *Eustachio Dègola, il clero costituzione e la conversione della famiglia Manzoni*, Florence, 1882; *Alessandro Manzoni. Sudio biografico*, Florence, 1879.

De Lollis, C.: *Alessandro Manzoni e gli storici liberali della Restaurazione*, Bari, 1926.

De Robertis, G.: *Primi studi Manzoniani*, Caserta, 1949.

De Sanctis, Francesco: 'Manzoni. Saggi e lezioni,' Bari, 1926. (In Vol. I of *La letteratura italiana nel secolo demimonono.*)

De Simone, J. F.: *Alessandro Manzoni, Aesthetics and Literary Criticism*, New York, 1946. (The only full study on the subject in English.)

Di Collegno, Margherita Provana: *Diario, a cura di Aldebrandino Malvezzi*, Milan, 1926.

D'Ovidio, F.: *Nuovi studi manzoniani*, Caserta, 1928.

Fabris, C.: *Memorie manzoniane*, Milan, 1944. (See under Giardini, C.)

Fauriel, Claude, and Clarke, Mary: *Correspondance. Publiée par Ottmar de Mohl*, Paris, 1911.

Flori, Ezio: *Voci del mondo manzoniano*, Milan, 1932; *Alessandro Manzoni e Teresa Stampa*, Milan, 1930.

Fossi, Piero: *La conversione di Alessandro Manzoni*, Bari, 1938 (for the anti-Jansenist view); *La Lucia del Manzoni*, Bari, 1937.

Gabbutti, Elena: *Il Manzoni e gli ideologici francesi*, Florence, 1936.

Gallavresi, Giuseppe, and Sforza, Giovanni: *Carteggio di Alessandro Manzoni*. Vol. I, 1803–21, Milan, 1912; Vol. II, 1821–31, Milan, 1921.

Galletti, A.: *Alessandro Manzoni, il pensatore e il poeta*, 2 vols., Milan, 1927. (The most complete work on Manzoni's theories and influences.)

Garnett, Richard: *History of Italian Literature*, London, 1898.

Gentile, Giovanni: *Manzoni e Leopardi; saggi critici*, Milan, 1828.

Giardini, C. (editor): *Colloqui col Manzoni di N. Tommaseo, G. Borri, R. Bonghi. Seguite da Memorie manzoniane di C. Fabris*, Milan, 1944.

Giorgini-Manzoni, Vittoria: *Memorie (a cura di Michele Scherillo)*, Milan, 1923.

Locatelli, Milesi: *La Signora di Monza nella realtà*, Milan, 1924.

Lombroso, Cesare: *Nuovi Studi sul genio*, 2 vols., Palermo, 1902. (For Manzoni as psychopath.)

Lugli, Archimede: *Alessandro Manzoni e gli insegnamenti della sua vita*, Milan, 1923. (The official view for schoolchildren.)

Marcazzan, M.: *Foscolo, Manzoni, Goethe*, Brescia, 1948. (Includes Giovita Scalvini's notes.)

Masi, R.: *Alessandro Manzoni. Studi e ricordi*, Lanciano, 1893. (For Manzoni's friendships, 1802–5.)

Momigliano, Attilio: *Alessandro Manzoni*, Messina, 1948. (The subtlest biographical study of Manzoni.)

Neri, Nicoletta: *La fortuna di Manzoni in Inghilterra*, Turin, 1939. (With examples of English mistranslations.)

Nicoletti, L.: *I Personaggi dei Promessi Sposi*, Florence, 1939.

Nicolini, F.: *Peste e untori nei Promessi Sposi e nella realtà*, Bari, 1937. (For Manzoni's historical inaccuracies.)

Novati, F.: 'Tra gli autografi. Il matrimonio Manzoni-Beccaria,' Milan, 1912. (In *Il Libro e la Stampa*, Jan.–Feb.) (For Donna Giulia's affairs and Manzoni's birth.)

Parenti, Marino: *Bibliografia manzoniana*, Florence, 1936 (for editions of *I Promessi Sposi*); *Immagini della vita e dei tempti di Alessandro Manzoni*, Milan, 1942 (portraits, photographs, and documents illustrating Manzoni's life).

Passerin d'Entrèves, Alessandro: *Alessandro Manzoni* (annual lecture of the British Academy, 1949), London, 1950.

Petrocchi, Policarpo: *La prima giovanezza di Alessandro Manzoni*, Florence, 1938.

Poe, Edgar Allan: Article on 1834 translation of *I Promessi Sposi* written for *Southern Literary Messenger* of May 1835, reprinted in Vol. VIII of his complete works. New York, 1902.

Premoli, O. M.: *Vita di Alessandro Manzoni*, 2 vols., Rome, 1925–6. (A biography by a priest.)

Reforgiato, V.: *Shakespeare e Manzoni*, Catania, 1898.

Reynolds, Barbara: 'Alessandro Manzoni and Leopold II, Grand Duke of Tuscany,' Cambridge, 1947–8 (in *Italian Studies*, Vol. III); 'W. E. Gladstone and Alessandro Manzoni,' Cambridge, 1951 (in *Italian Studies*, Vol. VI); *The Linguistic Writings of Alessandro Manzoni. A Textual and Chronological Reconstruction*, Cambridge, 1950.

Rondani, A.: *Scritti manzoniani*, Rome, 1950. (See 'Socialismo Manzoniano.')

Rosmini, Antonio: *Carteggio fra Alessandro Manzoni e Antonio Rosmini, raccolta e annotata da Giuseppe Bonola*, Milan, 1901.

Ruffini, Francesco: *La vita religiosa di Alessandro Manzoni, con documenti inediti, ritratti, vedute, e facsimili*, 2 vols., Bari, 1931.

Russo, Luigi: *Personaggi dei Promessi Sposi*, Bari, 1931.

Sainte-Beuve, C. A.: *Portraits contemporains*, Paris, 1847. (See the essay on Fauriel and Manzoni.)

Salvadori, Giulio: *Enrichetta Blondel e il Natale del '33*, Milan, 1929.

Sapegno, Natalino: 'Manzoni e il primo Risorgimento,' Milan, 1945 (in *Risorgimento*, No. 1, Anno 1, 15 April. Manzoni seen from the modern Left); Introduction to his edition of *Lettre à M. Chauvet*, Rome, 1947.

Scalvini, Giovita: For his notes on Manzoni and *I Promessi Sposi* see under Marcazzan, M.

Scherillo, M., and Gallavresi, G.: *Manzoni Intimo*, Milan, 1923. (Family letters in later life.)

Settembrini, Luigi: *Lezioni di letteratura italiana. Dialoghi*, Naples, 1909. (Attacks on Manzoni.)

Sforza, Giovanni, and Gallavresi, G.: *Carteggio di Alessandro Manzoni.* (See under Gallavresi, G.)

Stampa, Stefano: *Alessandro Manzoni, la sua famiglia, i suoi amici*, Milan, 1885–9. (Scattered reminiscences, mainly written to refute those of Cantù.)

Stendhal (Henri Beyle): *Souvenirs d'égotisme*, Paris, 1892 (for remarks on Fauriel and Mary Clarke); *Correspondance, 1800–42*, 3 vols., Paris, 1908.

Stoppani, Antonio: *I primi anni di Alessandro Manzoni. Spigolature*, Milan, 1874.

Tissi, S.: *Humour dialogico leopardiano e dramma manzoniano. Il dramma dell' uomo nel Leopardi e d'un uomo nel Manzoni*, Milan, 1920. (A metaphysical confrontation.)

Tommaseo, Niccolò: *Colloqui col Manzoni*, Milan, 1944. (See under Giardini, C.)

Tonelli, Luigi: *Manzoni*, Milan, 1928. (One of the few full biographies.)

Traversi, Derek Antona: 'The Significance of Manzoni's *Promessi Sposi*.' (In *Scrutiny*, Boston, 1940.)

Vidari, G.: *Manzoni*, Turin, 1936.

Young, M. V.: 'Alessandro Manzoni, Romanticist.' (In *Rerum Italicum*, Vol. XIII, 1922.)

Zibordi, G.: *Divulgazioni manzoniani*, Milan, 1933. (Particularly for criticism of the ending of *I Promessi Sposi*.)

Ziino, M.: 'Voltaire, Rousseau e I Promessi Sposi,' Milan, 1933. (In *Giornale Storico della Letteratura Italiana*, Vol. CI.)

Zottoli, A.: *Umili e potenti nella poetica di Alessandro Manzoni*, Rome, Milan, 1931. (Particular emphasis on Manzoni's democratic sympathies.)

SOME BOOKS ABOUT THE BACKGROUND

Alfieri, Vittorio: *Memorials of the Life and Writings of Vittorio Alfieri, Written by Himself*, translated from the Italian, London, 1810.

Andryane, Alexandre: *Memoirs of a Prisoner of State*, translated by Fortunato Prandi, London, 1840. (On the Lombard Carbonari.)

Ashbourne, Lord: *Grégoire and the French Revolution*, London, 1933; (as Hon. W. Gibson) *The Abbé de Lamennais and the Liberal Catholic Movement in France*, London, 1896.

Baldasseroni, Francesco: *Il rinnovamento civile in Toscana*, Florence, 1931. (For Vieusseux's movement in Florence.)

Bancroft, George: 'Diary' (of Italian journey, including a visit to Manzoni), New York, 1905. (In *Scribner's Magazine*, Vol. XXXVIII.)

Baretti, Giuseppe: *An Account of the Manners and Customs of Italy*, London, 1709.

Barthélemy Saint-Hilaire, J. M.: *Victor Cousin, sa vie et sa correspondance*, Paris, 1895.

Barzelotti, Giacomo: *L'idea religiosa negli uomini di stato del Risorgimento*, Milan, 1904.

Battaglia, F.: *L'Opera di Vincenzo Cuoco e la formazione dello spirito nazionale*, Florence, 1895.

Beccaria Bonesana, Cesare: *An Essay on Crime and Punishment, with the Commentary by Voltaire*, London, 1801; Venturi, G. A.: *Cesare Beccaria e le lettere di Pietro ed Alessandro Verri*, Milan, 1882.

Bedarida, Henri: *L'Influence française en Italie au dix-huitième siècle*, Paris, 1934.

Berthold, Baron: *Memoirs of the Secret Societies of the South of Italy, particularly the Carbonari*, translated from the French, London, 1821.

Blennerhassett, Lady: *Mme de Staël*, 3 vols., translated by J. E. Cuning, London, 1889. (See also 'The Doctrinaires' and 'The Papacy and the Catholic Church,' in Vol. IX of the *Cambridge Modern History*, Cambridge, 1907.)

Borgese, G. A.: *Storia della critica romantica in Italia*, Milan, 1920.

Botta, Carlo: *History of Italy during the Consulate and Empire*, translated from the Italian, London, 1828.

Bourg, E. T. (alias Saint-Edmé): *Constitution et organisation des Carbonari*, Paris, 1821.

Bouvier, Felix: *Bonaparte en Italie*, Paris, 1899.

Bouvry, Eugène: *Le Comte Pietro Verri, ses idées et son temps*, Paris, 1889.

Braga, C. Capone: *La filosofia francese ed italiana nel settecento*, Arezzo, 1920.

Calleri, F.: *Les idées religieuses de Manzoni et de Lamennais*, Paris, 1877.

Cantù, Cesare: *L'Abate Parini e la Lombardia nel secolo passato*, Milan, 1854; *'Il Conciliatore' e i Carbonari; Episodio*, Milan, 1878.

Casati, Gabrio: *Memorie e lettere di Federigo Confalonieri*, Milan, 1889.

Church, E. M.: *Chapters in an Adventurous Life. Sir Richard Church in Italy and Greece*, London, 1895.

Citanna, G.: *Il Romanticismo e la poesia italiana dal Parini al Carducci*, Bari, 1935.

Corio, L.: *Federigo Confalonieri e gli uomini del Conciliatore*, Milan, 1900.

Costa de Beauregard, A.: *Un Homme d'autrefois*, Paris, 1877. (Italian campaigns, 1796–7.)

Croce, Benedetto: 'La Definizione del Romanticismo,' Paris, 1921 (in *La Critica*, Vol. IV.); *Uomini e cose della vecchia Italia*, Bari, 1927 (see 'Della religiosità populare ai Giansenisti').

D'Azeglio, Massimo: *I miei ricordi*, Florence, 1920.

Dejob, C.: *Mme de Staël et l'Italie. Avec une bibliografie de l'influence française en Italie 1796–1814*, Paris, 1890.

Della Torre, A.: *Il Cristianesimo in Italia dai filosofici ai modernisti*, Palermo, 1908.

De Sanctis, Francesco: *La letteratura italiana nel secolo decimonono*, Bari, 1926.

Didier, Charles: *Rome Souterraine*, Paris, 1833.

Fabry, J. G. A.: *Histoire de l'armée d'Italie* (1796–7), Paris, 1844.

Fay, B.: *La Massoneria e la rivoluzione intellettuale del secolo XVIII*, Turin, 1939.

Ferrari, M. A.: *La preparazione intellettuale del Risorgimento italiano*, Milan, 1923.

Ferri, Luigi: *Essai sur l'histoire de la philosophie en Italie au dix-neuvième siècle*, Paris, 1869.

Gallarati-Scotti, Tomasso: *The Life of Antonio Fogazzaro*, translated from the Italian, London, 1922.

Galley, J. B.: *Claude Fauriel, membre de l'Institut*, St Étienne, 1909.

Gazier, A.: *Études sur l'histoire religieuse de la Révolution*, Paris, 1887; *Histoire générale du mouvement janseniste depuis les origines jusqu'à nos jours*, Paris, 1922.

Gentile, Giovanni: *Rosmini e Gioberti*, Pisa, 1898; *Vincenzo Cuoco*, Venice, 1927.

Gorani, Giuseppe: *Mémoires. Première Édition française publiée par A. Casati*, Paris, 1944; Monnier, Marc: *Un Aventurier italien du siècle dernier*, Paris, 1884.

Gramsci, Antonio: *Il Risorgimento*, Turin, 1950.

Guillois, A.: *La Marquise de Condorcet, 1762–1822: Sa famille, son salon, ses amis*, Paris, 1897; *Le Salon de Mme Helvétius. Cabanis et les Idéologues*, Paris, 1894.

Hazard, Paul: *La Révolution française et les lettres italiennes*, Paris, 1910.

Jemolo, Arturo Carlo: *Il Giansenismo in Italia prima della Rivoluzione*, Bari, 1928; *Chiesa e stato in Italia negli ultimi cento anni*, Turin, 1949.

Johnstone, R. M.: *The Napoleonic Empire in Southern Italy and the Rise of the Secret Societies*, London, 1904.

King, Bolton: *A History of Italian Unity. Being a Political History of Italy from 1814 to 1871*, 2 vols., London, 1899; *The Life of Mazzini*, London, 1906.

Labande-Jeanroy, T.: *La Question de la langue en Italie de Baretti à Manzoni*, Paris, 1925.

Lamennais, H. F. Robert de: *Words of a Believer*, translated by L. E. Martineau, with a memoir by Mazzini, London, 1891; *Essay on Indifference in Matters of Religion*, translated by Lord Stanley of Alderley, London, 1895.

Lee, Vernon (Violet Paget): *Studies of the Eighteenth Century in Italy*, London, 1880.

Lemmi, F.: *La restaurazione austriaca in Milano nel 1814*, Bologna, 1902.

Leti, Giuseppe: *Carboneria e Massoneria nel Risorgimento italiano*, Genoa, 1925.

Luzio, A.: *La Massoneria ed il Risorgimento italiano*, 2 vols., Bologna, 1925.

Mazzoni, G.: *L'Ottocento*, 2 vols., Milan, 1930.

Melegari, Dora: *La Giovine Italia e la Giovine Europa, dal carteggio inedito di Giuseppe Mazzini*, Milan, 1906.

Meredith, George: *Vittoria*, London, 1889. (Historical novel about Milan in 1848.)

Momigliano, Attilio: 'Rinascimento italiano e illuminismo francese.' (In *Rivista d'Italia*, 31 August 1918.)

Morandi, Carlo: *Idee e formazione politiche in Lombardia dal 1748 al 1814*, Bari, 1928.

Muoni, G.: *Ludovico de Breme e le prime polemiche intorno a Madama de Staël e il Romanticismo in Italia (1816)*, Milan, 1902.

Nievo, Ippolito: *Confessioni di un Italiano*, Florence, 1949.

Omodei, Enzo: *Orientamenti politici dei cattolici italiani dell' ottocento*, Milan, 1948. (With introduction by Don Sturzo.)

Omodeo, Adolfo: *L'Età del Risorgimento italiano*, Messina, 1932.

Ossoli, Margaret Fuller: *Memoirs*, London, 1852.

Pagani, G. B.: *Life of Antonio Rosmini*, translated from the Italian, London, 1907.

Parisi, A.: *I reflessi del Giansenismo nella letteratura italiana*, Catania, 1919.

Picavet, Francis: *Les Idéologues*, Paris, 1891.

Pingaud, Albert: *La Domination française dans l'Italie du Nord, 1796–1805*, Paris, 1914.

Prezzolini, Giuseppe: *Come gli Americani scoprirono l'Italia (1750–1850)*, Milan, 1933. (An entertaining account of American travellers, including several visits to Manzoni.)

Probyn, John Webb: *Italy; from the Fall of Napoleon in 1815 to the Year 1900*, London, 1891.

Ridley, F. A.: *The Jesuits*, London, 1938.

Robertson, J. G.: *Studies in the Genesis of Romantic Theory in the Eighteenth Century*, Cambridge, 1923.

Romanes, Ethel: *The Story of Port Royal*, London, 1907.

Rosenthal, D. A.: *Convertitenbilder aus dem neunzehnten Jahrhundert*, Weissenberg, 1866. (Describes nineteenth-century conversions similar to Manzoni's.)

Rota, E.: 'La Società dell' Caffè nelle sue relazione con l'enciclopedismo francese,' Pavia, 1915 (in *Bolletino della Società Pavese di Storia Patria*, Vols. I and II); *L'Austria in Lombardia*, Marciano, 1911.

Sainte-Beuve, C. A.: *Port Royal*, 5 vols., Paris 1840–61.

Sargent, H. H.: *Napoleon Bonaparte's First Campaign*, London, 1895.

Séché, L.: *Les Derniers Jansenistes (1710–1870)*, 2 vols., Paris, 1891; *Les Amitiés de Lamartine*, Paris, 1911.

Sedgwick, Catherine: *Letters from Abroad to Kindred at Home*, New York, 1841.

Segrè, Carlo: Chapter 4, on Italy after 1815, in Vol. IX of the *Cambridge Modern History*, Cambridge, 1907.

Smith, Marion E.: *Une Anglaise intellectuelle en France sous la Restauration: Miss Mary Clarke*, Paris, 1927.

Stendhal (Henri Beyle): *Souvenirs d'égotisme*, Paris, 1892 (for Fauriel and Mary Clarke); *Racine et Shakespeare*, Paris, 1925; *Journal*, 5 vols., Paris, 1923–34.

Ticknor, George: *Life, Letters, and Journals*, Boston, 1876.

Tivaroni, Carlo: *L'Italia prima della rivoluzione francese (1735–89)*, Turin, 1888; *L'Italia durante il dominio francese (1789–1815)*, Turin, 1889.

Trompeo, P. P.: *Nel Italia Romantica sulle orme di Stendhal*, Rome, 1924; *Rilegature gianseniste*, Rome, 1930.

Vanucci, A.: *I martiri della libertà italiana del 1794 al 1848. Memorie raccolte*, Milan, 1876.

Verri, Carlo: 'Sugli avvennimenti di Milano 17–20 Aprile 1820,' Milan, 1879. (In *Biblioteca Storica del Risorgimento italiano*, No. 3.)

Verri, Pietro: *Storia di Milano*, with continuation by Pietro Custodi, Milan, 1834.

Verri, Pietro and Alessandro: *Carteggio*, 13 vols., Milan, 1910.

Weil, W. M.: *Le Prince Eugène et Murat (1813–14)*, Paris, 1902.

Wilson, Sir Robert: *Private Diary of Travels, Personal Services, and Public Events, during Missions and Employment with the European Armies in the Campaigns of 1812, 1813, 1814*, London, 1861.

Witt, Jean: *Mémoires secrets relatifs à l'état de la révolution de Piemont, de l'esprit qui regne en Italie et de ses sociétés secrets*, Paris, 1831.

Zadei, Guido: *L'Abate Lamennais e gli Italiani del suo tempo*, Turin, 1921.

Zanella, G.: *Storia della letteratura italiana della metà del settecento sino ai nostri giorni*, Milan, 1880.

INDEX

271

Manzoni, Donna Giulia Beccaria, character, 14, 20, 22; marriage, 19, 21; and Giovanni Verri, 19–20; family quarrels, 19, 26, 27; with Imbonati, 21, 57; position in Paris, 57; friendship with Mme de Condorcet, 57, 67, 72; son's devotion, 70–1; encourages friendship with Fauriel, 73, 74; seeks wife for son, 75, 77; arranges his marriage, 77–80; her conversion, 95; longings for Paris, 115, 130, 145; in Paris 1820, 131, 134; in Florence, 212; and Manzoni's second wife, 235, 236–8; death, 239, 240–1

Manzoni, Donna Teresa Stampa Borri, character, 235–7; marries Manzoni, 236; criticisms of marriage, 236–7; quarrels with Donna Giulia, 237–8; relations with Manzoni, 240–1; death, 257

Manzoni, Don Pietro, marriage, 21; character, 22; quarrels with Donna Giulia, 26–7; relations with Alessandro, 28–9; death and will, 76

Manzoni family: history, 22; standing, 22–4; effect of family pride, 24–5

Manzoni, Giovanni, in Venice, 52–3

Manzoni, Giulietta (afterwards d'Azeglio), significance of baptism, 91; on I Promessi Sposi's progress, 177; on Scott's Woodstock, 187; marriage to Massimo d'Azeglio, 232; death, 239

Manzoni, Henriette Blondel, Manzoni's requirements in a wife, 76, 78; wedding, 80; religious interests, 81; her and Manzoni's conversion, 83, 84, 91–3; coolness with parents, 98–9; childbearing, 103, 130, 231–232; nurses Manzoni's health, 113–114, 136, 145; her own ills, 156, 203, 232; as Ermengarda, 156, 235; in Florence, 212; on I Promessi Sposi corrections, 217–18; effect of death, 234–5; as Lucia, 235

Manzoni, Monsignor, applies for patent of nobility, 22; watches Donna Giulia, 26; his sister, 38–9

Manzoni's daughters: Vittoria, 93, 240; Sofia, 115, 239; Clara, 234; Matilde, 234, 239; Cristina, 234, 239

Manzoni's sons: education, 31–2; Pietro, 231; Filippo, 239–40; Enrico, 239–40, 259

Marchetti, Abate Salvagnoli, attacks Inni Sacri, 105–6; attacks I Promessi Sposi, 182

Marescalchi, Count, his set in Paris and Manzoni's conversion, 84

Maria Carolina, Queen of Naples, Manzoni's attacks, 43–4

Maria Teresa, Empress, Verri's and Parini's comments, 6

Marie Antoinette, Queen of France, and Grégoire, 132; and Manzoni, 250

Marmontel, Jean-François, 196

Marzo 1821, 142–3; in 1848, 144, 257

Massillon, Jean-Baptiste, and Manzoni's style, 193

Mazella, Cardinal, and Modernist controversy, 227

Mazzini, Giuseppe, defends Manzoni, 184; and Young Italy, 243; relations with Manzoni, 243–5; and Jansenism, 244; Manzoni's opinions, 244, 245

Melzi d'Eril, Francesco, 35; and Donna Giulia, 36, 69; Custodi's comments, 37; and Italian Republic, 37–8; in 1814, 109

Metternich, Prince, and Il Conciliatore, 118; and Carbonari, 140; offers Manzoni decoration, 242

Mirabeau, Vicomte de, Cabanis's friendship, 60

Molina, Luis de, and Jansenists, 87–8, 89, 96

Momigliano, Professor Attilio, on Manzoni's conversion, 82; on Manzoni and Leopardi, 209; on Manzoni and art, 213